The Culture of the Sound Image in Prewar Japan

The Culture of the Sound Image in Prewar Japan

Edited by
Michael Raine
and Johan Nordström

Routledge
Taylor & Francis Group
LONDON AND NEW YORK

First published in 2020 by Amsterdam University Press Ltd.

Published 2025 by Routledge
4 Park Square, Milton Park, Abingdon, Oxon OX14 4RN
605 Third Avenue, New York, NY 10158

Routledge is an imprint of the Taylor & Francis Group, an informa business

ISBN: 9789089647733 (hbk)
ISBN: 9781041187592 (pbk)
ISBN: 9781003705727 (ebk)
NUR 670

Cover illustration: Advertisement for P.C.L.'s *Sakura ondo* (1934). *Kinema junpō*, 11 March 1934.
Cover design: Coördesign, Leiden

DOI: 10.5117/9789089647733

for Arthur and Simon

Table of Contents

Introduction

Michael Raine and Johan Nordström

In his call for a new film history Thomas Elsaesser questions 'notions of origin and teleology' in existing accounts of cinema and asks, 'Have we been fixated too exclusively on "the image", and forgotten about sound; have we been concentrating on films as texts, and neglected the cinema as event and experience?'[1] This book takes up these caveats, and others raised by the recent turn to media archaeology, in order to refocus attention on cinema as a changing intermedial field during the conversion to synchronized sound in Japan around 1930.[2] Each chapter traces a specific, sometimes vanishing, mediation of sound in the cinema and related media, seeking to restore complexity to a new media transition in Japan that is often described simply as slow and reluctant, or as obstructed by traditional oral culture. In fact, technologically mediated sound was an object of fascination and excitement, part of a rapidly modernizing popular culture. As these essays tell us, audiences first heard film stars speak on the radio, sound films were tied to developments in popular music, and filmmakers developed new styles in response to the new sound cinema technology. In the histories laid out here, mediated sound is both live and recorded, voice or sound effect, and cinema is an institution, a mode of narration, and an architectural space. Taken together, they approach Japanese cinema as what Christian Metz, borrowing from Marcel Mauss, called a 'total social fact', embedded in technological and economic changes and framed by wider fears and aspirations.[3] The extended transition to sound in Japan, full of interstitial and unremembered elements, is more common than the relatively rapid conversion in Germany, Great Britain, and the United States.[4] In this larger view the complex mix of emerging, dominant, and residual technologies

1 Elsaesser, 'The New Film History as Media Archeology', p. 77.

2 See for example Huhtamo and Parikka (eds.), *Media Archaeology*.

3 Metz, *Language and Cinema*, p. 9.

4 The transition was rapid in India, too, which may perhaps be explained by the size and literacy rate of the local market.

Raine, M. and J. Nordström (eds.), *The Culture of the Sound Image in Prewar Japan*.
Taylor & Francis Group 2020
DOI: 10.5117/9789089647733_INTRO

and practices, and the multiple forms of 'sound' and 'talking' cinema in Japan, are not so different from the cinemas of Latin America, Asia, and the European margins with their undercapitalized but cosmopolitan and intermedial mix of *films sonore* and *films parlant*.[5]

During the transition to sound Japanese cinema was subject to what Elsaesser has called '"media-interference" from radio as well as the co-presence or competition of the gramophone industry'.[6] In this introduction, we describe the technological, economic, industrial, and political contexts for the interrelated growth of the recording industry, radio, and sound cinema in Japan around 1930. Rather than claim a special cultural sense in which Japanese cinema is made up of 'commingled media' (the silent film image plus the live narrator, or *benshi*) we argue that all electronic media are 'commingled' in this period, sharing technology, personnel, and sounds.[7] Although this anthology focuses on the cinema, intermedial relations between the record industry, radio, and cinema constitute an extensive field of diverse sound practices that we are calling the 'culture of the sound image'. It is a *culture* because it concerns embodied practices that go beyond the text of film and the physical space of the theatre – an extended idea of cinema that incorporates radio broadcasts, theme songs, publicity materials, and the printed programmes provided at every screening. It is a *sound image* because in the age of computer data the deep etymology of 'image' as 'likeness' no longer refers only to vision. In this sense, the phrase 'visual image' is not redundant, and 'sound image' is its aural equivalent. The sound event's technical reproduction depends on its registration on a material substrate such as a shellac record or the celluloid soundtrack, or in its one-to-many mediation through an apparatus, as on the radio. As the chapters show us, these intermedial connections, forged in the midst of an economic crisis, furthered the trend toward a unified experience in the cinema that changed labour relations and even the architecture of the cinemas themselves. That extended and uneven transformation of the

5 See the discussion in O'Brien, *Cinema's Conversion to Sound*. For the transition to sound in the USSR, see Miller, 'Soviet Cinema 1929-41'. For China, see Bao, *Fiery Cinema*. For India, see the materials on sound cultures in Indian cinema at http://sounds.medialabju.org/ (Accessed 20 April 2020). O'Brien argues that *films parlant* were focused on reproducing the actor's sound performance on film, while *films sonore*, which relied less on the technology of synchronization pioneered in the USA, used sound expressively. Those films did not simply record a profilmic moment but employed counterpoint and incorporated music and sound effects into the film's narration.

6 Elsaesser, 'Discipline Through Diegesis', p. 209.

7 For the claims about 'commingled media', see Anderson, 'Spoken Silents in the Japanese Cinema'.

cinema soundscape in Japan also brought to the foreground aesthetic issues in film, from the incorporation of popular song and other sound practices into sound films to the importance of the frame line and the changing semiotic relation between onscreen and offscreen.

The peculiarities of the transition to sound in Japan are sometimes explained as the result of different stages of economic or cultural development: as a non-western country, Japan is assumed to have lagged behind Europe and America. That sense of a 'geopolitical incline' between East and West was certainly part of many contemporary discussions about new sound media in Japan, but we should also recognize that Japan around 1930 was a rapidly developing country. In 1932, when Tokyo City expanded to accommodate its newly developed suburbs, it became the second largest city in the world, exceeding London proper and smaller only than New York. Japan was the dominant power in East Asia, the fifth largest country in the world by population, with a growing corps of scientists and strong connections across the Pacific with the most technologically advanced country, the USA. Cinema was part of that story of development: Japan was the world's largest producer of feature films in the 1930s, by number if not by capital investment. It had the world's fourth largest box office income in 1929, and in 1930, it had about 1,400 cinemas, among the top ten countries in the world.[8] Drawing on Marilyn Ivy and Harry Harootunian's theorizations of 'co-eval modernity', we argue that the transition to sound in Japan was also 'co-eval' with similar developments in the West: conditioned by the same forces, at almost the same time, but situated differently, and so following a somewhat different path.[9] Steve Wurtzler has shown how the large industrial combines headed by General Electric and AT&T in the USA created 'culture industries' out of the shared technology of telephone, records, radio, and film.[10] Cinema was just one part of an umbrella of technology research, like the European Tobis-Klangfilm partnership, in which the manufacturing arm was largely owned by Siemens and AEG. The Japanese film industry was not so vertically integrated but one consequence of the sound transition was the closer engagement of film studios with the industrial and capital structure of the modernizing nation.

8 The *Kinema shūhō* trade paper claimed that Japan had the fourth largest box office in the world in 'Nihon no eigakai wa sekai dai yon', p. 16. Data on the number of cinemas from the *Kokusai eiga nenkan* (1934), compiled in Kinoshita, 'The Benshi Track', p. 7. That yearbook also lists Japan in ninth place in a graph of countries with the largest number of cinemas printed in an unpaginated front section.

9 See Ivy, *Discourses of the Vanishing* and Harootunian, *Overcome by Modernity*.

10 Wurtlzer, *Electric Sounds*.

Phonograph Records

Mechanical sound recording was introduced to Japan in the nineteenth century. Until around 1910 most records, even of Japanese artists recorded in Japan, were pressed abroad and imported. A domestic industry manufacturing 78-rpm 'SP' records with 3-5 minutes of recording per side was sustained by genres such as classical music and military marches, local vocal arts such as *gidayū* chanted narration, comic *manzai* spoken-word performances, and *benshi* narration of famous scenes from the cinema, often performed with actors from the film. Popular songs consisted mostly of Japanese folk songs and other popular songs in '*yonanuki*' (omitting the fourth and seventh notes) pentatonic scales, played on both western and Japanese instruments, as well as western folk tunes with Japanese lyrics that used similar scales and were included in the grade school curriculum.[11] The incorporation of western-style marching bands into the Japanese military (and, as we will see, the cinemas), as well as the growth of steamship lines between Japan and the west coast of North American increased Japanese familiarity with western popular music. The increased popularity of social dancing in the 1910s motivated the import of records and live musicians playing the ragtime, foxtrot, and occasional improvisation that came to be known as 'jazz' in Japan.[12] Records were luxury goods but recorded popular music was already a staple of cafes and upper-middle-class households by the 1920s. Luxury taxes on imports raised to pay for reconstruction from the 1923 Great Kanto Earthquake led to large foreign investments in Japanese record companies and a boom in the local production of records in the late 1920s.[13] As Sasagawa Keiko and Hosokawa Shuhei discuss in Chapters 1 and 2, those records included comic and romantic songs backed by orchestral jazz bands, sometimes sung in English as well as Japanese.

The newly established Nihon Victor and Nihon Columbia record companies were among the top ten Japanese companies by foreign capital investment and brought to Japan the new technology of electronic sound recording (*denki fukikomi* or *denki rokuon*) that developed out of telephone research in the USA, and that underpinned the development of sound recording in the cinema. Production of record players increased, and record sales tripled as prices fell drastically. New recordings with greater dynamic

11 See Kitahara, 'Kayokyoku'.

12 For an overview of this music see Atkins, *Blue Nippon*.

13 See Mitsui Tōru, '"Sing Me a Song of Araby" and "My Blue Heaven"' for an incisive overview of this period.

range and frequency response sustained the culture of college jazz groups and dance halls, which played records during the day and featured live bands in the evening. The boom in manufacturing commodified the new popular music, shifting the labels' commercial strategy from exploiting songs popularized by stage shows or sung in the pleasure quarters by more or less anonymous geisha and street entertainers to the planned promotion and release of popular songs with celebrity singers, supported by promotional campaigns in magazines, bars, and cafes. The style of the music also changed, shifting toward up-tempo and romantic melodies, although minor key 'blues' and 'new folk songs' were also popular.

Miriam Silverberg has written extensively on modern Japanese urban culture, which she calls by its Japanese pronunciation, *modan*, to indicate both its global filiations as well as the local specificity of the relations between technological and economic modernization, modernism as a more or less oppositional cultural phenomenon, and modernity as a philosophical category that attempts to name those new conditions.[14] In particular, Silverberg indicates the double-edged nature of the Japanese *modan*: both partaking of the exhilarating loosening of social roles amidst a surge of new material goods and cultural practices and at the same time enabling the new demands a state could make on citizen-subjects by virtue of the extended range and finer grain of bureaucratic systems of control, including new communications technologies. The new media of records, radio, and sound cinema were all enlisted from their inception as part of a capitalist economy but also as part of an imperial and militarist political project. The flipside of the flourishing culture of cafes and dance halls, mediated even more widely by jazz records, were the bestselling record collections, often offered by newspapers on a subscription model, of military marches and *nagauta* (a form of narrative singing associated with kabuki) celebrating Japan's colonial adventures in China.[15]

Radio

In December 1926, news of the illness and death of the Taishō Emperor was broadcast through the new medium of radio by the three stations of the nationalized NHK radio network. The broadcasts drew on the

14 See Silverberg, 'Constructing the Japanese Ethnography of Modernity', and 'Remembering Pearl Harbor, Forgetting Charlie Chaplin', summarized in her book *Erotic Grotesque Nonsense*.
15 Kurata, *Nihon rekōdo bunkashi*, p. 179.

development of a series of technologies over the previous fifty years: microphones that could register the human voice and other sounds as an electronic signal; the telephone system through which the radio stations were directly connected to the Imperial Household Agency; amplifiers and broadcast equipment to transmit that signal; and radios, whether crystal sets with headphones or vacuum tube receivers with loudspeakers that could produce recognizable sounds. Although the subscriber base was still small, Takeyama Akiko argues that the regular broadcasts of the Emperor's condition, and the announcement of the Emperor's death by station chiefs that doubled as a ceremonial commemoration, were the first media events in Japan that depended on the electronically mediated voice.[16] Hori Hikari shows that the state encouraged the spread of radio and staged the Shōwa Emperor's enthronement ceremonies in November 1928 so that they could be experienced through a newly established radio network linking major cities throughout the length of Japan. These scripted 'live' broadcasts complete with sound effects were then released as records that were sometimes played alongside silent newsreels of the ceremonies.[17] In sum, there was already a dense culture of the sound image in Japan by the time that mediated sound in Japanese cinema became technologically and economically possible.

Modelled on the BBC and started only three or four years after broadcasting in Britain, NHK radio soon embedded itself in the media environment of Japan. In 1925 Japan was the largest purchaser of radio receivers from the USA, increasing the number of licensed sets in Japan from 5,455 to 338,204.[18] Domestic production by Sharp and other companies also took off and the number of receivers doubled every three years, reaching 50% of Tokyo homes by 1934. What did Japanese audiences want from the radio? Early opinion polls give a sense of the range of preferences. In 1926, the major newspaper *Asahi Shimbun* reported a poll on radio conducted at a girls' school in Osaka. One of the respondents said it was no longer the age of *gidayū* (chanted puppet theatre narration) and other Japanese vocal arts and asked for more western music programmes, suitable to a 'modern girl'. That was the first time the newspaper had used the phrase, which would come to characterize the dangerous and exciting image of a new generation of women in Japan.[19] As radio spread further into the Japanese middle class,

16 Takeyama, *Rajio no jidai*, pp. 80-83.

17 Hori, *Promiscuous Media*, pp. 51-52.

18 Mitsui, 'Interactions of Imported and Indigenous Musics in Japan', p. 158.

19 'Chihōga', p. 6

the preferred programming also shifted toward more conventional tastes. Later, broader-based polls revealed the popularity of older vocal and musical forms such as *rakugo* (comic storytelling), *naniwabushi* (melodious narrative recitation accompanied by a shamisen), and *manzai* (comic repartee). Between the old vocal arts and the new jazz culture, alternative genres of vocal entertainment emerged, from sports broadcasting to drama on the radio, which relied on the creative construction of soundscapes. Even more popular than radio drama were two other forms of drama that drew on audience familiarity with the conventional soundscape of the cinema. Both forms presented the stories of silent cinema, accompanied by live music and a live *benshi*. As Niita Chie explains in Chapter 3, in the *eiga monogatari* (film story) the *benshi* explained the plot of a film and did character voices to a backing of music and sound effects. The *eigageki* (film drama) went one step further in using actors, typically from the cast of the film, to perform alongside the *benshi* even before those actors' voices could be heard in the cinema.

The one-to-many format of radio broadcasting encouraged the incorporation of individual Japanese into a larger community. For example, to commemorate the Shōwa Emperor's enthronement in 1928, the insurance arm of the Japanese Post Office introduced radio calisthenics on the model of radio broadcasts sponsored by the Metropolitan Life insurance company in the USA, which were in turn based on the revanchist mass calisthenics of the Czech Sokol movement.[20] Kurata Yoshihiro reports that after the Manchurian Incident of 1931 the radio calisthenics broadcasts were accompanied by military songs.[21] In the same decade, radio was the first medium to report Japanese successes in the Olympic games of 1932 and 1936. Also in the 1930s and early 1940s the radio networks were used for short wave 'exchange broadcasts' (*kōkan hōsō*) that tied Japan to the Asian colonies and Axis allies. In less than twenty years, radio spanned an enormous range of uses, bridging high and low culture, entertaining audiences with sports and drama, and uniting all Japanese as citizens of an expanding Empire. All mass media, by virtue of their ubiquity, become absorbed and naturalized as infrastructure but before radio sank into the background, a mere channel for coordinated exercise, information, or propaganda, Japanese listeners

20 See the Japan Post company history at http://www.jp-life.japanpost.jp/aboutus/csr/radio/abt_csr_rdo_history.html (Accessed 20 April 2020).

21 Kurata, *Nihon rekōdo bunkashi, p.* 178. For a history of a similar illiberal modernist use of radio technology, see Birdsall, *Nazi Soundscapes*. For the Japanese case, see Robbins, *Tokyo Calling*.

were presented with a range of possibilities for how radio might contribute to the human sensorium as it was constructed in Japan.

As a state-controlled enterprise, radio tended toward education more than entertainment, and music tended toward the classical rather than the popular. Nagahara Hiromu argues that Japanese elites tried, and failed, to preserve a space for high culture within Japan's emerging mass culture by limiting the rotation of popular songs on the radio, but that even radio was swept up in the media event that was 'Tokyo March' in 1929.[22] Popular novelist Kikuchi Kan serialized a story of that name, starting the previous year, in the top-selling monthly magazine *Kingu*. In the middle of the serialization, Victor Records released a song 'Tokyo March' with lyrics by Saijō Yaso and music by Nakayama Shinpei, perhaps the top lyricist and composer of popular tunes at that time. The record was a phenomenal hit, selling at least 150,000 copies on the back of its jaunty lyrics about a potential affair between a male bohemian and one of the 'modern girls' mentioned above.[23] The song was banned from the radio but an adaptation of Kikuchi's story was broadcast by NHK's Osaka station in May 1929, quickly followed by a film from the Nikkatsu studio, directed by Mizoguchi Kenji.[24] The multimedia promotion had been planned as a tie-up between Victor and Nikkatsu, the first such joint planning between film and record companies, and was intended to commemorate Nikkatsu's first talkie using the Mina Talkie (*Mina tōkī*) sound-on-film system. In fact, the system, a licensed version of Lee de Forest's Phonofilm, failed and the film was released silent with the song played on a record player in the cinema. Nevertheless, the project indicates the increasingly close relation between cinema, radio, and the recording industry during the transition to synchronized sound.

Sound in Japanese cinemas

The American and European films that dominated early Japanese film exhibition were accompanied by local instruments and musical genres, as well as by brass bands playing western marching tunes. Hosokawa Shuhei has reconstructed the musical accompaniment in Japanese cinemas of

22 Nagahara, *Tokyo Boogie-Woogie*.

23 Hosokawa Shuhei, in this volume, cites what he regards as a dubious estimate of 300,000 in sales. Kurata Yoshihiro claims that the record was not an immediate success but was promoted by Nikkatsu actresses who toured cafes and bars, encouraging the owners to play the record. See Kurata, *Nihon rekōdo bunkashi*, p. 156.

24 Kinoshita, 'The Edge of Montage', pp. 124-146. See also Hosokawa Shuhei's article in this volume.

the 1920s, the decade in which audiences for local films for the first time exceeded that for imported films. The film programme for both Japanese and western films included a live orchestra playing light classical music with a combination of western and Japanese instruments, interludes of classical standards between the films, and occasional appearances by live, usually female, singers that were replaced by records when the singers were banned for immodesty.[25] Kurata Yoshihiro argues that the cue sheets for foreign films familiarized Japanese musicians, and Japanese audiences, with western light classical music. One sociologist even claimed that you could hear kids in the slums playing classical melodies on their harmonicas, thinking it was 'movie music'.[26]

The live narrator or *benshi* was a crucial element of the cinema soundscape during the silent period.[27] As already mentioned, *benshi* made highlight records and performed film stories on the radio so that audiences could relive the sonic experience of the cinema. However, Fujiki Hideaki has shown that with the rise of the star system and the development of a more Hollywood-style *découpage*, audience attention shifted from the *benshi* to the actors. Rather than a free interpreter, the *benshi* was constrained by the proliferating intertitles of early 1920s films and by an approved censorship script after 1925.[28] In effect, like the musicians with their cue sheets, the *benshi* was part of a sonic *dispositif*, an apparatus increasingly focused on narrative and emotional effects centred on the screen.[29]

Even before electronic amplification, Japanese film exhibitors attempted to replace the *benshi* and live musicians with recorded sound. The Kinetophone and other mechanical playback systems had a brief success in the early 1910s, but the main use of recorded sound was to play popular songs in the cinema. One brief exception was Lee de Forest's Phonofilm system that was shown in Japan by Minagawa Yoshizō in 1925. Minagawa's Shōwa Kinema Co., Ltd. licensed Phonofilm as the 'Mina Talkie' system, and used it to produce several short sound subjects as well as the first Japanese talkie feature film, *Reimei/Dawn*, directed by Osanai Kaoru in 1927. Although the

25 Hosokawa, 'Sketches of Silent Film Sound in Japan'.

26 Kurata, *Nihon rekōdo bunkashi*, p. 140

27 See Dym, *Benshi* for a rich account of the 'forgotten narrative art of *setsumei*'.

28 Fujiki, '*Benshi* as Stars'.

29 See Foucault, *Power/Knowledge*, p. 194 for a discussion of the *dispositif* as an apparatus that links discursive and non-discursive structures in ways that discipline human behaviour. Foucault was interested in more powerful institutions than the cinema but the pattern of norm and exclusion, of technical and architectural materiality affecting consciousness, and of effects produced without definite subjective intention, is similar.

films received some press attention, the screenings failed to turn a profit or make any impact on Japanese filmmakers. As we will see in the next section, the introduction of Hollywood talkies in 1929 revived Japanese efforts to make synchronized sound films.

In the 1920s, cinemas played the radio and records in their lobbies to attract audiences and sometimes played the theme song of silent films before and during the film, with the lyrics and often the catalogue number for the record printed on souvenir postcards distributed with the ubiquitous film programmes. Film studios and record companies, along with cinemas, collaborated to advertise their products: posters advertised the records as well as the films, and the poster design was re-used for record advertisement handouts, with record stores sometimes offering discounted tickets or free passes to the movies with the purchase of a record. The record companies created advertising records containing the theme song and dialogue from the film, which played at the cinemas during the intermission, and when the actual film was screened its theme song was often played so that it could be heard in the street in front of the cinema.[30]

In one of the most widely discussed instances, Paramount and Victor promoted the 1931 release of Josef von Sternberg's talkie *Nageki no tenshi/ The Blue Angel* (1930), by inserting an advertisement for the record into the weekly programme handed out in cinemas and attaching an advertisement for the film to the record in all Victor record stores in Tokyo.[31] The All-Kanto Film Study Circle, sponsored by the Asahi newspaper, showed the silent version of the film in the company's cinema, narrated by famous *benshi* Tokugawa Musei.[32] The English talkie version was given a wider release, praised for its sparse dialogue and cinematic values, despite the fact that almost 400 metres was cut by the censors. The Kobe Shōchikuza staged a live revue of the film, though it is not clear whether this was to familiarize audiences with the plot or just to allow them to enjoy the popular songs from the film.[33] Later in the year, those songs were the main feature of an *eiga monogatari* (see Niita Chie's discussion in Chapter 3) broadcast on the radio, in which several *benshi* narrated the story of *The Blue Angel* and three other films, and a singer gave a recital of the songs.[34]

30 Ōnishi, 'Eiga shudaika "Gion kouta" kō', p. 158.

31 Minami, 'Rekōdo kaisha to no tai appu senden', pp. 21-22. See also 'Eiga to shohin no teikei senden', p. 10-12.

32 See 'Dai 35-kai kenkyūkai *Nageki no tenshi* no yoru', *Asahi Shimbun*, 6 May 1931, p. 7 and '*Nageki no tenshi* no yoru', *Asahi Shimbun*, 9 May 1931, p. 11.

33 See the programme for the Kobe Shōchikuza, 29 May 1931.

34 'Eiga fuan oatari no kon'ya', p. 5.

As Michael Raine argues in Chapter 5, western talkies, linked technologically and commercially to the modern media of radio and recorded music, threatened to make Japanese cinema seem backward in comparison. However, the exhibition of western films posed many problems, from the practical (how to help audiences understand dialogue in a foreign language?) to the theoretical (what is the proper relation of image and sound?).[35] *Benshi* shouted over the English dialogue or turned down the recorded sound, and some cinemas took to advertising *benshi*-free 'after dinner cinema' – screenings in which one could hear living English unencumbered by interpretation. In other attempts to assist audiences unfamiliar with subtitles, or struggling without them, Paramount even translated the story and key phrases for *Thunderbolt* and *Mysterious Dr. Fu Manchu* and published them as books. However unlikely, local editorials claimed the books sold well as examples of 'real "man" talk' in English.[36] Business suffered from the collision of foreign dialogue and *benshi* explanation, and many cinemas that specialized in western films went back to showing silent classics, cut out dialogue scenes from musical films and showed compilations of the musical numbers, or incorporated live stage shows into the programme.[37]

Critics at the time debated whether the talkies offered an improvement over *benshi* cinema, criticizing talking pictures for losing the aesthetic stylization of the silent film and for destroying cinema's international appeal. Although it was an extreme minority opinion, some even drew on Soviet film theory to criticize Hollywood films' slavish interest in synchronization and looked to the divided channels of *kabuki* narration for inspiration.[38] When translating Hollywood films, they debated the merits of the *benshi* over practices such as side titles (slides projected alongside the screen), X-titles (intertitles cut into a sound film), subtitles, and dubbing.[39] Most of those attempts failed – according to one article, the dubbing of *The Man Who Came Back* was so bad that audiences thought Janet Gaynor and Charles Farrell had dubbed themselves in Japanese – but the successful screening

35 See the discussions in Mori Iwao's regular column 'Kabin to hanataba' in *Kinema shūhō* from early 1931, and the many round-table discussions in *Kinema shūhō*, *Kinema junpō*, and other important film journals.

36 Cited in 'The Talkies, a Medium of English Study', p. 17.

37 See 'Kaku eiga kaisha ga neru seika o mukaete no kisaku' for examples.

38 See the survey of Japanese sound theory in Mori, et. al, 'Nihon tōkī taikan'. The Eisenstein, Pudovkin, and Alexandrov proposal on sound was introduced to Japan in *Kinema junpō* in 1930. Ogino, 'Film Criticism in Japan' also cites a T. Shigeno as proposing that the sound film should be modelled on the divided channels of kabuki in *Kinema junpō* in 1931.

39 These alternatives were widely discussed in January and February of 1931. For example, in Mori Iwao, 'Kabin to hanataba 8', p. 18.

of subtitled prints of *Morocco* in February 1931 settled the practical if not the aesthetic argument.[40] For the rest of the year, audiences could choose whether to watch films such as René Clair's *Sous les toits de Paris/Under the Roofs of Paris* with subtitles or with a *benshi* speaking over and between the French dialogue, but after a series of strikes in 1932 *benshi* were seldom listed in the programmes for cinemas showing western films. Apart from a few experiments with dubbing, films were shown with subtitles (usually scratched onto the right side of the frame) that gave the gist of the scene if not all the dialogue.

Japanese sound films and talkies

The introduction of Hollywood talkies, both sound-on-film and sound-on-disc, in May 1929 galvanized attempts to emulate the new sound film medium in Japan. That was no easy feat for cash-strapped Japanese studios. Talkies increased the cost of production, and that cost could not be amortized across multiple prints and global distribution as it could for Hollywood films. Japanese studios struck less than ten prints of most films and had essentially no export market outside the colonies of Taiwan and Korea and some expatriate communities in Brazil, Hawai'i and the west coast of the USA. The Japanese economy in the late 1920s was already shaky due to a financial crisis in 1927, made worse by fiscal tightening in 1929 and a return to the gold standard in 1930 just as the global depression hit. Agricultural prices fell by almost half, as did wages in the cities and the prices of many other goods.[41] With a fixed exchange rate, Japanese exports were decimated as the whole world was caught in a recessionary vicious circle. The crisis was only relieved by the fiscal expansion caused by Japan's military adventures on the continent and the decision to leave the gold standard at the end of 1931, after which the yen collapsed by 60% against the US dollar.

That reduction in purchasing power slowed the transition to sound even further as the studios could not afford to pay import taxes and the increased cost of foreign technology, reinforcing existing strategies of reverse engineering and import substitution. Stopgaps abounded: for example, cinemas would use turntable systems for silent film exhibition that channelled the

40 See Mimura, 'Western Electric Records "Namiko"', p. 7 for the *Man Who Came Back* anecdote, and Nornes, *Cinema Babel*, especially Chapter 4, for a rich historical and theoretical account of *Morocco* and the introduction of subtitling to Japan.

41 For a lucid survey of this period see Gordon, *A Modern History of Japan* Chapter 11.

sound through the projectors to the cinema speakers, as if the film itself had sound.[42] Minagawa Yoshizō restructured the Mina Talkie company and secured a distribution deal with Nikkatsu, supplying Nikkatsu cinemas with six machines for playback and releasing films starting in late 1929. Minagawa's former employees developed the Vitaphone-like sound-on-disc Eastphone system and the Phonofilm-like sound-on-film Eion system, but both were regarded as low quality and struggled to find commercial acceptance.

Hundreds of different sound playback systems were sold all over the world, including dozens in Japan, but when the patent wars were settled there were few exceptions to the sound recording tripoly of Western Electric, RCA, and Tobis-Klangfilm. The essential technologies for the incorporation of sound and image onto a single filmstrip – ribbon light valves and responsive photoelectric cells, triode (and more) vacuum tube amplification, separate but synchronized film- and sound-recording motors, flywheels to reduce sound flutter, frequency profiles and psychoacoustic research, and so on – were the product of major industrial research programmes that could not be emulated where patents applied. Japanese studios, however, developed two successful sound recording systems: the sound-on-film Tsuchihashi system at Shōchiku in 1931, followed by the sound-on-film system at Photo Chemical Laboratory (P.C.L.) in 1932. Nikkatsu signed a contract to use the P.C.L. system but soon reneged in favour of a Western Electric recording system that the studio used for dubbing films shot silent until it completed the sound stages at the new Nikkatsu Tamagawa studio in 1934.

Even before Nikkatsu and Shōchiku, whose Ōfuna sound studio was completed in 1936, could produce a full slate of talking pictures, they found ways to incorporate sound in their films. Although they made some talkies, Shōchiku also used the Tsuchihashi system to create 'sound versions' (*saundo-ban*) from 1932 – films shot silent and released with music and sound effects but without synchronized dialogue on the soundtrack. Unlike western sound versions, which also combined images with a musical soundtrack and intertitles, Japanese sound versions were almost always accompanied by a *benshi*, either live or recorded on the soundtrack. Even though that combination of music, voice, and occasional sound effects matched the sonic environment of Japanese silent films, the power relation between the music and the *benshi*, and the nature of their mutual performance, shifted with the creation of the sound version. Like the *benshi*, the conductor or bandleader of a live musical performance could respond to the audience, and maintain

42 For descriptions of these systems see the Chapter 5 in this volume.

communication with the *benshi* at the front of the auditorium. Yet the introduction of recorded soundtracks fixed the synchronization of sound and image, and control of the volume generally shifted to the projection booth. Adjusting the soundtrack volume according to the *benshi*'s performance now depended on buttons or telephones linked to the auditorium. *Benshi* did not use microphones so they would have to speak over the music or wait for the pauses that sound versions incorporated into the soundtrack before they could summarize the film's narrative.

From 1932, Shōchiku increased the number of synchronized sound films it produced and Nikkatsu switched from Mina Talkie to P.C.L. and then Western Electric equipment to dub some films that were shot silent. The resulting talkies played in the increasing number of contract cinemas that the studios had wired for sound. Also, the P.C.L. studio, after being spurned by Nikkatsu, produced its own films, the first of which were shown in Shōchiku chain cinemas while later films were released in cinemas run by the Tōhō exhibition company. In 1937, Tōhō would absorb P.C.L. and the smaller J.O. studio to create the vertically integrated Tōhō studio that is still a major presence in Japanese cinema. Johan Nordström traces the development of the sound-on-film P.C.L. system in Chapter 6, arguing that the company's inability to provide Nikkatsu with matching playback systems caused the established studio to renege on their contract, and so forced P.C.L. to enter film production. The history of Japanese sound systems and their relation to western precursors demonstrates the complexity of a technological transition constrained by cultural and economic forces that produced the extended and uneven transition to sound in Japan.

Unevenness in Japanese film culture

Technological catch-up is only one reason for the complexity of this period of Japanese film history, a complexity sometimes obscured by the tendency of national cinema studies to hypostatize Japanese culture as both distinct and unitary. Neither of those assumptions holds in this period: the technology, techniques, personnel, and arguments involved in the transition to sound all crossed national borders, while the exhibition environment of Japanese cinemas was radically uneven. If we track the cultural geography of the sound transition, we can identify multiple forms of unevenness in Japanese cinema – for example, between Japan and the West, city and country, and between audiences for films made by different studios and shown in different cinemas.

For all the cultural permeability of silent cinema there was still a gulf in capital investment between Japanese and western film industries, and the cinema was subject to different cultural pressures in different locations. The *Japanese Cinema Labour Yearbook* in 1933 estimated the capital formation of the Japanese film industry as only 3% of the capitalization of Hollywood studios. Only in 1927 did Japanese audiences watch more Japanese than Western films, by a 7:3 ratio (lower in the more cosmopolitan cities and higher outside), a ratio that did not change despite the troubled introduction of talkies from Europe and America. As part of contemporary capitalist culture, Japanese films had much in common with Hollywood cinema. Even period films (*jidaigeki*) were often modelled on outlaw westerns and experimented with European film styles. Yet as the 1930s wore on there was official pressure to 'nationalize' Japanese popular culture. Records of traditional *nagauta* and military marches sold in large numbers and 'decadent' songs were gradually restricted. Cinemas specializing in Japanese films increasingly showed topical features and documentaries based on Japanese military adventures. Some aspects of the cinema experience converged in the 1930s, reducing the differences between Japan and the West. However, in other ways the experience of the cinema in those different contexts diverged as film programmes, like records and radio programmes, became major vehicles for cultural nationalism in Japan.

In many ways, the unevenness between city and country was more pronounced than the difference between Tokyo and other global cities. Cinemas in the provinces were concentrated in regional cities; smaller locations were serviced by traveling projectionists. Quality was always a problem: if the talkie made silent film seem backward then any sound would do. To save money provincial cinemas used Japanese systems such as Nitta and Rola that, coupled with the lower fidelity of the Japanese recording systems and the much greater wear on each print, often rendered the dialog for Japanese films incomprehensible.[43] After a great deal of industrial unrest, starting with cinemas for western films and shifting from city to country, musicians disappeared from all but the largest cinemas, which used live music and stage shows as an attraction. The *benshi* were relegated from being fixtures at particular cinemas to itinerant and

43 See *Kinema junpō*, 1 January 1935, p. 17 for the claim that Japanese films were incomprehensible on rural projectors. In Mori, et. al., '*Madamu to nyōbō* o meguru', the chief Western Electric engineer in Japan, Kobayashi Kichijirō, claimed that prints sound best after a protective layer has worn off the film, when they have been projected between 22 and 36 times. According to Kobayashi, the prints are designed to be shown 150 times but prints for Japanese films are screened 500 times!

sometimes freelance workers who would follow the dwindling number of silent and sound version films from cinema to cinema. This situation speaks not so much of a reluctant transition to sound as the co-presence of emergent, dominant, and residual aspects to Japanese film exhibition dictated by the specific material conditions of technological change during the depression.[44] If we include non-synchronized recorded sound films along with talkies, and count the number of cinema seats and the size of audiences, not just the number of cinemas and films, by the early 1930s Japanese cinema was already deeply embedded in a culture of the sound image.

Cinemas in the 1930s were organized into chains, with only a small number in the largest cities specializing in western films. The remaining 1,300 or so, rising to about 1,600 by 1936, were evenly split between showing mixed programmes and showing only Japanese films. The larger cinemas were typically directly owned by or affiliated with specific studios. Cinemas that showed western films or first-run Shōchiku and Nikkatsu films typically installed sound projectors made by Western Electric or RCA, sometimes Tobis-Klangfilm, that were connected to sophisticated record playback devices in the projection booth. These cinemas featured the most powerful and highest fidelity sound systems in the country, though these most prestigious and expensive cinemas often also included live stage shows in the programme. Admission prices ranged from 2 yen for the best seats at the prestigious Teikoku Gekijō (Ozu Yasujirō's regular cinema, which showed almost exclusively western films) to less than a tenth of that price in the cheapest cinemas.

In Tokyo in the early 1930s, there was also a dramatic difference in the level of sound integration among cinemas that catered to audiences for western films and films from the four main studios: Shōchiku, Nikkatsu, Shinkō, and Kawai (which became Daito in 1933). Shōchiku, the most economically successful studio, gradually bought up or otherwise controlled those rivals during the 1930s, seeking to create a monopoly until thwarted by Tōhō in 1937. The various studios maintained product differentiation through highly variable production budgets and uneven sonic conditions at their affiliated cinemas. Shinkō and Daito specialized in sword fighting period films (*chanbara*) that were popular with children and working-class audiences. There, the *benshi* still reigned supreme. Even in the late 1930s, audiences in those cinemas could hear '*benshi*

44 Raymond Williams explores the concepts of dominant, emergent, and residual "structures of feeling" in *Marxism and Literature*, pp. 121-135.

sound versions' of films shot silent with a soundtrack of *benshi* backed by recorded music.[45] Some scholars claim that a cultural preference for the *benshi* was an obstacle to synchronized sound cinema in Japan. While it is undeniable that there was an audience for the distinct vocal art of the *benshi*, based on a history of oral storytelling forms, it is also clear that Shōchiku and Nikkatsu, joined by the new studios P.C.L and J.O., which were amalgamated into the Tōhō studio in 1937, were determined to make talking pictures. They also found a receptive audience. By 1932, commentary in trade magazines such as *Kinema shūhō* recognized that even western talkies drew larger audiences than silent films and the studios would have to shift to sound and talkie production if they were not to lose their audience.[46]

Even the date of the 'end' of silent cinema is uneven: for much of the supposedly 'delayed' transition, sound in Japanese cinema was both 'already' and 'not yet'. Some studios made and circulated silent films in Japan even after Ozu Yasujirō, the last major holdout, made his first talkie in 1936. 1936 was also the year that the number of talkies finally exceeded the number of silent films, but if we add the intermediary category of the sound version to the totals then films with recorded soundtracks already constituted a majority of productions by 1935. If we consider not just the number of films but also the size of the audience then 1934 is the first year that sound films exceed silent films from Shōchiku, the best-capitalized studio with the largest chain of contract cinemas and the most popular films. We could even argue that the transitional point is 1933, the last year that a silent film took top spot in the *Kinema junpō* Best Ten poll, and the year that talkies and sound versions produced by the studios were some of the top draws, even though they were still in the minority.[47] The essays in this volume are further evidence for the media historical argument that there is no single dimension by which to measure the 'transition to sound' in Japan. Rather than a miraculous 'advent' the transition to sound was a long-anticipated and seldom-resisted achievement in difficult economic circumstances, a development that was realized at different moments, depending on whether we consider the number of films, the number of people who heard them, or their cultural significance to critics and regular filmgoers.

45 Kitada, 'Tōkī jidai no benshi'.

46 'Kōkyūteki kanosei jūbun naru ka: Nikkatsu no gaiga tōkī joei mondai', p. 5.

47 Chika Kinoshita argues that 1934 was the last year a silent film was ranked top by *Kinema junpō* but that film, Ozu Yasujirō's *Story of Floating Weeds*/*Ukikusa monogatari*, was released as a sound version that played with a recorded soundtrack that competed with the live voice of the *benshi*. See Kinoshita, 'The *Benshi* Track', p. 6.

The historiography of the transition to sound

There is a history to the historiography of Japanese cinema's transition to sound. Japanese writers published an abundance of richly textured material on the technology and aesthetics of talking pictures during the late 1920s and the 1930s.[48] Just as the arrival of electronically recorded sound brought about questions of medium specificity in Western classical film theory, Japanese critics were preoccupied with delineating the difference between the talkie and silent cinema through extended theoretical and critical reflections on film language and *mise-en-scène*. Chika Kinoshita has convincingly argued that the prolonged coexistence of the silent and the talkie in both production and exhibition in Japan, as well as the close personal connections between critics and filmmakers, fostered a 'media-conscious' film culture in the early 1930s:

> First, the media-conscious critics tried to identify the essence of the talkie medium in contrast to the silent medium, as European filmmakers/theorists did. Secondly, however, the media-conscious did not seek to purify each medium, but to create silent films that reflected talkie aesthetics. Most critics and filmmakers were concerned with the talkie's influence on the use of intertitles in relation to the flow of images. Third, the problem of intertitles was reflected back to the question of how to deal with the tangible duration of filmic discourse brought by synchronized sound. In other words, the question of interval and duration (*ma*) occupied a central place.[49]

A network of specialist publications sustained that film culture, which was perhaps the most extensive in the world. Throughout this period, *Kinema junpō* (1919-) was one of the main venues for sustained discourse on the theoretical implications and practical applications of sound film for film as art and industry. *Eiga hyōron* (1926-1975) also printed critical reflections on sound film style, often from an auteurist point of view, whereas industry-oriented trade publications such as *Kokusai eiga shinbun* (1927-1937) and *Kinema shūhō* (1930-1939) frequently featured articles penned by filmmakers, studio representatives, and film technicians. Short-lived journals such as *Eiga kagaku kenkyū* (1928-1932) and *Eiga geijutsu kenkyū* (1933-1935) explored issues relating to film production and film aesthetics, respectively. Film journals

48 See for example the articles collected in Gerow, Iwamoto, and Nornes, *Nihon senzen eiga ronshū*, chapter 6.

49 Kinoshita, *Mise-en-scène of Desire*, p. 243.

specifically dedicated to issues of sound and music, such as *Tōkī ongaku* (1934-1937) and *Eiga to ongaku* (1937-1940), also carried highly theoretical articles on the nature of talkie aesthetics and talkie film production, with close analysis of sound films' constituent parts in relation to film music.

As Johan Nordström has shown, the debates were led by film scholars, critics and theorists such as Iijima Tadashi and Iwasaki Akira; pioneering film-maker, theoretician and prolific writer Kaeriyama Norimasa; scholar and musician Nakane Hiroshi, one of the foremost contemporary writers on the theoretical aspects of sound cinema; and Kakeshita Keikichi, prolific writer on sound cinema and talkie music who spearheaded the journal *Tōkī ongaku* and later became head of the music division at P.C.L.[50] Both Nakane and Kakeshita frequently advanced technologically determinist readings of talkie music's development from the classical accompaniment of silent cinema to the jazz-infused soundtrack of the talkie, remaining sensitive in their analysis of origin and aesthetic application to the specificities of technology and musical development. Many producers and studio representatives also took an active part in these discourses, perhaps none more so than Mori Iwao, arguably one of the most important and influential figures in the history of the Japanese talkie, especially in his role as head producer at P.C.L., later Tōhō. Mori's voluminous writings touch on almost all aspects of the sound transition, from early theoretical considerations on the viability of sound cinema as artistic form, to later discussions on sound cinema's industry-wide implications for film production.

That many Japanese filmmakers, such as Mizoguchi Kenji, Gosho Heinosuke, and Kimura Sotoji, often doubled as critics and theoreticians during the transition to sound indicates that from the time of the Pure Film Movement onwards representatives of the Japanese film industry systematically investigated their medium. Similarly, the regularly-updated corporate histories of production companies such as Shōchiku, Nikkatsu, and Tōhō attest to how the Japanese film industry has continuously documented itself in ways that, for example, Hollywood studios did not. In the context of the sound transition, those studio histories, especially the editions published during the Pre-War era, offer detailed accounts of how each respective studio dealt with the logistic, economic and technological challenges of sound film. These corporate narratives also serve, by omission, to illustrate the studio's frequent self-censorship, or selective memory, when faced with politically sensitive issues such as workers' rights, left-leaning political

50 For a detailed discussion on contemporary discourses concerning Japan's transition to sound, see Norström, 'Chapter 10: Technology', pp. 151-163.

affiliations, and the effects of state censorship. Pertinent historical incongruities surface when comparing these 'official' narratives with postwar interviews and memoirs by producers, directors, actors, scriptwriters and technicians. These first-hand accounts of the industries transition to sound often prove invaluable for a deeper, albeit highly subjective, understanding of the technological and aesthetic transitions within the industry. In the context of the sound transition Mori Iwao's *Watakushi no geikai henreki* and Shōchiku producer Kido Shirō's *Nihon eigaden: Eiga seisakusha no kiroku* are particularly important accounts of the sound transition from the viewpoint of two of the industry's most important producers. Gosho Heinosuke's *Waga seishun: Denki Gosho Heinosuke* and Yamamoto Kajirō's *Katsudōya jitaden: Denki Yamamoto Kajirō* also offer important insights from the point of view of two directors who were instrumental in shaping the Japanese talkie cinema of the 1930s. Likewise, Iwamoto Kenji and Saeki Tomonori's collection of long-form interviews *Kikigaki kinema no seishun* serves as an important resource.

The post-war era saw the publication of several multi-volume Japanese film histories that gave detailed accounts of the Japanese film's development. Tanaka Jun'ichirō's multi-volume *Nihon eiga hattatsushi*, begun before the war as serialized instalments in *Kinema junpō*, was one of the first histories based on documents that the author had collected since his early days as a journalist, supplemented by interviews with contemporary filmmakers and producers. The second volume provides an industry-focused, densely detailed history that firmly establishes the industrial, economic, and personnel-based reasons for the corporate restructurings entailed by the transition to sound. Satō Tadao's more narratively-oriented four volume *Nihon eigashi* shifts the focus to the tone and content of the films that were produced and the people who created them, building on his previous account of the transition to sound era published as the chapter 'Tōkī jidai: Nihon eigashi 3' in the third volume of the important anthology series *Kōza Nihon eiga*. That series is rich with interviews and eyewitness accounts from the rise of the talkies.

Another short but succinct historical account of the transition to sound can be found in *Nihon eigashi: Jissha kara seichō konmei no jidai made*, published by *Kinema junpō* as volume 31 of the *Sekai no eiga sakka* series.[51] As Aaron Gerow and Markus Nornes point out, this volume was groundbreaking in that it was the first Japanese film history compiled by university trained film scholars such as Iwamoto Kenji and Chiba Nobuo.[52] The authors

51 Chiba, *Nihon eigashi*.

52 Abé Mark Nornes and Aaron Gerow, *Research Guide to Japanese Film Studies*, p. 136.

set out to not merely give a descriptive history, but to continuously problematize that history in their analysis of the transition to sound not only within the specificities of the Japanese film industry, but also in relation to issues of colonialism, imperialism and the politics of inter-war Japan.[53]

There is a wealth of historical information drawn from first hand sources and documents in these and other postwar accounts of the sound transition in Japan but, when compared to the richness of the theoretical discussions in the prewar, there is a striking lack of theoretical consideration given to the sound transition. Although many Japanese film historians have given detailed versions of the technological, industrial and artistic shift that occurred during the transition, until recently few have focused on the wider implications of what these changes might entail for the nature of the cinematic apparatus, its social and political implications, and artistic potential. Iwamoto Kenji's work stands out as one of the few exceptions in this context. His sustained interest into the field of sound and the switch from silent to sound has repeatedly gone beyond mere historicism to the intersections between technology, art and industry.

Iwamoto is also editor for the anthology series *Nihon eigashi sōsho*, which across its volumes has included several articles that help inform our understanding of the sound transition. For example, Daibō Masaki's analysis of early Japanese attempts at sound-film synchronization, up until those by Minagawa Yoshizō with the Lee de Forest's sound-on-film technology during the 1920s, calls into question teleological narratives while illuminating the divergent audio-visual experience that these attempts embodied.[54] More recently, Sasagawa Keiko's foray into the intertextual field of musical films and the intersection between popular song and film has boldly staked out new territory for consideration when it comes to re-assessing the historical context of various transmedial forms of cinema. Sasagawa shows how the introduction of radio and the proliferation of phonographic records, together with the further development of the record companies' business model, changed previously established patterns of song consumption. The cinema and sound media industries collaborated more closely, with the *kouta eiga* eventually giving way to the artistic inflections of 'theme song films' (*shudaika eiga*) and 'popular song films' (*kayō eiga*).[55]

In English-language film criticism, occasional articles in contemporary newspapers or film magazines alerted western readers to the importance

53 Chiba, p. 348.

54 Daibō, 'Musei eiga to chikuonki no oto'.

55 Sasagawa, 'Kouta eiga ni kan suru kiso chōsa'.

of the *benshi* to Japanese silent films, but those articles tended to play up the exoticism of the practice and give very little sense of the stakes of the sound transition in Japan.[56] Major critic Iwasaki Akira provided the most reliable account in *Sight and Sound* in 1937, emphasizing the enthusiastic reception of sound films in Japan, which forced Japanese studios to invest in sound production.[57] Japanese cinema was not 'discovered' by western critics until after world war two, and the first silent and sound-transition films shown were early works by auteurs such as Ozu Yasujirō and Mizoguchi Kenji. Those films were almost invariably shown silent or with a simple musical accompaniment. That some of those films were originally released as 'sound versions' with a complicated relation to the *benshi* was not part of the discussion.

Later scholarship in English paid less attention to the technological, architectural, and social aspects of the sound transition, than to the cultural background and aesthetic consequences of the relatively slow transition, and in particular to the fate of the *benshi*. For example, Noel Burch, supported by a renewed attention to the cultural difference of Japanese cinema by Japanese interlocutors such as Iwamoto Kenji, insisted that Japanese culture had never supported the 'ideology of transparent representation' typified by the 'bourgeois' sound cinema. Sound for Burch was an instance of western cinema's original sin of attempting to create seamless 'codes of illusionism'.[58] In his 'hypothetical explanation', directors such as Ozu and Naruse resisted the introduction of sound, taking advantage of the long transition and accepting the interference of the *benshi* as part of a 'unified cultural practice' in which 'the aesthetic values of Japan's past came to be fully reincarnated in cinema'.[59] Although less extreme, Joseph Anderson also focuses on the traditional nature or avant-garde potential of the splitting of sound and image in silent Japanese cinema narrated by the *benshi*.[60]

Film historians have long recognized the inadequacy of Burch's deconstructive account of Japanese cinema. He misunderstands the role of the *benshi* in the 'ideology of transparent representation' of silent Japanese cinema, does not recognize the prevalence of intertitles and visual narration in films of the period, and makes ahistorical claims about the connection

56 See for example Venebles, 'The Cinema in Japan' and Byas, 'From Oriental Screens'. Though see Byas, 'News of Japan's Films' for a more sympathetic account of the tensions raised by the arrival of sound films in Japan.

57 Iwasaki, 'Honourable Movie-Makers'.

58 Burch, *To the Distant Observer*, p. 66.

59 Burch, *To the Distant Observer*, p. 145-150.

60 Anderson, 'Spoken Silents in the Japanese Cinema'.

between contemporary cinema and ancient Japanese aesthetics.[61] Reacting against this version of Japanese film as 'our dream cinema' David Bordwell insisted on the importance of primary research into Japanese film style, industry, and social institutions that gains in explanatory power what it loses in exoticism.[62] Bordwell's auteur monograph on Ozu Yasujirō incorporates one of the best English-language overviews of the transition to sound. More recently, scholars based both inside and outside Japan have contributed to the increasingly dense historiography of the sound transition in English.[63]

The chapters in this volume continue that work, contributing to what Bordwell called for forty years ago: a view of 'film style, the film industry, and the social matrix in one complex whole'.[64] They take a broad view of sound in the cinema, attentive to its limits and unexpected effects. For example, in Chapters 1 and 2 Sasagawa Keiko and Hosokawa Shuhei trace the aesthetic as well as industrial connections between cinema and popular song. In Chapter 3, Niita Chie shows how the ways in which film stories were told on the radio developed audience familiarity with talkies. In Chapter 4, Ueda Manabu explores the spread of a new architecture for the cinema auditorium in reciprocal relation to the development of sound technology. In Chapter 5 Michael Raine traces how the growth of electronically mediated sound in the middle of an economic crisis disrupted the soundscape of the cinema and its labour relations. In Chapter 6 Johan Nordström demonstrates that the new P.C.L. studio drew on the performers and the style of the Asakusa revue for the audio-visual style of its films. Finally, in Chapters 7 and 8 Nagato Yohei and Itakura Fumiaki analyse the effects of sound technology and technique on the visual style of filmmakers sensitive to those changes in the medium. We are honoured to be able to present the work of these established and emerging scholars of Japanese cinema in English, often for the first time.

61 Contrary to Burch's argument in *To the Distant Observer*, p. 80, the number of *benshi* were reduced in later silent films, not increased, and the goal of *benshi* performance was often precisely the kind of illusionism that Burch deprecates. See Fukuchi Gorō. 'Musei no deshi to shite' for an account of elite *benshi* Tokugawa Musei's illusionist ambitions. See also Raine, 'A New Form of Silent Cinema' for an account of Ozu's relation to transitional sound film. Burch's argument for the traditional mode of *benshi* narration as avant-garde was anticipated in English by Koch, 'Japanese Cinema', p. 296.

62 Bordwell, 'Our Dream Cinema'.

63 Bordwell, *Ozu and the Poetics of Cinema*. For an excellent overview of the current state of research see Gerow, 'Japanese film and television'. Specialized monographs in English that deal in whole or in part with the sound transition in Japan include Dym, *Benshi*; Fujiki, *Making Personas*; Kinoshita, *Mise-en-scène of Desire*; and Nornes, *Cinema Babel*.

64 Bordwell, 'Our Dream Cinema', p. 58.

In Chapter 1 Sasagawa Keiko reviews the sonic conditions of early cinema screenings, in particular the changing relation between cinema and popular ballads (*kouta*) before the production of Japanese sound films. Film followed the song when the *kouta* first appeared, around the time of the Great Kanto Earthquake in 1923. The songs were released as sheet music and phonograph records, played in cafes and advertised in magazines. Film studios would then release silent romantic melodramas titled after the most popular songs, in which the *benshi* was partially displaced by records that played over scenes superimposed with the song lyrics. With the boom in production and the fall in prices of records at the end of the 1920s, *kouta* films that showcased songs with more western rhythms and scales became even more prominent. Sasagawa interprets this as a response by the film industry to the threat of western musical talkies, showing how the bonds between the film and record industries grew closer as the exploitation cycle for popular music tightened. She argues that those tie-ups prepared the way for the more reciprocal relation between cinema and popular music in the creation of theme songs (*shudaika*) that became ubiquitous in Japanese cinema, along with the new sound genre of the popular song film (*kayō eiga*).

In Chapter 2 Hosokawa Shuhei outlines a history of Japanese popular song and its 'one-way' relationship with cinema to show how the former geisha Katsutarō was produced as a new musical celebrity and then incorporated into *Shima no musume/The Island Girl* and *Tokyo ondo*, two Shōchiku sound films made in 1933, and *Sakura ondo*, made at P.C.L. in 1934. Hosokawa demonstrates the multivalent relationships between sound and image in early Japanese sound films by identifying three different modes to the integration into the diegesis of Katsutarō's title song for each film. In the first film, it serves as a kind of commentary on the feelings of the characters, more aligned with the narrative than the typical *kouta* film. In the second film, Katsutarō's hugely popular song colours and thereby links scenes with a similar emotional valence. In the third film, Katsutarō appears only at the beginning, inoculating Kimura Sotoji's dark melodrama against censorship with an upbeat and pro-military title song.

Turning from records to the radio, in Chapter 3 Niita Chie shows how *eiga monogatari* (film stories), narrated by *benshi* on the radio, advertised films and produced intermedia entertainment for their listeners. In the early 1930s, *eiga monogatari* were displaced by *eigageki* (film dramas) that featured the voices of actors who could not yet be heard in the cinema. Niita's exploration of different radio genres shows how the medium was linked to cinema as part of the culture of the sound image. She argues that *eigageki* prepared the audience for synchronized Japanese talkies, even as the genre dissolved into radio dramas featuring film actors after the transition to sound.

In Chapter 4 Ueda Manabu shows how cinema architecture responded to the demands and affordances of the film medium during the silent period and the transition to sound. It traces a series of developments in the orientation, size, and distribution of cinemas in Japan and argues that they contributed to the tendency toward a unified and synchronized presentation of films in the 1920s and 1930s. Purpose-built cinemas changed their layout from the wide and shallow theatre format to box-like spaces oriented around a long axis that focused audience attention on the screen. With the introduction of amplification and recorded sound, cinemas also increased in size and spread around the country, enabling a standardized cinema experience through the creation of uniform seating and the production of sound films.

In Chapter 5 Michael Raine traces the growth of electronically mediated sound in the middle of an economic crisis that disrupted the soundscape of the cinema and its labour relations. Even before Japanese studios were equipped for talkie production, cinemas showing Japanese films displaced the musicians with recorded sound and 'sound versions'. The introduction of talkies also displaced the musicians and then the *benshi* from cinemas showing western films. That development also threatened the *benshi*, who had been the main attraction of Japanese film exhibition. They became the central figures in the industrial actions that were billed as a struggle against machine civilization, a struggle that played out in the cinemas and in journalism against a wider background of economic and political instability in 1930s Japan.

In Chapter 6 Johan Nordström traces the development of P.C.L. as a new sound studio that employed progressive filmmakers, some with experience in Hollywood, and a more rationalized set of production practices than the established studios. The studio specialized in light musical comedies that combined influences from Hollywood musical films and local live entertainments, in particular the revue form known as Asakusa opera. Nordström shows that the early P.C.L. films featuring the performer Enomoto Ken'ichi emulated the comic interactivity of the stage shows for which the star was famous, distancing the films from their Hollywood intertexts and testing the illusionism of standard forms of film narration.

In Chapter 7 Nagato Yohei questions the historical judgment that *Madamu to nyōbō/The Neighbour's Wife and Mine*, made with the Tsuchihashi

Shōchikuphone system and released in 1931, was the first commercially and aesthetically successful sound film in Japan. He shows that *Furuoato/Hometown*, a part-talkie made with the Mina Talkie system and directed by Mizoguchi Kenji for Nikkatsu, played for weeks in major cinemas in 1930 and was widely praised by film critics. Nagato explores the subtle sound design of the film and discovers a concept of 'counterpoint' and a technique of 'cutaway within the shot' that anticipates Mizoguchi's intense 'one scene, one shot' long take style in his later films, in which the moving camera articulates an undivided *mise-en-scène*.

Finally, in Chapter 8 Itakura Fumiaki approaches the transition to sound from the perspective of its material substrate. He shows that many Japanese films in the transitional period used the 'early talkie frame', in which the soundtrack was added to 35mm silent film without modifying the top and bottom of the frame. Drawing on the importance of a concept of 'authenticity' in archival studies and on his experience at the National Film Archive of Japan, Itakura argues that many well-known films, including Japanese films, cannot now be seen in the correct aspect ratio without access to archival sources. The narrowed horizontal dimension changed the aspect ratio of the image, which prompted some filmmakers to reflect on their film style. Through a close analysis of the original negatives Itakura shows that Ozu Yasujirō's use of the early sound aspect ratio coincided with his increased interest in visual composition, in particular with arranging objects along the bottom frame line, a development that has gone unrecognized because of the faulty reprinting of the original films.

The editors would like to acknowledge these authors, not only for their contribution to the field and to this volume but as mentors and colleagues who have sustained us throughout the long gestation of this project. We would also like to thank the many, many others who have helped us in our research, and to bring this project to completion. No acknowledgment could express in full the debt we owe them as teachers, advisers, interlocutors, and supporters of our research, so we can only list them here: Rick Altman, Daibō Masaki, Roland Domenig, Alexander Jacoby, Kamiya Makiko, Kimata Kimihiko, Chika Kinoshita, Komatsu Hiroshi, Kondo Kazuto, James Lastra, Makino Mamoru, Matsuzaki Masataka, Mark Nornes, Charles O'Brien, Okada Hidenori, Tochigi Akira, Yamanashi Makiko, Yamada Chika, Kerim Yasar, and Yasui Yoshio.

Note on names and transliteration: Japanese names in this volume are given in Japanese name order (family name first), unless the author publishes regularly in English in western name order. Macrons are used to indicate long vowels in all Japanese words, including personal, company, era, and place names, except for words commonly used in English, such as Tokyo,

Osaka, Kyoto, and Hyogo. Film titles in each chapter are introduced with the Japanese title followed by the common English title, and are thereafter mentioned by the English title. Japanese words used in the text, such as *benshi* and *eigagaku*, are italicized unless they are commonly used in English. Japanese book titles and names of institutions are not translated, unless relevant to the argument of the essay.

Bibliography

Abé Mark Nornes and Aaron Gerow. *Research Guide to Japanese Film Studies* (University of Michigan Press, 2016).

J. L. Anderson. 'Spoken Silents in the Japanese Cinema; or, Talking to Pictures: Essaying the *Katsuben*, Contexturalizing the Texts'. In *Reframing Japanese Cinema: Authorship Genre, History*, edited by Arthur Nolletti, Jr. and David Desser (Bloomington: Indiana University Press, 1992), pp. 259-311.

Taylor Atkins. *Blue Nippon: Authenticating Jazz in Japan* (Durham: Duke University Press, 2001).

Weihong Bao. *Fiery Cinema: The Emergence of an Affective Medium in China, 1915–1945* (Minneapolis: University of Minnesota Press, 2015).

Carolyn Birdsall. *Nazi Soundscapes: Sound, Technology, and Urban Space in Germany, 1933-1945* (Amsterdam: Amsterdam University Press, 2012).

David Bordwell. 'Our Dream Cinema: Western Historiography and the Japanese Film'. *Film Reader* 4 (Chicago: Northwestern University Press, 1979), pp. 45-62.

David Bordwell. *Ozu and the Poetics of Cinema* (London: BFI, 1988).

Noël Burch. *To the Distant Observer: Form and Meaning in the Japanese cinema* (Berkeley and Los Angeles: University of California Press, 1979).

Hugh Byas. 'News of Japan's Films'. *New York Times* 3 July 1932, p. X2.

Hugh Byas. 'From Oriental Screens'. *New York Times* 2 July 1933, p. X2.

'Chihōga'. *Asahi Shimbun* 5 March 1926, p. 6.

'Dai 35-kai kenkyūkai *Nageki no tenshi* no yoru'. *Asahi Shimbun*, 6 May 1931, p. 7.

Daibō Masaki. 'Musei eiga to chikuonki no oto'. In *Nihon eiga no sōsho 15: Nihon eiga no tanjō* (Tokyo: Shinwasha, 2011), pp. 329-366.

Jeffrey A. Dym. *Benshi, Japanese Silent Film Narrators, and Their Forgotten Narrative Art of Setsumei: A History of Japanese Silent Film Narration* (Lewiston, N.Y.: Edwin Mellen Press, 2003).

'Eiga fuan oatari no kon'ya: rebyū-shiki ni hōsō sareru ninki eiga yonhen'. *Asahi Shimbun*, 8 July 1931, p. 5.

'Eiga to shohin no teikei senden: tai appu shushusō'. *Kinema shūhō* 64 (5 June 1931), p. 10-12.

Thomas Elsaesser. 'The New Film History as Media Archeology'. *Cinémas: revue d'études cinématographiques/Cinémas: Journal of Film Studies* 14.2-3 (2004).

Thomas Elsaesser. 'Discipline Through Diegesis: The Rube Film Between "Attractions" and "Narrative Integration"'. In *The Cinema of Attractions Reloaded*, Wanda Steuven, ed., (Amsterdam: Amsterdam University Press, 2006).

Michel Foucault. *Power/Knowledge: Selected Interviews and Other Writings, 1972-1977* (New York: Pantheon, 1980).

Hideaki Fujiki. '*Benshi* as Stars: The Irony of the Popularity and Respectability of Voice Performers in Japanese Cinema'. *Cinema Journal* 45.2 (2006), pp. 68-84.

Hideaki Fujiki. *Making Personas: Transnational Film Stardom in Modern Japan* (Cambridge, MA: Harvard University Asia Center, 2013).

Aaron Gerow, Iwamoto Kenji, and Mark Nornes. *Nihon senzen eiga ronshū: Eiga riron no saihakken* (Tokyo: Yumani Shobō, 2018).

Aaron Gerow. 'Japanese Film and Television'. In *Routledge Handbook of Japanese Culture and Society* (London: Routledge, 2011), pp. 213-225.

Fukuchi Gorō. 'Musei no deshi to shite'. In *Kōza Nihon eiga* v. 1, Imamura Shōhei et. al., eds., (Tokyo: Iwanami Shoten, 1985).

Andrew Gordon. *A Modern History of Japan: From Tokugawa Times to the Present, 4th Edition* (Oxford: Oxford University Press, 2019).

Gosho Heinosuke. *Waga seishun: Denki Gosho Heinosuke* (Tokyo: Ōzorasha, 1998).

Harry Harootunian. *Overcome by Modernity: History, Culture, and Community in Interwar Japan* (Princeton, Princeton University Press, 2002).

Hikari Hori. *Promiscuous Media: Film and Visual Culture in Imperial Japan, 1926-1945* (Ithaca: Cornell University Press, 2018).

Hosokawa Shuhei. 'Sketches of Silent Film Sound in Japan: Theatrical Functions of Ballyhoo, Orchestras and Kabuki Ensembles'. In *The Oxford Handbook of Japanese Cinema* (Oxford: Oxford UP, 2014), pp. 288-305.

Errki Huhtamo and Jussi Parikka (eds.). *Media Archaeology: Approaches, Applications, and Implications* (University of California Press, 2011).

Imamura Shōhei, et. al. (eds.). *Kōza Nihon eiga* (8 volumes) (Tokyo: Iwanami Shoten, 1985-1986)

Marilyn Ivy. *Discourses of the Vanishing: Modernity, Phantasm, Japan* (Chicago: University of Chicago Press, 1995).

Iwamoto Kenji and Saeki Tomonori. *Kikigaki kinema no seishun* (Tokyo: Riburo Pōto, 1988).

Iwamoto Kenji, et al. (eds.). *Nihon eigashi sōsho* (Tokyo: Shinwasha, 2004-).

Iwasaki Akira. 'Honourable Movie-Makers'. *Sight and Sound* 6.24 (1937-1938), pp. 194-197.

'Kaku eiga kaisha ga neru seika o mukaete no kisaku'. *Kinema shūhō*, 23 (25 July 1930), p. 7.

Kido Shirō. *Nihon eigaden: Eiga seisakusha no kiroku* (Tokyo, Bungei shunjū shinsha, 1956)

Chika Kinoshita. *Mise-en-scène of Desire: The Films of Mizoguchi Kenji* (PhD Diss. University of Chicago, 2007).

Chika Kinoshita. 'The Benshi Track: Mizoguchi Kenji's *The Downfall of Osen* and the Sound Transition'. *Cinema Journal* 50.3 (2011), pp. 1-25.

Chika Kinoshita. 'The Edge of Montage: A Case of Modernism in Japanese Cinema'. In *The Oxford Handbook of Japanese Cinema* (Oxford: Oxford UP, 2014), pp. 124-146.

Kitada Rie. 'Tōkī jidai no benshi: gaikoku eiga no Nihongo jimaku arui wa "Nihon-ban" seisei o meguru kōsatsu'. *Eiga kenkyū* 4 (2009), pp. 4-21.

Kitahara Michio. 'Kayokyoku: An Example of Syncretism Involving Scale and Mode'. *Ethnomusicology* 10.3 (1966), pp. 271-284.

Carl Koch. 'Japanese Cinema'. *Close Up* 8.4 (December 1931).

Kokusai eiga nenkan Shōwa 9 nen ban (Tokyo: Kokusai Eiga Tsūshinsha, 1934).

'Kōkyūteki kanosei jūbun naru ka: Nikkatsu no gaiga tōkī jōei mondai: Chūmoku subeki Shōchiku/SP no tōsaku to Kido-shi no hōkō 1'. *Kinema shūhō* 129 (14 October 1932), p. 5.

Komatsu Hiroshi. 'The Foundation of Modernism: Japanese Cinema in the Year 1927'. In *Film History* 17.2/3 (2005), pp. 363-375.

Kurata Yoshihiro. *Nihon rekōdo bunkashi.* (Tokyo: Tōkyō Shobō, 1992).

James Lastra. *Sound Technology and the American Cinema: Perception, Representation, Modernity* (New York: Columbia University Press, 2000).

Christian Metz. *Language and Cinema* (The Hague: Mouton, 1974).

Jamie Miller. 'Soviet Cinema 1929-41: The Development of Industry and Infrastructure'. *Europe-Asia Studies* 58.1 (2006), pp. 103-124.

Harry A. Mimura. 'Western Electric Records "Namiko"'. *International Photographer*, August 1932, p. 7.

Minamida Masatoshi. 'Rekōdo kaisha to no tai appu senden *Nageki no tenshi* Tokyo fūkiri no mae'. *Kinema junpō* 402 (1 June 1931), p. 21.

Mitsui Tōru. 'Interactions of Imported and Indigenous Musics in Japan: A Historical Overview of the Music Industry'. In *Whose Master's Voice? The Development of Popular Music in Thirteen Cultures*, edited by Alison J. Ewbank and Fouli T. Papageorgiou (Westport, CT: Greenwood, 1997), pp. 152-174.

Mitsui Tōru. '"Sing Me a Song of Araby" and "My Blue Heaven": "New Folksong," Hybridization and the Expansion of the Japanese Recording Industry in the Late 1920s'. *Popular Music History* 1.1 (2004), pp. 65-82.

Mori Iwao. 'Kabin to hanataba 8'. *Kinema shūhō* 50 (27 February 1931), p. 18.

Mori Iwao, et. al. '*Madamu to nyōbō* o meguru Nihon tōkī zadankai'. *Kinema shūhō* 73 (7 August 1931), pp. 8-10.

Mori Iwao, et. al. 'Nihon tōkī taikan'. *Kinema shūhō* 104 (1 April 1932), pp. 12-30.

Mori Iwao. *Watakushi no geikai henreki* (Tokyo, Seiabō, 1975).

Hiromu Nagahara. *Tokyo Boogie-Woogie: Japan's Pop Era and Its Discontents* (Cambridge, MA: Harvard University Press, 2017).
Nihon eiga rōdō nenpō (Tokyo: Rōdō keizai chōsajo, 1933).
Nihon eigashi: Jissha kara seichō konmei no jidai made (Tokyo: Kinema Junpōsha, 1976).
'Nihon no eigakai wa sekai dai yon'. *Kinema shūhō* 11 (25 April 1930), p. 16.
Johan Norström. 'Chapter 10: Technology – Sound and Intermediality in 1930s Japanese Cinema'. In *The Japanese Cinema Book*, edited by Hideaki Fujiki and Alastair Phillips. (London: British Film Institute, 2020), pp. 151-163.
Mark Nornes. *Cinema Babel: Translating Global Cinema* (Minneapolis: University of Minnesota Press, 2007).
Charles O'Brien. *Cinema's Conversion to Sound: Technology and Film Style in France and the U.S.* (Bloomington: Indiana University Press, 2005).
Ogino Yasushi. 'Film Criticism in Japan'. *Close Up* 9.2 (June 1932), pp.107-114.
Ōnishi Hidenori. 'Eiga shudaika "Gion kouta" kō'. *Āto risāchi kiyō* 3 (2003), pp. 157-164.
Michael Raine. 'A New Form of Silent Cinema: Intertitles and Interlocution in Ozu Yasujiro's Late Silent Films'. In *Reorienting Ozu: A Master and His Influence* (Oxford: Oxford UP, 2018), pp. 101-117.
Jane M. J. Robbins. *Tokyo Calling: Japanese Overseas Radio Broadcasting 1937-1945* (European Press Academic Publishing, 2001).
M. Ruot. 'The Motion Picture Industry in Japan'. *Journal of the Society of Motion Picture Engineers*, 18.5 (May 1932).
Sasagawa Keiko, 'Kouta eiga ni kan suru kiso chōsa: Meiji makki kara shōwa shoki o chūshin ni'. *Engeki kenkyū sentā kiyō* 1 (2003), pp. 175-96.
Satō Tadao. *Nihon eigashi* (Tokyo, Iwanami Shoten, 1995).
Miriam Silverberg. 'Constructing the Japanese Ethnography of Modernity'. *Journal of Asian Studies* 51.1 (1992).
Miriam Silverberg. 'Remembering Pearl Harbor, Forgetting Charlie Chaplin, and the Case of the Disappearing Western Woman: A Picture Story'. *Positions* 1.1 (1993).
Miriam Silverberg. *Erotic Grotesque Nonsense: The Mass Culture of Japanese Modern Times* (University of California Press, 2009).
Takeyama Akiko. *Rajio no jidai: rajio wa chanoma no shuyaku datta* (Kyoto: Sekai Shisō-sha, 2002).
'The Talkies, a Medium of English Study'. *Paramount Around the World*, December 1929, p. 17.
Tanaka Jun'ichirō. 'Nihon ni okeru tōkī jigyō hatten no rekishi'. *Kinema shūhō* 104 (1 April 1932), pp. 16-18.
Tanaka Jun'ichirō. *Nihon eiga hattatsushi* Vols. 1-3 (Tokyo, Chūōkōronsha, 1957).
Tsuchihashi Takeo. 'Eiga ga koe o hasshita toki (Tsuchihashi Takeo)'. In *Kikigaki Kinema no seishun*, edited by Iwamoto Kenji and Saiki Tomonori (Tokyo: Riburopoto, 1988), pp. 286-316.

E. K. Venables. 'The Cinema in Japan: A Visit to the Pictures in the Far East'. *Sight and Sound* 2.7 (1933), pp. 87-88.

Raymond Williams. *Marxism and Literature* (Oxford: Oxford University Press, 1977).

Steve J. Wurtzler. *Electric Sounds: Technological Change and the Rise of Corporate Mass Media* (New York: Columbia UP, 2008).

Yamamoto Kajirō. *Katsudōya jitaden: Denki Yamamoto Kajirō* (Tokyo, Ōzorasha, 1998).

1 A Genealogy of *Kouta eiga*

Silent Moving Pictures with Sound

Sasagawa Keiko

Abstract

This chapter reviews the sonic conditions of early cinema screenings, in particular the changing relation between cinema and popular ballads (*kouta*) before the production of Japanese sound films. With the boom in record production and the fall in prices at the end of the 1920s, *kouta* films began drawing on songs with more western rhythms and scales. This response to the threat of western musical talkies shows the growing connection between the film and record industries as the exploitation cycle for popular music tightened. That process prepared the way for a more reciprocal relation between cinema and popular music in the creation of theme songs (*shudaika*) that became ubiquitous in Japanese cinema, along with the new sound genre of the popular song film (*kayō eiga*).

Keywords: film musicals, cinema and popular music, popular song films, theme songs, *shudaika*, *rensageki*, *kayō eiga*, *kouta eiga*

Kouta eiga (ballad films) was a genre of silent films that were inspired by and dramatized popular songs (*kouta*). The films were screened accompanied by songs at specific moments, played from phonograph records or performed by singers, or even by *benshi* in some cinemas, with the lyrics inserted as intertitles or superimposed against a background of people and landscapes. The *kouta* films were cooperative productions between the film and music industries. Even before the production of the actual film, *kouta* were marketed in the form of scoresheets and phonograph records, introduced in magazines and advertisements, and played at cafes and other stores to attract customers. The *kouta* films in turn were promoted through picture postcards with song lyrics, scoresheets for *kouta*, songbooks, phonograph records and other media.

Raine, M. and J. Nordström (eds.), *The Culture of the Sound Image in Prewar Japan*.
Taylor & Francis Group 2020
DOI: 10.5117/9789089647733_CH01

Mainstream Japanese historians have long held *kouta* films in low esteem. In Tanaka Jun'ichiro's *Nihon eiga hattatsushi*, for example, *kouta* films were mentioned but dismissed just as 'a makeshift *shinpa* style romance shot in four and a half days mainly on location' and 'one of the many attractions made to appeal to the masses'.[1] Other contemporary critics, such as Iijima Tadashi and Iwasaki Akira, merely observed that *kouta* films 'had the elegiac and nihilistic sentimentalism to appeal to people who were in despair after the Great Kanto Earthquake', that they 'attracted people by popular songs', not by their plots, or just that they 'represented the helpless mood of the times'.[2] Fujita Motohiko went so far as to say they were outright money-making schemes that began with *Kago no Tori/The Caged Bird* (Eiichi Matsumoto, 1924), were all similar, and destined to fall into oblivion soon. He concluded that they constituted an 'unfortunate phase in the irreparable degeneration of Japanese cinema'.[3] In short, those critics viewed *kouta* films as a temporary phenomenon arising after the great earthquake.

Although *kouta* films were 'commercial' and tried to boost their box office value by utilizing non-film media, the history of the *kouta* films is longer than those critics recognized, and connects to an even more extensive history of sound in Japanese cinema. The scorn directed at *kouta* films demonstrates that film was understood as a visual medium – after the introduction of the 'talkie', *kouta* films were called 'silent', though they were never silent, and were passed over in favour of synchronized recorded sound films produced in Japan and abroad. Approaching them from the standpoint of music history, Hosokawa Shuhei defined *kouta* films as 'a transitional form from silent films to talkies', and 'a rather unusual genre or form of screening silent films accompanied by songs'. He pointed out how deeply *kouta* films were embedded in popular songs among the masses, the spread of phonographs, and foreign owned major record labels.[4] We say that the soundscape of Japanese cinema changed with cinema's turn to sound. However, at what point and in what way did its sound conventions change? We must revisit the *kouta* film's multiplicity of forms that have

1 Tanaka, *Nihon Eiga hattatsushi* Vol. 2, pp. 20-21. Although *shinpa* ('new school') dramas were regarded as progressive in the nineteenth century, by the 1920s they were regarded as old-fashioned and melodramatic.

2 The Great Kanto earthquake struck the Kanto region on 1 September 1923. About 140,000 people died or went missing in the earthquake and subsequent firestorm, and 370,000 houses were damaged or destroyed. It was the largest and most destructive earthquake in Japanese history. See Iijima, *Nihon eigashi* Vol. 1, pp. 57-67. Iwasaki, *Nihon gendaishi taikei: eigashi*, pp. 41-43.

3 Fujita, *Gendai eiga no kiten*, p. 22.

4 Hosokawa, 'Kouta eiga no bunkashi', pp. 12-15.

until now been dismissed by Japanese film histories in order to clarify the genealogy of Japanese cinema's relation to sound and the way screening locations became connected to sounds otherwise mostly present in small theatres that presented live performances.

In sum, the purpose of this chapter is to give a fresh view of the historical process in which *kouta* films were created and that changed the relationship between sounds and moving pictures. *Kouta* films were not a temporary phenomenon that appeared and disappeared abruptly in the early 1920s, as has often been suggested, but a development of the ongoing relationship between sounds and moving pictures in the context of changes in the environment surrounding the films.

Sound and Image before the *Kouta* Film

Various forms of sound were used to accompany soundless films after cinema came to Japan in 1896. In Tokyo in 1897, the Hiromeya, an advertising company, provided a band with western instruments for a film screening in the Kinkikan.[5] In June 1899 at the Kabukiza, a screening of Japanese films such as *Tsuru kame/Crane and Turtle* (c.1899) was accompanied by popular songs from the late Edo Period (1603-1868). Likewise, in 1901 at the Kairyōza, films of geisha performances were accompanied by musical instruments such as shamisen, *taiko* (Japanese style drum), and *fue* (Japanese style flute), performed out of sight of the audience. Also, comedy films were accompanied with *atarigane* (traditional drums and gongs), *zokuyō* (a type of Edo period song) and dialog delivered by the *benshi* in synchronization with the movements of the actors.[6] These examples show that in the early period films were accompanied by sound according to the conventional rules of theatrical and popular entertainment at kabuki theatres, variety houses, and other theatrical spaces.

Experiments with Sound in the early Movie Theatre

Films were first screened for the most part in playhouses, theatres, and variety halls, which mainly staged *gidayū-bushi* (a type of narration, very popular from the Edo period to the Meiji era), *rakugo*, short dramas, dances,

5 Yoshiyama, *Nihon eigakai jibutsu kigen*, pp. 86-88.
6 Yoshiyama, 'Shoki no Nihon eiga (1)', p. 129.

and other live performances to general audiences. It was in 1907 that dedicated theatres for films started to spread. Increased competition led to sound being utilized in various ways to draw audiences to the films. Theatrical managers began to have *gidayū-bushi* or *naniwabushi* recited beside the screen, lines read by a number of *benshi*, or onstage performances between film showings. One example was the girls' kabuki version of *Sogakyōdai kariba no akebono/The Soga Brothers on the Hunting Ground at Dawn* (1908), featuring Nakamura Kasen, a 'pioneer who turned into a screen actress' from a female performer on stage.[7] This film was shown with live music and dialog read behind the screen by Hanai Hideo and other *benshi* who also appeared in the film.[8]

At other cinemas the *degatari* style of exhibition – the storyteller narrating not behind, but at the side of the screen, in sight of the audience, as in *ningyō jōruri* (puppet theatre) – was very popular. According to Yoshiyama Kyokō, on the Emperor's Birthday in November 1909, the Taishōkan screened *Sendaihagi* in the *degatari* style by a female *gidayū* performer 18 times, until she allegedly 'coughed up blood and collapsed', suggesting that human performers were treated like phonograph records.[9] Films imported into Japan were made popular by connecting them with sounds according to the taste of the Japanese masses.

Stage Performances with Moving Pictures – Theatre as a Site for Media Mix

From the end of the Meiji era to the early period of the Taishō era, in the urban entertainment districts there were various playhouses for *naniwabushi*, female *gidayū,* monkey performances, water juggleries by female divers, magic tricks, circuses and other shows. Imported films were added to the repertoire offered at such playhouses and created new forms of amalgamated performance. Among them, *jitsubutsu ōyo katsudō shashin* (using a film image in place of a theatrical backdrop) was particularly remarkable. The Operakan, a *shinpa* theatre, started performances in June 1909 that mixed theatre performance and film projection. It became more popular than any other theatre. This form of performance was introduced to Osaka, where it changed into the *rensageki,* which was later

7 Yoshiyama, 'Nakamura kasen jō', p. 62.
8 Hanai, 'Yo ga satsuei tōji no shinpageki ', p. 154. Yoshiyama, 'Nakamura kasen jō', p. 62.
9 Yoshiyama, *Nihon eigashi nenpyō*, p. 131.

reintroduced into Tokyo. When Tenkatsu, a film company, produced a *rensageki* with Nakano Nobuchika and Shibata Zentarō in Mikuniza in Asakusa, it created a sensation. After that, many other theatres staged *rensageki*.[10] The main difference between *jitsubutsu ōyo katsudō shashin* and *rensageki* was that the former used a film as background during the stage performance and the latter alternated the film screening and stage performance. Each medium, stage and screen, was chosen for its specific expressive ability to strengthen a scene. For example, when the scene called for the eloquent expression of emotion, it was performed on the stage and when scenes could not be enacted effectively on the stage, such as outdoor scenes and chase scenes, they were shown on the screen with sound provided by *benshi* or musical instruments.

Rensageki, called 'a half Japanese and half western cheap box lunch', was a play, but put on like a film in that admission fees were low, the audience were guided to their seats by female ushers and allowed to keep their shoes on inside the theatre. Also, set changes on the stage took place while a film was shown on the screen, which made it possible to tell the whole story in a shorter time than in a regular play. So *rensageki* could be understood as a new form of drama, a modernized and accelerated version of the conventional drama in the theatre, shown on the stage/screen, accompanied by musical instruments, with exciting parts extracted from often lengthy dramas of *shinpageki* or *kyūgeki*, and chained together (*rensa*). Such a hybrid style of showing peaked in 1917 and 1918 and faded away, but this style of narrating lyrical stories against beautiful landscapes of nature and giving poetic effects with sounds is what led to *kouta* films.

Phonograph based Sound Film Companies – Longing for Sound Synchronization

In their early period, films frequently used phonograph records, played on unamplified mechanical playback systems. In the spring of 1908, an '*ōgoe hatsuonki*', i.e. 'loud sound generator', was played behind the screen when *Sanjyamatsuri no tekomai/Steeplejack at the Annual Shrine Festival* (c.1908) was put on at the Denkikan in Asakusa.[11] In September 1909, the Yoshizawa Shōten film studio tried to take advantage of the popularity of Toyotake Roshō, a female *gidayū* performer, by asking the Sankodō record company

10 Shinoyama, 'Rensageki wa horobiyo', pp. 72-75.

11 Fumikura, *Tokyo ni okeru katsudō shashin*, p. 30.

of Ginza to produce a phonograph record of Roshō, then screening a film of her performing to the record.[12]

Several phonograph-based sound film companies were established in 1913. This showed not only that the exhibition of sound films was considered to be a form of entertainment worth investment, but also that there was a strong demand for 'synchronization' between films and sounds. The first company of this kind was Yamato Ōnei, which was established in 1913. Yamato Ōnei was engaged in manufacturing and selling phonographs, scores for phonograph records, and moving pictures, including the 'Naramaru type'. The Naramaru type moving pictures referred to the screening of films of Yoshida Naramaru chanting *naniwabushi*, while playing a phonograph record of *naniwabushi* performed by Narakatsu, an apprentice of Naramaru. Allegedly, however, sometimes phonograph records were not used in the theatre. The memoirs of Tokugawa Musei vividly showed how films were presented at the Shinjukuza in 1914:

> At the beginning, the screen is hidden by a curtain. It is raised. Naramaru appears and bows composedly to the audience. Then a shamisen starts playing 'tweng tweng' and then 'In the middle of March/From the skies of the city of seven-, eight- and nine-fold flowers, the imperial messenger arrives in the eastern provinces,' he chirps. In those days, there were no such things as vitaphones or talkies. At the side of the screen, the song was rendered by a close-cropped, 17- or 18-year-old *tayū*, or narrator, in a guttural drone. I was impressed by the synchronization. When the overture of the song ended, the drama started. The drama went exactly according to the *naniwabushi* by Naramaru, so the close-cropped narrator kept intoning from the beginning to the end.[13]

Contemporary audiences were fascinated by characters on screen speaking in others' voices, whether recorded or live, and it was only after the introduction of sound films that people gradually come to think it 'aesthetically' natural that characters on the screen should speak in their own voice or what seemed to be their own voice.

Around the same time, Nihon Kinetophon was established. The company had the exclusive right to import Edison's Kinetophone, employing Okabe Yoshirō, who had worked at the Edison Institute and Kaeriyama Norimasa, who later argued strongly for the abolition of *kowairo narimono* (mimic

12 Tanaka, *Nihon eiga hattatsushi* Vol. 1, p. 107.

13 Tokugawa, *Musei handaiki*, p. 189.

voiceover and music played at the side of the stage). In November 1913, a preview was held at the Kagetsu cinema and in December *Faust* and other foreign opera films were screened at the luxurious western-style Teikoku Gekijō and Yurakuza. Readers of *Kinema rekōdo* admired Kinetophon, saying 'it was natural, inspiring, high quality, and superb, both for drama and opera, much better than a *benshi*'s description'.[14] After that, the Asakusa Nihonza became a film theatre attached to Nihon Kinetophon.

The most successful Japanese Kinetophone was a recording of Matsui Sumako singing 'Katyusha's Song' from Tolstoy's *Resurrection*. Wearing a Russian apron and a ribbon, Matsui entered into a prison workshop with a bouquet under her right arm, sat in an armchair, and sang five melodies for about three minutes. However, the popularity of this attraction did not last. Along with Yamato Ōnei, however, Nihon Kinetophon's box office take declined in the spring of 1915, and it collapsed with huge debts in the spring of 1917.

Why did phonograph-based sound film companies get into financial difficulties so soon? As more and more film theatres featured live songs and accompaniment, the 'novelty' of phonographic sound films worn off and recorded sounds began to be received unfavourably, regarded as inferior to live sounds and voices, since the sound quality was quite poor with no electronic amplification. Furthermore, phonographs did not spread widely enough, making it difficult to earn profits from such a small market. Lastly, as films got longer and longer, the limited playing time of phonographs became a disadvantage. However, phonograph based sound films played a critical role in creating *kouta* films as they demonstrated the possibility of synchronizing sounds with characters on the screen, and explored the possibility of showing films independently, without the help of *benshi*.

Song in Drama: Narrative Song

When phonograph-based sound films became popular, films appeared with songs incorporated into the diegesis. Among the earliest examples of this kind was the immensely popular *Kachūsha/Resurrection* (Hosoyama Kiyomatsu, Nikkatsu, 1914), although it was later criticized as reeking of *shinpa* style. This film starred the *onnagata* (a male actor who impersonates a female character) Tachibana Teijirō as Katyusha, and Sekine Takuhatsu as Nekhlyudov. 'Katyusha's Song', sung in the film, was composed by Nakayama

14 B-sei. 'Shitsumon oyobi hagaki ran', p. 30.

Shinpei from the Tokyo Music School, in the *yonanuki* (tonal pentatonic) scale that was an 'intermediate' scale between scales used in Western music and in Japanese music. The song became popular probably because it was similar to *min'yō* (a type of Japanese folk song) and thus easy to sing, also because it was advertised extensively through films, records, magazines and other media. Cinemas used anyone who could sing to perform with the film, and the attraction of the song brought box office success. Nikkatsu, encouraged by those successes, released a sequel, *Nochi no Kachūsha/Katyusha Continued* (Kiyomatsu Hosoyama, 1915), and *Kachūsha zoku zoku hen/Second Sequel to Katyusha* (Kiyomatsu Hosoyama, 1915) in the next year, making huge profits and solidifying the new studio's corporate foundations. That *yonanuki* scale was applied to and transformed the tunes of *kouta* in general.

Patterned and Diversified Sounds

When it became usual for *naniwabushi*, *gidayū*, and *biwa* to be performed at the side of the screen, film projectionists were assigned, among other things, to synchronize pictures with those sounds. Some projectionists with little training in music were fired, which showed how much importance was placed on the sound rather than the picture. According to Somei Saburō, chief *benshi* of Asakusa Teikokukan, it was extremely fashionable around 1916 to perform 'highly emotional' *Chikuzen biwa* (a narration-type performance originating in the Meiji era) when a *shinpa* film was screened:

> In moving pictures, *biwa* is used to add striking effects to characters' emotions, scenes, and explanations of some middle and concluding parts, while explanations of other parts are given by the *benshi*. This is just like weaving words and melodies skilfully into one *naniwabushi*.[15]

This presumably means that the *biwa* players narrated, while playing the *biwa*, in scenes for expressing characters' emotions, for presenting scenic beauty, for giving explanations during the film, and at the end of the film; and that when the *biwa* was not played, just verbal explanations were given. So, it could be assumed that, as far as the sounds which accompanied soundless films in the theatre were concerned, (1) combinations of tuneful narration (like arias in the opera) and rhythmical narration by *benshi* (recitative) were popular; and (2) there were typical scenes where tuneful

15 Somei, 'Biwa ōyō no setsumei', p. 128.

narration was inserted. Sound was a major factor in attracting people who sought different kinds of auditory stimulation in the cinema, and a crucial determinant of the various cinemas' rank, genre, and clientele.

The Reformist Movement and the Popularization of Western Music

Around this time, people also became more interested in accompaniments of Western music because of *Cabiria* (Giovanni Pastrone, 1914), *Civilization* (Reginald Barker, Thomas H. Ince, Raymond B. West, 1916) and many other masterpieces were imported with their music scores. Film magazine articles carried titles such as 'The age of film music has come – music is the words of the films'.[16] High-class cinemas such as the Teikokukan and Musashinokan began to employ full-scale orchestras. Even so, conventional sound practices died hard in many other film theatres. Intellectual magazine critics, who preferred western accompaniment to what they regarded as obsolete conventional practices such as mimic voice-over, or onstage instrumental accompaniment and narration, began to play them down. Under such circumstances, Shōchiku, which was established with the goal to modernize Japanese films and raise them to the level of their American counterparts, overwhelmed other film companies by hiring Yamada Kōsaku, Shimada Harutaka and other top musicians and providing superior orchestral accompaniment to their films. It was Shōchiku, a new film company that placed importance on Western music accompaniment, that gave birth to *kouta* films.

In sum, it is clear that films were introduced into Japan as projectors of moving images first, and then were connected in the Japanese theatrical space with the rich sound culture of Japan. Japanese films readily responded to overseas trends and incorporated new elements. This environment in which novelty and tradition were mixed in a complex and dramatic manner in the early 1920s prepared the development of *kouta* films. The relationship between live sound and moving pictures, which had been cultivated in theatrical space since their introduction, gradually disappeared with the arrival of the sound films, taking more than a decade. It should be remembered, however, that during the approximately three decades from the first combination of sound and film until the category of 'soundless' films came to be recognized, there were distinct relationships between sounds and moving pictures that were quite different from the relationships of today, in which filmmakers have control of all sound in the cinema.

16 'Katsudo ongaku no jidai kitaru'.

Shōchiku Modernism and the *Kouta* Film

The first film categorized as a *kouta* film was *Sendō kouta/The Boatman's Song* released by Shōchiku in 1923. Called 'a new experiment by Itō Daisuke', Itō created the film from a popular song with lyrics by Noguchi Ujo, a pastoral lyricist, and music by Nakayama Shinpei, a darling of the popular music world.[17] The song was put on sale in the form of sheet music in 1919, in the form of phonograph record in 1922 on the Orient and other labels in the Kansai region, and became a big hit. The film is about Okimi (Kurishima Sumiko), a beautiful girl in a riverside district, and Ritsuta (Iwata Yukichi), a boatman in love with Okimi, tying the knot as a happy couple.[18] In the last scene, Ritsuta is rowing a boat cheerfully in the breeze on the Tone River, and beautiful Okimi is singing 'Sendō kouta' in the boat. This is not a tearful story in which many incidents happen one after another until they get entangled and the film ends in an unnaturally dramatic scene on the shore, nor is it a conventional family tragedy in which a wife or a child is bullied by step-family members. It is a romance between a young man and a woman who love each other of their own free will and marry happily in the end.

Kouta films were a kind of 'photoplay' in which innovation and conservatism were inextricably intertwined. For *kouta* films to come into existence required two currents flowing in parallel during the early days of the Shōchiku studio. One was the *shinpageki* films (a kind of photoplay that evolved from *shinpa* drama) from the Shōchiku Kamata Studio, and the other was the innovative film form that the Shōchiku Cinema Institute, led by Osanai Kaoru, advocated. The former was initiated by Nomura Hōtei from the Hongōza, the base of *shinpa*, who lead the Kamata Studio with the motto 'Aim high, cater to the masses'. Splitting the difference between the too lofty film play and the old-fashioned *shinpa* film, he sought subject matter in *shinpa*, but broke the old moulds and produced innovative *shinpageki* films. The *shinpageki* films aimed to get away from the influence of the theatre and identify itself as an independent innovative medium by attaching importance to subtitles, actresses, and on location filming, full scale orchestral accompaniment, plain commentary by *benshi* instead of synchronized voiceover and shamisen music played at the stage-side, and by applying cross-cutting and other film-specific methods of expression. The followers included Murata Minoru, Ushihara Kiyohiko, Shimazu Yasujirō

17 'Kamata satsueijo dayori…', p. 41.
18 Yumeno, 'Sendō kouta', pp. 118-122.

and Itō Daisuke who were to produce *kouta* films afterwards. The Shōchiku Cinema Institute closed within one year because its films were regarded as 'hardly profitable', but its spirit was inherited by others and later expressed in the production of *kouta* films.[19] Those two different innovative currents, one by Osanai and the other by Nomura, eventually converged into *kouta* films. In addition, *kouta* films were innovative in preventing the *benshi* from giving an arbitrary account of the action, since some scenes were accompanied by phonograph records or by singers, and the lyrics of songs were superimposed on the screen.

Kurishima Sumiko could be called the heroine who embodied the dual nature of *kouta* films. Like those films, she projected two contradictory images of 'oldness' and 'newness'. She was taught by Henry Kotani to look gorgeous and act naturally like Hollywood actresses and appeared as a new type of actress. Her debut was in *Denkō to sono tsuma/The Electrician and his Wife* (released on 6 May 1921, after censorship revision) by Henry Kotani, who introduced the board reflector for directional lighting to Shōchiku. Her second film, *Gubijinsō/Red Poppy* (Henry Kotani, 29 April 1921), was released along with *Rojō no reikon/Souls on the Road* (Murata Minoru, 1921), the first film by Shōchiku Cinema Institute, and *Kyokkō no kanata e/Beyond the Aurora* (1921), an action film directed by Tanaka Kaneyuki (a.k.a. Edward Tanaka), creating a sensation. Kurishima was highly regarded as very 'Japanese' with sorrowful but handsome and impassive features. Since early childhood, she had learned Japanese dancing, and performed at the theatre of *shinpa* with her father, Kurishima Sagoromo. With her elegant postures that she had attained through her training in Japanese dance, she distinguished herself from other *shinpa*-style actresses who merely affected a European manner.

When *The Boatman's Song* was released it was praised by the audience as a Japanese film that broke away from Western imitation, yet *kouta* films were nothing but ingenious Western imitations.[20] It is a variety of *shinpa* film that contains many elements similar to contemporary Hollywood films: a combination of the typical *shinpa* film narration of mixing lyrical scenes, which had hardly anything to do with the plot, and constructing the whole story in prose; and the Hollywood style narration of constructing a romance-centred story adroitly while interweaving its details in clear causal relationships. The 1920s was a period when lyrical *shinpageki* films became popular again, in reaction to the haughty, innovative Pure Film

19 Kaeriyama, 'Iwayuru eigageki to shinpahigeki', p. 41.
20 Ogura, 'Jojō eiga ni tsuite', p. 50.

Movement that sought to bring Japanese films closer to Western cinema. It seems Shōchiku created *kouta* films as a new type of film that combined an innovative Hollywood-style narration with *shinpa*-style narration in order to attract the mass audience.

The Earthquake and the Teikine Studio

On 1 September 1923, the Great Kanto Earthquake devastated Tokyo and relocated the centre of the film industry to Kyoto and Osaka in the Kansai region. In a sense, this was necessary for Shōchiku's new type of *kouta* films to be imitated by other film companies and spread. Of course, the earthquake was a catastrophe to the film industry in Tokyo, but it brought unprecedented growth to the industry in Kansai. According to a survey by Osaka Prefecture, after the quake, many factories were built in rapid succession, the number of young factory workers increased rapidly, and they eagerly spent their disposable income on new forms of consumption. As they were inexpensive and did not take up too much time, films were a popular entertainment among workers who toiled long hours at low wages.

During this boom, Yamakawa Kichitarō, who quit as head of the Osaka branch of Tenkatsu, a rival of Nikkatsu, set up the Teikine studio in 1920, the same year that Shōchiku was established. Teikine took over the studio at Kosaka and the film distribution network in western Japan and Korea from Tenkatsu. After the earthquake, Teikine went into volume production, sometimes producing as many as 18 films in a month, and became the third largest film company, following Nikkatsu and Shōchiku. *Kouta* films were among the low cost, quickly produced films Teikine preferred. One reason Teikine suddenly started producing *kouta* films was that Itō Daisuke, one of the originators of *kouta* films, joined the Teikine Ashiya Studio in Kansai. Itō quit Shōchiku in July 1923 after he wrote *Onna to kaizoku/Woman and the Pirate* and *Mizumo no hana/Aquatic Plant*, the second *kouta* film released by Shōchiku. He joined the Teikine Sugamo Studio in Tokyo, where Kaeriyama Norimasa was working. However, as the studio was closed by the earthquake, he transferred to Ashiya. There, he wrote the scenario of *Rurō no tabi/Wanderings* (1924), a *kouta* film. He was assigned to write scenarios of eight films for Matsumoto Eiichi, who was to be acclaimed as Teikine's *kouta* director. Itō himself directed *Jōgashima* (1924), a sentimental *kouta* film about a ruined father and son. However sloppily made, *kouta* films were more or less successful because the songs attracted young adults.

Figure 1.1 Film frame printed on a lyric card included with the Orient Records three-disc 78rpm version of 'The Caged Bird' song. A poster advertising the song is displayed on the left of the image. The lyric card identifies the frame as from the Teikine version of *The Caged Bird*. However, since the film does not survive this cannot be confirmed. From the collection of Honchi Haruhiko.

Even if they were box office disappointments, *kouta* films had a low risk of loss, since they were made at low cost with only three or four days of shooting. This was very convenient for Teikine, which had shifted into mass production at short notice.

The Caged Bird, mentioned as a representative of the genre in the Japanese film history, is one of the *kouta* films mass-produced by Teikine. Its eponymous song was a countrified *enka,* a Japanese balladic popular song. It became so popular that even elementary school students took to singing it, so much so that it was heavily criticized by educators as dangerous to the State and prohibited. The film, based on the theme of that song, elegiacally depicted urban young people longing for free love. One day, a young daughter (Sawa Ranko) from a long-established store meets a college student (Satomi Akira) and falls in love with him at first sight. They eventually come to love each other. However, she is obliged to marry another man of her parents choosing, but she does not love the man and kills herself in despair. *Kinema junpō* referred to it as 'a faddish film produced overnight', but 'a film highly likely to attract young adults as it ingeniously describes some facets of the real life of young men and women'.[21]

This film became an unprecedented hit, giving rise to live stage versions and records (Fig. 1.1), as well as novelizations (Fig. 1.2), and sheet music (Fig. 1.3), all of which gave rise to outspoken criticism against *kouta* films.

21 Yamamoto, '*Kago no tori*', p. 17.

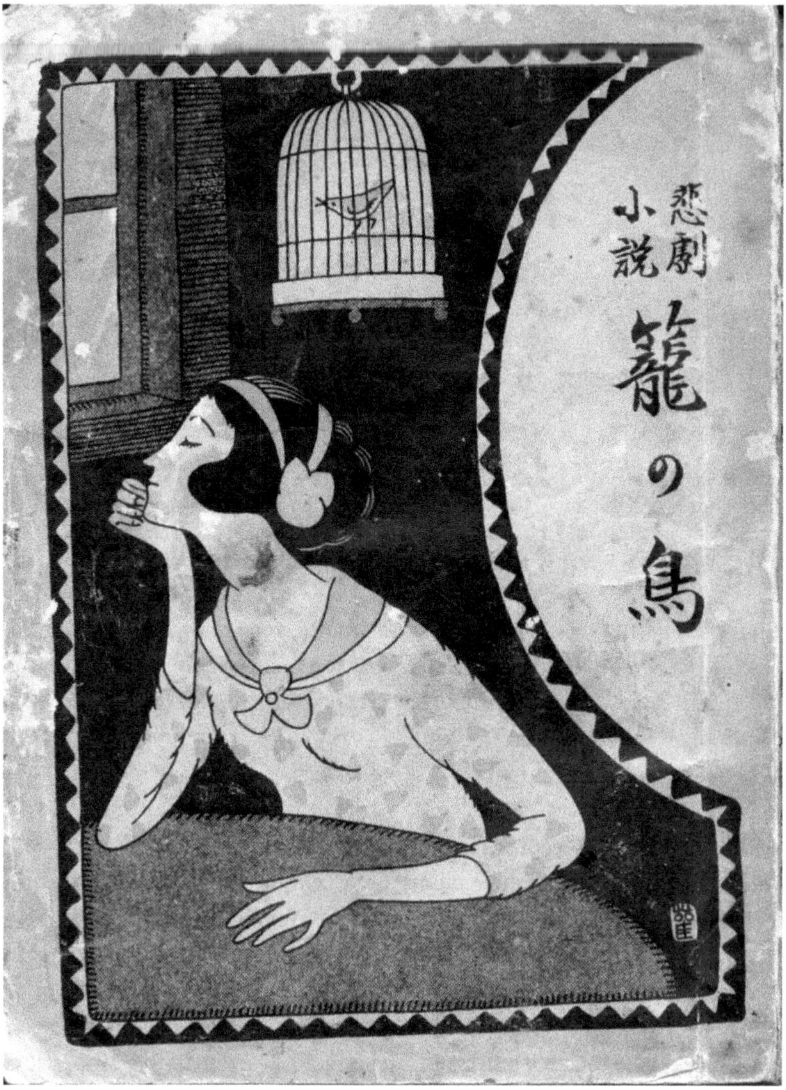

Figure 1.2 A novelization of the film *The Caged Bird*. Published by Bunmeikan shoten, Osaka in October 1924, price 20 zeni. From the collection of Honchi Haruhiko.

Two months after *The Caged Bird,* Teikine 'revived' the heroine who was supposed to have died, releasing a highly profitable sequel *Kago no tori Kohen/The Caged Bird, part 2* (1924), starring Sawa Ranko and Utagawa Yaeko, and a spin off, *Hatsukoi no koro/Days of First Love* (1925) directed by Matsumoto Eiichi and starring Utagawa Yaeko. At the same time, other companies released similar films in quick succession. The commercialism of these film companies came under attack, which damaged the image of

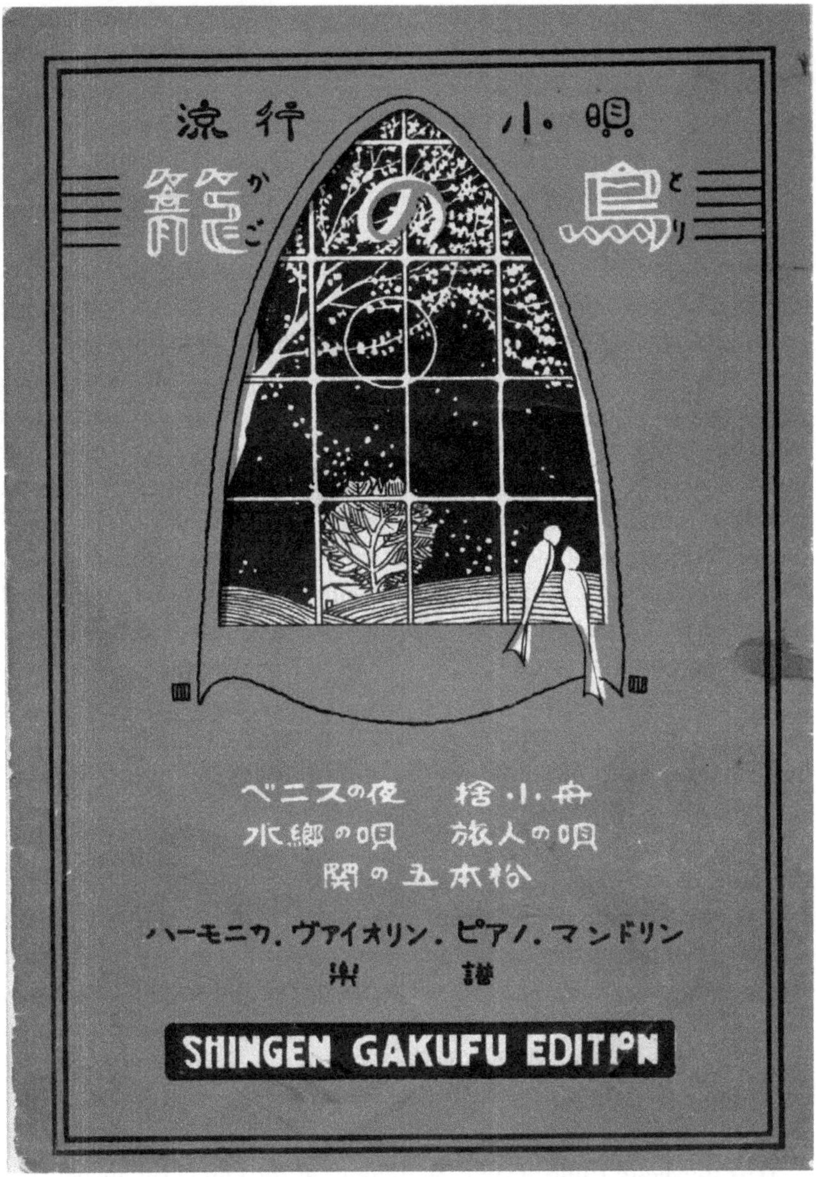

Figure 1.3 Sheet music for the theme song 'Kago no tori'/'The Caged Bird'. Published by Shingen Gakufu Shuppansha, Osaka in September 1924, price 10 zeni. From the collection of Honchi Haruhiko.

kouta films further. Moreover, because they depended on the attraction of songs, *kouta* films were regarded as compromising the film medium.

Shōchiku, which originated *kouta* films, was treated quite differently by critics. In response to Teikine's move, Shōchiku released *Kouta shū/*

Kouta Collection (1924) under the direction of Ushihara Kiyohiko, Ikeda Yoshinobu, and Shimazu Yasujirō, including *Kago no tori/The Caged Bird*, a tragic love story in emulation of Teikine's *The Caged Bird*. These films impressed critics as 'masterfully capturing something flowing through the minds of contemporary audiences', albeit 'ignoble and slipshod', and achieved extraordinary success at the box office.[22] After that, Shōchiku produced *Kangeki jidai/Exciting Days* (1928), a cheerful students' sports film which starred Suzuki Denmei and into which *kouta* songs were inserted, and *Kokkyō no uta/Song at the Border* (1927), a military film accompanied by songs, and other genre-mixing *kouta* films. At the same time, Shōchiku judiciously produced elegiac and serene *kouta* films. One of them was *Benisu no funauta/Boat Song in Venice* (1926) by Ōkubo Tadamoto, which was considered as very lyrical for Ōkubo, who had been 'notorious for his vulgar tastes', and regarded as 'the crown jewel of *kouta* films'.[23] Film critic Kitagawa Fuyuhiko praised this film highly, describing it as 'tranquil', and 'cleverly made'.[24] Nevertheless, the high reputation of *kouta* films by Shōchiku was overshadowed by the unfavourable reaction to *kouta* films in general, and in the end *The Caged Bird* by Teikine went down in the Japanese film history as the representative *kouta* film.

The Environment of Sound Media and Changes in *Kouta* Films in the late 1920s

The label of the '*kouta* film' appeared, without definition, just before the Great Kanto Earthquake, but it was at the height of its popularity, from the end of 1928 into 1929, that *kouta* films became established as a genre. Fukuro Ippei, who analysed *kouta* films in the historical context of film culture, defined them as 'taking their theme from a *kouta song* and inserting it at an appropriate moment' and 'playing the *kouta song* [...] when an appropriate scene appears on the screen' with 'the purpose of conveying the atmosphere of the *kouta*, whatever the story might be'.[25]

Why did *kouta* films become so popular at the end of the 1920s? One important reason would be the many articles about the arrival of talkies in Japan. A Japanese legend from the 12th century has it that the soldiers of the

22 Okamura, et al., 'Sakunen eigakai no kaiko (2)', p. 30.
23 Nakamura, 'Reisan subeki *Benisu no funauta*', p. 78.
24 Kitagawa, '*Haru no ame*', p. 63.
25 Fukuro, 'Kouta eiga hayaru', p. 19.

Heike clan mistook the sound of water birds taking off for the advancement of a massive enemy force from its rival, the Genji clan, and ran away. Fukuro compared talkies to 'water birds', and *kouta* films to the soldiers of the Heike clan. He meant that the fear of incoming talkies made Japanese film companies hurriedly produce *kouta* films as a way to counter talkies, and those *kouta* films became popular. More critically, Kaeriyama Norimasa referred to the rage for *kouta* films in the following way:

> My friends, you should not regret that Japanese talkies are not perfect when *kouta* films are popular. The mission of talkies is not to play *kouta* songs in films.[26]

Kaeriyama thought that *kouta* films were popular as a substitute for talkies. His comment could be understood as meaning it should be unnecessary to make do with *kouta* films because artistic films could be produced when talkies became full-fledged. The perception of *kouta* films as immature talkies is understandable, considering both the sensational boom of talkies in the U.S. and the situation prevailing in Japan. By 1929, the U.S. had moved into the age of 'all talking, all singing, and all dancing', while *Broadway* (1929) and many other Hollywood sound films were released and much discussed in Japan. It was a fact that the talk of talkies rattled the film industry of Japan. It could be assumed that many *kouta* films were produced as a substitute for talkies in Japan, where 'there was a lot of talk about talkies, but no facilities for them'.

It should be noted, however, that in this period the critics consciously ignored the fact that *kouta* films had existed since around the time of the Great Kanto Earthquake, and instead focused on those *kouta* films produced in the late 1920s. In this regard, Sugimoto Akira was not different from Kaeriyama, though he appreciated *kouta* films as a new type of entertainment film. He referred, among others, to *Habu no minato/The Harbour of Habu* and *Kimi koishi/I Miss You* (both 1929) and pointed out that 'the phenomenal appearance of *kouta* films this year should be particularly noted in film history'. However, he dismissed the preceding 'several kinds of similar films' as 'not deserving the name of *kouta* film'.[27]

Such undue dismissal of the past shows not only the sense of fear and inferiority people felt toward talkies, but also the changes in mode that *kouta* films were undergoing during that period. As Fukuro Ippei commented:

26 Kaeriyama, 'Hassei eiga kaihatsu jidai', p. 86.

27 Sugimoto, 'Uta to eiga', p. 10.

> Where can we find the lyrical atmosphere of *kouta* films? Probably no atmosphere of *kouta* whatever could be found in any part of films these days. Rather, they do not have even one scene that should allow any *kouta* song to be inserted at all.[28]

Fukuro referred to competing versions of *The Harbour of Habu* by Nikkatsu and Teikine, and criticized them as not dramatizing the subject or atmosphere of a *kouta* song, but merely 'going on a filming trip to a convenient shore somewhere, having readily available actors act unnaturally, and superimposing words of a *kouta* song at the beginning and end of the films'.[29]

In the same year, Sugimoto Akira made similar comments about *kouta* films by Shōchiku:

> Their scenarios are originally made without considering the possibility of inserting songs in them. The films in themselves do not particularly need songs to be included. However, songs fundamentally unrelated to their contents are superimposed on the screen.[30]

Both critics insisted that unlike those in the Taishō era (1912-1925), *kouta* films in 1929 had little connection with songs and played *kouta* songs unrelated to their subject in several scenes, which means the mode of *kouta* films had changed.

The change in mode of *kouta* films were related to the fact that new sound media such as radio and phonograph records appeared, and the consumption patterns of songs changed. In the mid-1920s, when radio broadcasting started, many new phonograph companies such as Pioneer, Tokkyo and Naigai, developed new markets. The system of phonograph recording changed from acoustic to electrical recording, improving the quality of sound dramatically. Moreover, Polydor, Columbia and other foreign-affiliated companies started production in Japan, the price of a record dropped from between 3 and 7 yen to 1.5 yen, and new records were released frequently. As a result, the consumption cycle of songs became shorter and shorter. In 1927, 100% American-owned Victor Company of Japan appeared and conducted business in the American way, with popular singers under exclusive contracts. Under such circumstances,

28 Fukuro, 'Kouta eiga hayaru', p. 20.
29 Ibid.
30 Sugimoto, 'Uta to eiga', p. 12.

'Habu no minato'/'The Harbour of Habu', a new folk song of which the words were written by Noguchi Ujō and the music was composed by Nakayama Shinpei, was released in May 1928 and made a great hit, selling more than one hundred thousand records. Satō Chiyoko, its singer, became one of the first 'record' singers in Japan. There were other songs that sold tens or hundreds of thousands of records, such as 'Arabia no uta'/'Sing Me A Song of Araby' and 'Aozora'/'My Blue Heaven', jazz *kouta* songs sung by Futamura Teiichi, who was an ex Asakusa Opera star and became a pioneer Japanese Jazz singer. Also popular were 'Mon Paris', a song sung by the Takarazuka Kagekidan (a Japanese all female review company), 'Kimi koishi'/'I Miss You', and 'Tokyo kōshinkyoku'/'Tokyo March', which were jazz-style *kouta* songs.

As the pattern of song consumption changed and the amount of consumption increased steeply, the production process of *kouta* films also changed. At the end of the Taishō Era, *kouta* songs were put on the market in the form of sheet music or picture postcard first, then in the form of a phonograph record, and finally were cinematized. In the early days of the Shōwa era, when record companies started to compete intensely, existing songs were not only sold in the form of phonograph records, but also new songs originally made for records were released in succession every month, and at the same time advertised by radio and many other media. As a result, popular songs spread much more quickly than before and the cycle of their life became shorter. In response to such changes, *kouta* films were released shortly after the records were released in order to make the most of the advertising effect of *kouta* songs.

If a song became a huge hit, film companies competed to produce films based on that same song. This old business practice of several rival companies concurrently releasing films under the same title was very often adopted for *kouta* films particularly in the beginning of the Shōwa era. For example, 'The Harbour of Habu' was cinematized by four companies: Kawai, Nikkatsu, Teikine and Tōa. 'I Miss You' was adapted by six companies: Makino, Shōchiku, Morimoto, Nikkatsu, Tōa and Kawai. Just as several singers' release records of the same song, so several film companies produced films based on the same song. People compared different films made from the same song, and enjoyed looking for the film that best fitted the image they had conjured up from the song.

Under such circumstances, *kouta* films began to be produced quickly with a *kouta* song just inserted, not necessarily with the subject of a *kouta* visualized. As Kifuji Shigeru, the director of *Sabaku ni hi ga ochite/Sunset on the Desert* (1928), said, 'The most important thing about *kouta* films, like films on current topics, is to release as soon as possible'.[31] Kifuji claimed they had had to shoot the film 'really fast because they were falling far behind the fashion in *kouta* songs'. What he meant was that when the cycle of fashions in *kouta* records became short, it was important to create a café setting or other scenes where a *kouta* song could be played in the film, rather than to make a narrative out of the subject of a *kouta* song. As Fukuro and Sugimoto suggested, the subject of a *kouta* song and the narrative of a *kouta* film became less connected. Probably along this line, some companies began to tie in with record companies to make a new *kouta* song for a *kouta* film and advertise it. One example of this kind was *Tokyo March* (1929) directed by Mizoguchi Kenji. It could be assumed that this development led to *shudaika eiga*, i.e. 'theme song films' for which new songs were composed based on the film theme and played in important scenes, and *kayō eiga*, (popular song films) for which some existing popular songs which would fit scenes of the film were selected and sung by characters in the film.

Songs used for *kouta* films also changed. The lyric of 'Sunset on the Desert' was translated by Horiuchi Keizō from an American jazz song. It was a fast, modern piece not limited by conventions such as the pentatonic scale or the seven and five syllable meter of earlier *kouta*. Moreover, its cheerful accompaniment and Futamura Teiichi's carefree singing created a bouncy atmosphere, far from being suggestive and elegiac. Such outspoken Americanism in Japanese film disagreed with the conventional association of *kouta* films with elegiac and nihilistic sentimentalism, perhaps creating a sense of discordance but also amusement that attracted the mass audience. Hayashi Itsuma, a reader of the film journal *Eiga jidai*, commented on the relationship between *kouta* films and Americanism:

> The characteristics of modern people are fatigue, nervous breakdown, and insomnia. [...] Americanism suddenly came in from a country far off over the sea. It was cheap, cheerful optimism like 'It would be OK to sing and dance without thinking deeply.' Then, *kouta* films suddenly caught on here in this country.[32]

His comment that a large amount of Americanism 'came' in 1929 is noteworthy. Around this year, many revue companies, like Casino Follies joined by Enoken (Enomoto Kenichi, the king of Japanese comedy then), were established to produce a powerful cultural current mainly in Asakusa

31 Kifuji, 'Kinsaku no kansō', p. 21.

32 Hayashi, 'Kouta eiga no ryūkō ni tsuite', p. 106.

and Shinjuku. Revue performances became popular and were staged in film theatres. In the meantime, Takarazuka drew attention by showing the first line dance in Japan and beautiful revues on steps that spanned the width of the stage in *Mon Paris*. Cafés and dance halls which were frequented by 'modern boys and girls' (westernized fashionable young adults of those days called *Mobo* and *Moga*) came into vogue. With these various entertainments interrelating with each other and reshaping mass culture, *kouta* films followed the fashion of the day, incorporating jazz and attracting young people, who were particular about sound and music.

Conclusion

This paper has traced the developing history of the relationship between sound and moving pictures through the lens of the *kouta* film. Contrary to some film histories, those films were not a temporary phenomenon that appeared around the time of the Great Kanto Earthquake and disappeared in a little more than a year. *Kouta* films were silent films, but like all silent films they cannot be separated from sound. Since they were first imported into Japan, films became associated with various forms of sound such as *nagauta, gidayū, naniwabushi, biwa, kyūgeki, shinpa, shingeki* and other rich performing arts that were performed regularly in Japanese popular theatres. Meanwhile, Japanese films, including *kouta* films, eagerly adapted the American popular culture represented by Hollywood films. In the late 1920s, *kouta* films absorbed the new jazz music and became a popular film genre that continued to develop in the sound period. The history of *kouta* films shows that to clarify the deep relationships between sound and image in the cinema we cannot be limited to binaries such as silent/sound, film/theatre, and song/narration. Historical studies of Japanese cinema should go beyond such conventions and retrace the relationships between sounds and images. Putting various media and their relationships in a broader spatial and temporal context, as in *Kouta* films, we can rescue film history from the evolutionary history that has been dominant until now. Previously unseen connections become clear, leading to a change in the dominant historical perception.

* This paper is based on my Japanese paper, 'Kouta eiga ni kan suru kiso chōsa: Meiji makki kara shōwa shoki o chūshin ni'. *Engeki kenkyū sentā kiyō* 1 (Waseda University, 2003). We are grateful to Waseda University Tsubouchi Theatre Memorial Museum for permission to revise and reprint this article.

Bibliography

B-sei. 'Shitsumon oyobi hagaki ran'. *Kinema rekōdo* 20 (February 1915), p. 30.

Fujita Motohiko. *Gendai eiga no kiten* (Kinokuniya Shoten, 1965).

Fukuro Ippei. 'Kouta eiga hayaru'. *Eiga jidai* 6.10 (October 1929), pp. 18-20.

Fumikura Heizaburō. *Tokyo ni okeru katsudō shashin* (Tokyo: Anonymous, 1918).

Hanai Hideo. 'Yo ga satsuei toji no shinpageki'. *Katsudō shashin zasshi* 3.1 (January 1917), p. 154.

Hayashi Itsuma. 'Kouta eiga no ryūkō ni tsuite'. *Eiga jidai* 6.12 (December 1929), p. 106.

Hosokawa Shuhei. 'Kouta eiga no bunkashi'. *Cinema don don* 1 (2002), pp. 12-15.

Iijima Tadashi. *Nihon eigashi* Vol. 1 (Tokyo: Hakusuisha, 1955).

Iwasaki Akira. *Nihon gendaishi taikei: eigashi* (Tokyo: Tōyō Keizai Shinpōsha, 1961).

Kaeriyama Norimasa. 'Iwayuru eigageki to shinpahigeki'. *Katsudō gahō* 5.9 (September 1921), p. 41.

Kaeriyama Norimasa. 'Hassei eiga kaihatsu jidai'. *Eiga ōrai* 5.4 (April 1929), pp. 85-86.

'Kamata satsueijo dayori...'. *Kamata* 2.1 (January 1923), p. 41.

'Katsudo ongaku no jidai kitaru: Ongaku wa eigageki no bushi de aru'. *Katsudō shashin zasshi* 6.10 (October 1920), pp. 130-132.

Kifuji Shigeru. 'Kinsaku no kansō'. *Eiga shunjū* 1.1 (April 1929), p. 21.

Kitagawa Fuyuhiko. 'Haru no Ame'. *Kinema junpō* 267 (11 July 1927), p. 63.

Nakamura Suiko, 'Reisan subeki *Benisu no funauta*'. *Kamata* 5.11 (November 1926), p. 78.

Ogura Shūro. 'Jojō eiga ni tsuite'. *Kamata* 3.6 (June 1924), p. 50.

Okamura Shihō, et al. 'Sakunen eigakai no kaiko (2)'. *Eiga to engei* 2.2 (February 1925), p. 30.

Shinoyama Ginyō. 'Rensageki wa horobiyo'. *Katsudō gahō* 1.9 (September 1917), pp. 72-75.

Somei Saburō. 'Biwa ōyō no setsumei'. *Katsudō shashin zasshi* 2.10 (October 1916), p. 128.

Sugimoto Akira. 'Uta to eiga'. *Eiga jidai* 6.10 (October 1929), pp. 8-12.

Tanaka Jun'ichirō. *Nihon eiga hattatsushi* Vol. 1 (Tokyo: Chūōkōronsha, 1975).

Tanaka Jun'ichirō. *Nihon eiga hattatsushi* Vol. 2 (Tokyo: Chūōkōronsha, 1976).

Tokugawa Musei. *Musei handaiki* (Tokyo: Shibundō, 1929).

Yamamoto Rokuha. '*Kago no tori*'. *Kinema junpō* 169 (21 August 1924), p. 17.

Yoshiyama Kyokkō. 'Nakamura kasen jō'. *Katsudō shashin zasshi* 1.12 (December 1915), p. 62.

Yoshiyama Kyokkō. 'Shoki no Nihon eiga (1)'. *Eiga jidai* 4.1 (January 1927), pp. 128-129.

Yoshiyama Kyokkō. *Nihon eigakai jibutsu kigen* (Tokyo: Shinema to Engeisha, 1933).

Yoshiyama Kyokkō. *Nihon eigashi nenpyō* (Tokyo: Eiga Hōkokusha, 1940).

Yumeno Shūko. 'Sendō kouta'. *Katsudō gahō* 7.3 (March 1923), pp. 118-122.

About the Author

Sasagawa Keiko is Professor of Film and Media Studies at Kansai University, Osaka. Her research engages with the aesthetic, cultural, and industrial history of Japanese and Hollywood cinema in Japan and across East and South East Asia during the first part of the twentieth century.

2 Katsutarō's Trilogy

Popular Song and Film in the Transitional Era from Silent Film to the Talkie

Hosokawa Shuhei

Abstract
This chapter outlines a history of Japanese popular song and its 'one-way' relationship with cinema to show how the former geisha Katsutarō was produced as a new musical celebrity and then incorporated into *Shima no musume/The Island Girl* and *Tokyo ondo*, two Shōchiku sound films made in 1933, and *Sakura ondo*, made at P.C.L. in 1934. Through close analysis of specific scenes, it demonstrates the multivalent relationships between sound and image in early Japanese sound films. It identifies three different modes to the integration into the diegesis of Katsutarō's title song for each film: as a commentary on the narrative; as emotional colouring; and as a separate performance of an upbeat and pro-military song that inoculates the film's dark melodrama against censorship.

Keywords: *kouta* film, musical celebrity, *Shima no musume/The Island Girl, Tokyo ondo, Sakura ondo.*

Introduction

The transition from silent to talkie was neither smooth nor unidirectional. It involved a great deal of 'trial and error' until the all-talkie system became established and industrialized in Japan. The first commercially successful talkie, *Madamu to nyōbō/The Neighbour's Wife and Mine* (Gosho Heinosuke, 1931), did not yield immediate follow-ups due to technical difficulties both in the studio and in the cinemas. For several years, the new films were produced as silents, *saundo-ban* ('sound versions'), or talkies, dependent on

Raine, M. and J. Nordström (eds.), *The Culture of the Sound Image in Prewar Japan.*
Taylor & Francis Group 2020
DOI: 10.5117/9789089647733_CH02

the budget, the genre, the studio, and other conditions.[1] Though the process was irreversible, the films in this transitional period show how production teams adapted the new sound technologies while applying the ideas and practices of filmmaking established during the silent period. The popular song came to play a crucial role in this process, since it could be used either on phonograph (with silent films), unsynchronized on the soundtrack (with sound versions) or synchronized with the spoken words (the talkie). For example, in the 1920s cinemas that showed silent films that had a theme song, generally called *kouta eiga* ('ballad films'), would play phonograph records of the theme song during particular scenes.[2]

This chapter will discuss the role of the popular song and its singer, focusing on three films featuring hit songs recorded by the most popular female singer of the 1930s, Katsutarō.[3] Those three songs – 'Shima no musume'/'The Island Girl', 'Tokyo ondo' and 'Sakura ondo' – were undeniably significant in the history of popular song both musically and commercially. The films are not a 'trilogy' in its strict sense (having a common production or plot) but merely three separate films inspired by songs recorded by the same artist. However, they reveal several important aspects of narrative technique and sound technology in the transitional era of 1933-1934, especially the commercial and narrative importance of the 'title song', the tie-up strategy, and the star-song association. These songs were not only 'theme songs' but were also 'title songs' in the sense that their titles were utilized for the title of the film and played during the title sequence (over the credits). The title song is a special type of theme song – such a straightforward tie-up between the song and the film was common in the earlier *kouta eiga*. Rene Clair's *Sous les toits de Paris/Under the Roofs of Paris* (1930, Japan premiere in 1931) and Erik Charell's *Der Kongress Tanzt/Congress Dances* (1931, Japan premier in 1934) have title songs in this sense (both of them were recorded in Japanese by several singers) but not all film theme songs were titled in this way. The title song system, or title-song association, suggests the centrality of song

1 Sound versions were films featuring recorded soundtracks of music and sound effects but with no synchronized dialog.

2 See Sasagawa Keiko, 'A Genealogy of Kouta eiga: Silent Moving Pictures with Sound' in this volume.

3 The artist name of a geisha is composed of the name of the area she worked in and her proper stage name. In Katsutarō's case, 'Yoshichō Katsutarō' was her official name authorized by the Yoshichō Union of Entertainment. After she left the profession, she called herself 'Kouta Katsutarō' (kouta, literally 'small song', is a broad term for ditties but also the name of a vocal genre developed in the pleasure quarters). To avoid the trouble of the complicated name system of Japanese traditional performing arts, I refer to her simply as Katsutarō in this paper.

in the marketing campaign and the strong interdependence between the commercial sectors of the entertainment business. The film public would have recognized the song before they went to the cinema because the song could be heard on radio, in public spaces, and at home, intentionally or not. The song motivated audiences to see the film and not the other way around. The identification of song and film by the title song was crucial both for the industry and the public. Katsutarō's three films will serve to illustrate the relationship between the popular song and the soundtrack, and between the music industry and the film studio during this era.

Katsutarō in the History of the Record Industry

Katsutarō (1904-1974) was a singer signed to the Victor record label, who came from the pleasure quarter of Yoshichō, Tokyo, where she had been hired as a geisha to sing with shamisen accompaniment. She made her recording debut in 1930 and signed a contract with Victor in 1931. Just after 'Tokyo ondo' became a hit, she left Yoshichō to work exclusively for Victor, also appearing on the radio, in live concerts, and other events. Since the seventeenth century, the pleasure quarters – generally called *hanamachi* ('flower town') – were the most vital place for popular song. The pleasure quarters were controlled by the government, which licensed entertainment businesses. The geisha (or *geigi, geiko*) artists were strictly affiliated with the hierarchical order of a specific pleasure quarter and they performed in *ozashiki* (a Japanese-style parlour with tatami mats on the floor) with shamisen accompaniment when requested by customers. This 'semi-private' party was the basic form of their performance and their repertoire of rural and urban vernacular ditties and pieces passed down in certain schools was orally transmitted. Geisha were devalued as erotic playthings during the Edo period (1603-1868) and modern-oriented Meiji (1868-1912) elites continued to reject them, claiming that they were vulgar and obsolete. On the other hand, the recording industry, when established at the turn of the twentieth century, depended on these musically trained geisha and some of them became the first stars of popular song.

The recording industry changed drastically in 1927-1928 with the injection of capital by foreign labels that created Japan Victor, Japan Columbia and Japan Polydor. The new labels invested in modern electronic recording systems, utilized aggressive advertisement, established a business model in which they made exclusive contracts with specific composers, lyricists and singers, and began producing Western-styled popular songs, often labelled as 'jazz'. Furthermore, they rapidly created a market oligopoly together with the new domestic labels King and Teichiku. The entire sonic field of entertainment was radically changed in this period with the start of government radio broadcasts (1925) and the introduction of various synchronized sound systems in the cinemas (1929). The new labels commercialized *shin min'yō* ('new folk songs'), folk-like tunes composed and written by the Tokyo-based professionals and recorded by geisha singers. These songs were often commissioned by rural commercial or tourist bureaus, and the lyrics celebrate the provincial landscape, its festivals and people, or love affairs situated in these settings. The new songs were effective in industrializing a stereotypical ruralism, or folk taste. Many geisha artists actively recorded in this genre, spreading their vocals through radio, live shows, and other media outside of the pleasure quarters. Katsutarō started her recording career with new folk songs but had her breakthrough with 'The Island Girl' (1933). It not only boosted her fame but created the very format of popular song.

'The Island Girl': The Illustrative Function of the Theme Song

'The Island Girl', composed and arranged by Sasaki Shun'ichi, was Katsutarō's first national hit and reportedly sold 200,000 copies.[4] It successfully mixed the melodic movement and rhythmic oscillation of *ozashiki* songs with all-Western orchestration, without shamisen. Katsutarō's voice was so adaptable to the modernized folk style that she was accepted by a wider audience. Her refined, high-register vocal style was seen as a little peculiar for the conservative audience of geisha but it was well-suited to the new electronic recording systems (like the 'crooner' among male singers). That vocal style insulated her from claims of vulgarity (although conservatory-schooled singers of Western classical music still publicly refused to sing on the same stage with her). Soon, Katsutarō disaffiliated from the pleasure quarter hierarchy and established herself as a Victor artist.

Because of the unexpectedness of the song's success, it had no planned film tie-up. As a result, four films were produced to take advantage of its sudden popularity: productions by Kawai Eiga, directed by Ozawa Tokuji; Henry Kinema, directed by Ōsawa Torao; Terao Cinema (the director is

4 Statistics for the record industry in pre-war Japan is rather unreliable. An influential yet hasty music journalist reported that Katsutarō's trilogy, discussed in this article, sold a million copies each but it seems to me exaggerated, given his comic writing style. See Yoshimoto, 'Naze ryūkōka wa sanshinsuru?', p. 286.

unknown); and Shōchiku, directed by Nomura Hōtei. The first three films were silent and enjoyed commercial success because of their rapid production while the song was popular. This situation of 'one hit, several films' was common with *kouta eiga* – a notorious case was the 1932 hit, 'Tengoku ni musubu koi'/'A Love Fulfilled in Heaven', which resulted in five eponymous films and a lawsuit. The film studios aimed to produce a film as quickly as possible to capitalize on the popularity of the hit song. Consequently, *kouta eiga* was often criticized as 'cheap faddish products' (*kiwamono*) by journalists. On the other hand, Nomura's film – his second sound version based on a popular song – was released a little later but the critics judged it to be the best.[5] One of those critics, Kitagawa Fuyuhiko, in the film magazine *Kinema junpō*, called it a 'sound version of the *kouta eiga*'. In many ways, Kitagawa was correct, as we will see in the film's continuation of the silent cinema practice of featuring popular songs.[6]

The Shōchiku version of *The Island Girl* is a sentimental story of Okinu (Tsubouchi Yoshiko), a girl on a small Japanese island loved by both the sailor Ichirō (Egawa Ureo) and the Tokyo student Ōkawa (Takeuchi Ryōkichi). To save Okinu from the broker who wants to gain a commission by contracting her to an inn in Tokyo, her fiancé Ichirō steals money from the post office and escapes from the island. However, he dies aboard the ship and is buried at sea. Meanwhile, Ōkawa, upon disembarking, finds out about Okinu's plight and pays off the broker. Knowing of her engagement to Ichirō, however, he gives up his new love and returns to Tokyo, marrying his fiancée soon afterwards. The narrative of the separation between an island girl and a sailor comes from the lyrics of the song and is similar to the scenario written by Ōsawa Torao for the Henry Kinema film. How the content of the lyrics would be turned into fiction was a principal concern for the scenario writers of the *kouta eiga*, and for the audiences of the films. As we can tell from the reference to 'snowfall' in the fourth verse of the song, the lyricist and writer of a stage drama under the same title, Nagata Mikihiko, imagined the island of the title as Sado Island near Niigata on Japan's Northern shore (Katsutarō was born in Niigata city). However, Shōchiku's team preferred Ōshima Island located near the Izu peninsula, south of Tokyo Bay. The island was notorious as well as fashionable, owing to a series of suicides of young

5 See '*Shima no musume*' [Shōchiku version], p. 57; '*Nagisani utau: Shima no musume*' [Kawai eiga version], p. 58; 'Tokyo eigakan: nigatsuyonshū, sangatsu isshū: bangumi no keishō chōsa "Kawai kinema"', p. 26; Kitagawa, '*Shima no musume*' [Shōchiku version], p. 125; Kitagawa, '*Shima no musume*' [Henrī kinema version], p. 125.

6 Kitagawa, '*Shima no musume*' [Shōchiku version], p. 125.

lovers at Mt. Mihara, a volcano, in the centre of the island.[7] In the café scene, a waitress tells the depressed Ichirō 'what if you went to Mt. Mihara', suggesting that he die by suicide. The shift of place was an effective means to make the narrative topical and attractive to the public.

The title sequence of *The Island Girl* is accompanied by the orchestral version of the title song, like the overture of opera and operetta films. The exhibition of silent *kouta eiga* also involved playing a phonograph of the song before the film or in the intermission to intensify audience interest. *The Island Girl*, however, uses an instrumental version in order to downplay the immediate association with the lyrics as well as to differentiate the filmic experience from the phonographic (vocal) one. It was also different from the typical Japanese sound film that, if it had a musical accompaniment, would use orchestral music unrelated to the theme song. Listening impatiently, expecting the song to begin in the first moments of the film, must have given the audience a peculiar experience of excitement and tension.

The first diegetic sound in *The Island Girl* is the whistle of a ship, followed by the sound of the anchor chain, and a bell announcing the arrival of the ship at Ōshima harbour. As several other essays in this anthology discuss, recorded dialog and sound effects were not widely used in Japanese film until after this period. The illustration of a scene by sound effects was a new experience specific to the sound film, although due to its presence in stage and radio drama it can be said that the film studios took over a set of pre-existing techniques. As the story develops, the film uses the sounds of a clock, a tempest, the seashore, and so on. The majority of sound effects do not require perfect synchronization, only strong and dramatic ones. When Ichirō jumps from the second floor of the post office, the sound of his landing is accurately synchronized. In the exhibition of silent film too, such strong sound effects, if necessary, could be synchronized and made by the percussionist looking at the screen. *The Island Girl* also features scenes with diegetic music, such as in the café and the pleasure quarter. In a scene at the café, a geisha recording is synchronized with a waitress playing the phonograph. This scene is likely intended to show off the effective synchronization of the sound-on-film soundtrack, compared to the rival sound-on-disc technology.

Of course, the soundtrack inherited the practices of silent film. Although the heritage of *geza* (background music in kabuki) stood out especially in

7 There were several popular songs on the theme of Ōshima and love affairs; the Kawai eiga version was also set in Ōshima. A magazine column claimed that in 1934 Ōshima received 150,000 tourists, who locally spent 750,000 yen. See Kita, 'Miharayama', p. 305.

the case of *jidaigeki* (period films), the modern feature film largely, if not entirely, adopted the Hollywood method (see Hosokawa 2014). As is well known, the music for silent cinema was usually underscored to illustrate the characteristics of specific scenes – romantic, agonistic, thrilling, happy, and so on. The music director of *The Island Girl*, Shimada Harutaka, a former navy bandleader, had worked in Shōchiku silent theatres for years and was therefore familiar with the practice of underscoring in live musical accompaniment. *The Island Girl* respects this convention, underscoring nearly all the scenes. Only one piece is repeated and used twice, once in the scene of Ichirō receiving a telegraph from Okinu and then again when Okinu is reading his will. The sorrowful melody expresses the narrative correspondence of these scenes, but it can be perceived only by the most attentive of audiences because the melody has no audibly distinctive shape.

Shimada composed or selected three types of non-diegetic music: popular song; Western music; and *shakuhachi* ('bamboo flute'). First, Shimada used two orchestral pieces, which must have been well known to the contemporary public – one is a local folk song, the other is a commercialized new folk song – that play under the arrival of Ichirō's ship at Ōshima harbour. They contribute to a change in the 'mood' of the narrative trajectory. Second, Western pieces are used in a date scene between Ōkawa and Okinu at the seaside, when a semi-classic piece known as 'Drigo Serenade' (Riccardo Drigo) is played. This was a standard number since the 1920s, both inside silent film theatres (used for romantic scenes) and elsewhere (it was loved by amateur musicians). Shimada simply adapted the musical cliché for this scene. In the end of the scene it is mixed with a fade-in of the diegetic sound of festive drums and shamisen played by the villagers in the image, as if the romantic suspension of time is over. Third, the first underscored music is a *shakuhachi* solo during Ōkawa's arrival scene. The *shakuhachi* became popularised during the eighteenth century, when it was used by Zen Buddhist monks, and so the *shakuhachi* solo is associated with loneliness. For contemporary viewers, simply hearing the sound of the *shakuhachi* in the cinema must have been novel since it was not a standard instrument in the orchestra pit. The director and music director had more alternatives in tone colour than before: unlike the live performance of silent film accompaniment, the studio-produced soundtrack enabled the use of different instrumentation, depending on the characteristics of each scene. This experiment with *shakuhachi* must have been seen as successful since one can hear it again in the next collaboration between Nomura and Shimada, *Tokyo ondo* (1933).

The first verse of the title song is played in a date scene between Ichirō and Okinu. He has to leave the next day and she will be 'sold' to Tokyo during his absence. It is their last chance to see each other. The soundtrack consists of Katsutarō's vocals, the underscored music (a stock piece and then the title song) and sound effects. The date is first underscored by a gloomy theme with strings and flute. Then, Katsutarō's solo version specially recorded for this scene is inserted accompanied by the low sound effect of the seashore:

Haaa… a girl grows up on an island
I reach sixteen, with romantic feelings in my heart
Hidden from the eyes of people
I meet with my man just for one fleeting night

Although the situation of the two lovers is not the same, the lyrics endorse their 'fleeting' relationship. *Kouta eiga* screenings would play the phonograph of the title song during the romantic climax of the film. *The Island Girl* adopts this method replacing the record with the soundtrack. The song functions like an aria in an operetta, highlighting the emotion of characters as if time stopped. The scenes with Katsutarō's singing are not interrupted by intertitles, except once at the beginning of the final scene, discussed below, since Nomura knew well that her performance was the film's most highly anticipated moment. This vocal fragment is followed up by the continuation of background music before the song. The date continues and the second vocal fragment enters:

Haaa… the lights on the island go out
Plovers on the rocky shore
Don't cry for me
I am a sad small boat, abandoned

This verse was unrecorded in the bestselling record, probably due to the time limit on SP records. In the film, the lovers walk along a rocky shore, passing a boat as the song literally illustrates (the plover is a frequent romantic topos in traditional poetry). The image visualizes or anchors the lyrics as was typical in *kouta eiga*. As the couple goes to the horizon, one hears faintly the bell from a Buddhist temple, so as to be nearly unperceivable. It is a common sound effect in traditional Japanese theatre to punctuate a scene, announce the sunset, or to anticipate the tragic fate of the characters. Nomura probably aimed at dramatizing this song's scene with this theatrical device. It is followed by the title song's flute solo that closes the scene like a postlude.

The next time one hears Katsutarō is the final scene where Okinu and her friend, who knows the whole situation, return to the same seashore to mourn the dead Ichirō. The phonograph arrangement, perhaps re-recorded for the film, is played:

Haaa... the sea was rough away off the shore
East wind was the last wind
My man was a sailor
He won't return, he is at the bottom of the sea

Haaa...you must feel cold
The waves are your pillow every night
The snow falls lightly
Plovers cry over the night

Again, the lyrics describe the situation, except for the snowfall. In the days of silent film exhibition, the *benshi* might have recited the most appealing text in the climactic scene, accompanied by sentimental music, but here it is the popular song that jerks tears from the audience. Furthermore, mixed up with the sound effects of the seashore, the popular song is more integrated in the diegetic world than in *kouta eiga*, and played through the theatre's speakers, which by 1933 usually had better sound quality than the phonographs used for the earlier films.

Ending with the theme song was not uncommon for American and European sound and talkie films. Nomura adopted this practice, in which the recurrence of a familiar melody endorses the filmic unity. Katherine Spring argues that the 'theme song of the transitional era, constituted the theme in three ways: by association, by structural function, or by synoptic value'.[8] The title song in *The Island Girl* completes these functions in a much simpler way than her examples. It merely contributes to raising the emotional level of the romantic climaxes in the film.

Tokyo ondo (1933): Exploiting National Pandemonium in the Soundtrack

The raucous sound of 'Tokyo ondo' was the most popular song across Japan in the summer of 1933. Etymologically, *ondo* refers to a form of call and

8 Spring, *Saying it With Songs*, p. 98.

response in Buddhist ceremony but it has been secularized for centuries in the folk culture to mean a type of joyful dance and music. The nation wide success of 'Tokyo ondo' caused local organizations across Japan to commission hundreds of similar *ondo* pieces. Today, *ondo* has become a near-synonym for dance music in the summer *obon* festival. It is often said that the government exploited the pandemonium as an outlet for the people's increasing anxiety as the war situation in China grew worse. Victor's sales propaganda aggressively exploited all the media available: radio; journalism; record shops; posters; free lessons in how to perform the dance, which often turned into impromptu parties; and *yukata* (a light cotton kimono suitable for outdoor festivals in the summer) with the song title printed on them. Contemporary intellectuals remarked on the hype, and eighty years later 'Tokyo ondo' is still popular during the summer *bon odori*, 'dance festivals', held all over Japan.[9] It is also played after home team home runs and in the seventh inning stretch by the Tokyo-based baseball team Yakult Swallows.

The lyrics celebrate Tokyo as a capital, the Imperial Palace in its centre, and consequently Japan as a nation at the centre of the world. Different from the 'new folk song' that advertised local colour, the lyrics of 'Tokyo ondo' were appropriate no matter where the festivals were held. The local and the national were mingled together, or confused. The dance performance was commonly accompanied by a phonograph, played through loud speakers, along with the strong beat of a live *taiko* drum. Under the exclusive contract between Victor and Shōchiku, the tie-in film was directed by Nomura Hōtei and released in the last week of September. Shimada Harutaka was again the music director.

The title sequence starts with the familiar introduction of the title song. After the company logo, the first title is for the Tsuchihashi-shiki Shōchikuphone sound system, which shows that Shōchiku considered it as a selling point. We next see the title 'Sponsored by Jiji Shinpō Newspaper', commissioner of 'Tokyo ondo', along with the writing credits for the song. Perhaps the newspaper's sponsorship supported the budget of this all-star cast film. Unlike *The Island Girl*, the title confirms Shōchiku's exclusive contract with Victor. An embossed art title follows, which contains a reference to Nomura as the director. The staff credits then appear in the order of recording, music direction, arrangement, and sound effects in advance of the names of the scenario writer, assistant directors, and so on. It is only when the vocals enter that we see the cast, while the image of lanterns with the text 'Tokyo ondo' written on them move horizontally. The film already evokes a festive mood.

9 Takada 1933; see also Hosokawa 2000.

Figure 2.1 Advertisement card for *Tokyo ondo*, featuring lead actress Fushimi Nobuko in dancing pose and song lyrics.

The song fades out with the end of the title sequence and fades in again with the first sequence of close ups of Yajima Nobuko (Fushimi Nobuko) appearing from the *noren* hanging curtain of her home. This is a slower instrumental version, performed with clarinet. This music smoothly leads the viewer into the story, satisfying their desire to see a filmic adaptation of the already-known tune. This initial use of 'Tokyo ondo' sets up a narrative frame in which it plays an important role. Different from *The Island Girl*, in which the title song is played only in the particular scenes that are linked with the content of the lyrics, *Tokyo ondo* exploits the theme song's recurrence in a more refined way. It is not the lyric that matters to the plot but the festive mood. For example, a date scene with Nobuko and her fiancé Saitō Susumu (Oka Jōji) is underscored by another instrumental version, with clarinet and guitar. In his room, they momentarily mimic the dancing that goes with this music as an expression of their happiness. Nobuko must have taught him the choreography since she has learnt it in her traditional dance class, as shown in the previous scene. Later he also dances it, accompanying dancers and drunken friends, in a dance hall with music from an unseen source (phonograph or band). In an earlier scene of a dance class, a shamisen solo version of the title song is played by a musician we see in the background. It is superimposed (though not synchronized) with the hand clapping of dancers in kimono. However, in the later dance class scene, we hear Katsutarō singing alone (without accompaniment but with hand clapping), though no singer appears. The singer could be understood as a singing master in the classroom outside the frame, but rather than justify such far-fetched logic the director simply incorporates the audible participation of the star singer in his film, like an audio cameo, although her singing lasts less than thirty seconds.

In many cases, diegetic/non-diegetic distinctions would be irrelevant for contemporary viewers, who were used to hearing live music in the cinema that was evoked by the image but not synchronized to it.[10] For the same reason, the strict synchronicity between image and sound was not required as we notice in all the dancing scenes – jazz, Japanese dance, or *ondo*. Synchronization is realized only in two moments: Saitō's punching of his son and the breaking of glass that accompanies a fight. As discussed in the case of Ichirō's landing in *The Island Girl*, synchronization is nearly compulsory for this type of strong sound effect.

Many scenes in the film are underscored with music matching the 'mood' of the narrative. Throughout a tense scene of the break of the two lovers from

10 Slowik, *After the Silents*, p. 56.

their fathers in Susumu's room, one hears a sorrowful melody lasting for seven minutes. The continuity of the music implies that Nomura considered the series of dramatic shots as a single narrative unit. The melody sounds like a commercial song and is played about ten times. In the subsequent scene, one violin solo (later with saxophone) in minor key underscores the crosscutting between Susumu's room and Nobuko's over the course of four minutes. It suggests how they share the same affection for each other. A melodic unit is repeated several times. Such repetition is basic to the music of silent film since it is not the duration of the melody but that of the image that determines the accompaniment.

There are other examples of musical accompaniment typical of silent films. Ten different themes can be identified in the film. None of them are repeated or musically impressive – they function well as unperceivable 'background' music. Intentionally or not, it is only the title song that can potentially remain in viewers' minds. Three romantic scenes, for example, have three similar yet different pieces. The two piano pieces (instrumentally distinct from the orchestra sound) are played in two scenes widely separated in the narrative. It is not known whether all of these pieces are from Shimada's stock or his new compositions, whether this music-story association/dissociation is creative or uneconomic. Interestingly, a piece in major key played in the scene of imagining a future house on Susumu's property was recycled from that used to underscore a date scene between Okinu and Ōkawa in *The Island Girl*. Shimada, I suppose, must have recycled his stock pieces when necessary.

In the final climax, however, Shimada seems to go beyond silent routines by using different music sources depending on the filmic space. The scene consists in an alternation between Susumu's apartment, where the lovers are about to die by double suicide, and the other spaces where their families and friends are approaching to try to stop them. In the apartment, a sorrowful melody with *shakuhachi* and violin plays continuously, whereas in the other spaces an orchestral number is played (Saitō's house, Yajima's house) or silence is kept (the car ride). In addition, a sequence of an *ondo* festival is inserted. The successive shifting in and out of different types of music would be difficult, if not impossible, in the silent film theatre. At the climax, the audience is suddenly relieved by the shot of a broken mirror, which indicates that Susumu did not kill his lover. Simultaneously, the instrumental intro of 'Tokyo ondo' recurs. The next scene shows the festival, where all the characters join in and dance as a group to Katsutarō's singing. It is a version of the song specially made for the film. Curiously, the singer makes a mistake at the beginning and starts again. It makes one wonder whether

her performance was recorded at the same time as the image or separately (in the Victor recording studio, for example). Finally, the end mark appears with the lanterns in the same pattern as in the opening title sequence.

In *Tokyo ondo* Nomura Hōtei, in collaboration with his sound engineers, shows a more sophisticated planning of sound-image construction than in his previous work. One example is offered by a scene when Nobuko receives a call from Susumu in her dance classroom. Nobuko and the other women dance upstairs to a shamisen song, but the music stops when she goes downstairs to receive his call. The silence, excluding the music upstairs, focuses on their affection as if they did not hear anything but their respective voices. The music returns when she goes upstairs. The same sound-space scheme reoccurs during a later call in which Susumu tells her farewell. As Slowik mentions, in films of this period 'the music's volume is "conveniently" raised, lowered, or kept steady in ways that assist the narrative. Most often this occurs during romantic portions of the film'.[11] This is also applicable to the scene of Susumu's decision to kill himself. He remains despairing and alone in his room but the dance version of 'Tokyo ondo' fades in. The audience would understand that it comes from a loudspeaker in the neighbourhood because of Katsutarō's vocals. He says to himself, 'everyone is dancing crazy'. However, this diegetic music stops with the sound effect of knocking at the door. Nobuko arrives. The silence signifies the urgency of the situation.

One interesting instance of sound-story design is heard in the collective singing of Edo (the name of Tokyo before 1868) folk songs during the conversation scene between Yajima and Saitō in the former's house. Since it ends with loud laughter, it is presumably diegetic sound from a party of neighbours (the song could be a 'field' recording). Such large-sized vocal performances were naturally impossible in the exhibition of silent film. Furthermore, the singing must have been chosen in order to suggest the Shitamachi location (the 'lower city' of Eastern Tokyo, occupied predominantly by working class people and small businesses), of which Yajima's knitwear business was typical. Actually, such businesses had declined after the 1923 Great Kanto Earthquake that destroyed Tokyo's Shitamachi but contemporary audiences could easily associate his business with that location. His Shitamachi house contrasts with Saitō's suburban house built in the Yamanote district of Western Tokyo, which developed enormously after the Great Kanto Earthquake. This spatial contrast corresponds to other contrasts, such as Yajima's bankrupt business and Saitō's booming one (such people were called 'Manchurian millionaires', as they gained

11 Slowik, *After the Silents*, p. 117.

their fortune in the colonies), the Yajima family in kimono and the Saitō family in Western clothes, the traditional tatami house and the house with modern floors, as well as folk song and jazz.

To summarize, *Tokyo ondo* offers both a 'transplant of late silent film accompaniment practices' and an experiment in associating sound and image that is only feasible by utilizing a recorded soundtrack.[12] In *Kinema junpō*, the film critic Kitagawa Fuyuhiko refers to the film's sound only in one sentence, stating that: 'this is certainly sound film'. Evaluating the smart narrative trajectory and the actuality implied in the plot, he found no fault in the sound.[13] Is this, however, sufficient acknowledgement of the work involved in making the sophisticated soundtrack analysed above?

Sakura ondo (1934): Music Prologue and Alternative Story

In the spring of 1934, the largest media synergy in pre-war Japan was created. It was the 'Sakura ondo' (Cherry Blossom Dance) campaign in which twelve songs and ten films of the same title were released, and at least sixteen stage dramas and revues in Tokyo and Osaka used one of those songs, while the tunes and dramas were broadcast on the radio at least twenty times. All the songs mentioned the striking beauty of cherry blossoms, the euphoric feeling of cherry-blossom viewing parties, and the hopeful march of the imperial armies in China. Just as with 'Tokyo ondo', the nationalistic content caused the song to be deemed appropriate anywhere in the empire. Traditionally, the dancing during cherry-blossom viewing was freewheeling and unrelated to a specific song or rhythm. Now the routines changed. All the record companies wanted to replay the 'Tokyo ondo' rage, which had been monopolized by Victor. However, among the twelve recordings the Victor version by Katsutarō (accompanied by two male singers) was the only success. In many large cinemas live performances titled 'Sakura ondo' was presented with one of the recordings as a prologue. None of the other films were successful because, as a trade article noted, the first production, by P.C.L. (Photo Chemical Laboratory), betrayed the general expectation of creating a film as uplifting as the song.[14] Among the ten films *Kinema junpō* commented on, five were produced by the established studios (some were full talkies, the others sound versions). Only the Shōchiku Kamata version,

12 Slowik, *After the Silents*, p. 56.
13 Kitagawa, 'Tokyo ondo', p. 88.
14 Kojima, 'Sakura Ondo Tomodaore'.

Figure 2.2 Advertisement for P.C.L.'s *Sakura ondo /Cherry Blossom Dance*. At the bottom left, Katsutarō is standing in the middle, flanked by the main actresses in the film. *Kinema junpō*, 11 March 1934.

directed by Gosho Heinosuke, was critically well regarded.[15] However, its title song, from Columbia records, failed commercially, as did Gosho's film.

Victor contracted with P.C.L., which appointed Kimura Sotoji as director. However, he did not write a new script inspired by the song but instead adapted a scenario he had already prepared. The title song was nothing but an excuse to sell the film. In opposition to the uproarious mood of the song, the film implies social criticism as the reviews noted: 'Very dark and soggy film. We do not understand at all why it is called *Sakura ondo*'; 'It hardly seems like a faddish product, but its dampness does not match with the expectation of audiences'.[16] Reviewers thus appreciated the serious content but failed to see the films connection with its title song.

Kimura's film begins with a close-up of the record label. It starts rotating, while the camera tracks out to show a girl next to the Victor record player,

15 The film critic Kishi Matsuo liked P.C.L.'s version except the incongruity between the prologue and the narrative. See Kishi, 'P・C・L eiga: *Sakura ondo*', p. 65.

16 Q, '*Sakura ondo*', p. 5; 'Tōto eigakan: nigatsuyonshū, sangatsu isshū: bangumi oyobi keikyō chōsa', p. 26.

Figure 2.3a-d From the opening sequence of *Sakura ondo*.

putting the needle to the disc. Then, she coquettishly smiles at the viewer. The well-known intro to the song starts and the image shows the credit of the record and the names of special guests, two actresses from the Tokyo Takarazuka Girls' Opera (an all-female revue troupe) and three recording singers. The image is of jewel-like blossoms, accentuating the festive mood. After the title sequence, we see touristic images of cherry blossoms and Mt. Fuji, then a track-in on a singing Katsutarō in front of a plain background. For viewers this was the most anticipated moment because it was the first time Katsutarō had appeared in person singing in a film. It is followed by alternating shots of the cherry blossoms and each of the two male singers (Mishima Issei and Tokuyama Tamaki).[17] They sing directly to the camera without lip-synch. Technically the synchronization of image with pre-recorded song should not be difficult but here the studio did not even attempt it.

The alternation of artists and cherry blossoms in the 'Sakura ondo' title sequence together with the sound of the song enhances the star-song-title

17 'Sakura Ondo' was in fact recorded with Mishima, a male singer from folk song society, who was lesser known than Katsutarō. We hear his part in the vocal version in the film. Tokuyama came from concert music scene. However, their presence is totally eclipsed by that of Katsutarō. The centrality of Katsutarō and the marginality of co-singers are obvious in the film.

association. The blossoms in full bloom are amplified by the use of mirrors and a kaleidoscope, the overlapping and other visual effects in correspondence with the lyrics celebrating the happiness of both people and the country. While the song continues, outdoor location shots of geisha dancing at an event labelled 'Meeting of Sakura ondo, Victor Records' alternate with studio shots of modern dancers (from the Kokka Dance Hall, Tokyo, where the dance hall scenes were shot) and the two special guests from Takarazuka dancing around a cherry tree. This six-minute' prologue (taking up both sides of the SP record) looks more like an American music short (which were not distributed in Japan) or even music videos from the 1980s than the 'overture' to a film. Much more explicitly than the previous two films, *Sakura ondo* clarifies the commercial value of the 'star-song association' and this opening scene at least fulfils the promise of the film's advertisement – 'special participation of Katsutarō' – which made the public expect to see her singing in the narrative (she is photographed next to the actors in publicity shots).[18] The Katsutarō-song association must have been the film's strongest selling point. However, this prologue is totally independent from the main part of the film. The special guests never return. The title song will be repeated six times but played by either *chindon-ya* or a dance band.[19] Katsutarō's vocal is hardly audible.

The story focuses on Shizue, a young girl living in the working class Shitamachi who is about to sell herself to Maki, a wealthy man in a dance hall, to get medical treatment for her dying mother. Her troublemaker elder brother left the family some time ago, while her wise younger brother is about to enter middle school. The plot is centred on Shizue's affection for family. The class opposition of proletariat and bourgeoisie is obvious from the first scene in which the camera pans from a jazz party in a hilltop house to the shantytown below the hill where Shizue's family lives. The sound of *chindon-ya* fades in, while American dance music fades out, to articulate these special characteristics. The little daughter of the bandleader says to her father in a sad voice, 'I was ridiculed [...] because I had such a funny face' (she is made up to look like a dog). Her father consoles her, 'You are doing a good job and will become a big singer one day'.

18 Spring, *Saying it With Songs*, p. 72ff.

19 *Chindon-ya* refers to a street band for advertisement common since the late twenties ('chindon' is both a handy combined percussion of small taiko and mini-cymbals appropriate for street performance, and its onomatopoeia). They played any popular melody in broken style but were often despised because of their bizarre costume and poor musicianship. Due to their strong association with the underclass, they were sometimes spotlighted as Shitamachi heroes in proletarian literature. For more information see Marié Abe's *Resonances of Chindon-ya*.

Shizue works at the ticket counter of the Cherry Dance Hall. In the 1930s the dance hall was regarded as one of the most modern and sensual spots where bourgeois customers could physically touch the professional ('taxi') dancers. The dancers were generally considered to be erotic and dangerous women, as in the attitude of Shizue's neighbours toward her dancer friend Akiko. Shizue is not a dancer herself but the ticket counter is a contact zone connecting the outside society and the enclosed ballroom. In the first scene at the ticket counter, we hear the instrumental version of 'Sakura ondo'. In the next scene inside the hall, the couples dance to the tune (though the band is not represented). The volume is augmented in order to express the closeness to the sound source. Then the music changes to an American tune. Similar to the opening scene, jazz and 'Sakura ondo' are juxtaposed yet this time not in a class hierarchy but as both part of bourgeois life. Perhaps the sequence is intended to show how one cheerful rhythm integrates the nation, bridging the two separate classes: the association of *ondo* with Shitamachi that we see in the opening scene should be revised. Is such a national unity, however, Kimura's intention or a compromise to hide his Marxist views? The film he made directly prior to joining P.C.L., *Kawamukō no seishun/ Youth Across the River* (Onga geijutsu kenkyūjo, 1933), was harshly censored and he had previously been arrested by the police for subversive activity. Therefore, Kimura and P.C.L. had to be sensitive to any political message. It seems to me that the gesture toward class harmony is a way to appease the political censors, just as his use of the musical prologue was a way to make his dark film more commercial. If the independent prologue changes the form of the feature film, the use of the title song in the dance hall scenes would alter its content.

Katsutarō's vocal version is played only once, almost imperceptibly, for several seconds in an important scene in which Shizue remembers Akiko saying that Maki is a good man. Shizue finally makes up her mind to accept his proposition in order to help her mother. The song can be associated with its earlier playing in the Cherry Dance Hall, though the words and Katsutarō's voice have no particular function. In another scene in which she meets with her older brother, who is pursued by the police, one can also hear the loose collective singing of the title song, probably from a drunken cherry blossom party off-screen. Their wild singing makes a contrast to the intense situation, although the singing is recorded too low to be dramatic. These are the only vocal versions of the song in the film, none of which are effectively integrated into the narrative.

As with the two previously discussed examples, this film ends with the title song. The *chindon-ya* playing of 'Sakura ondo' fades in over an exterior shot of Shizue's house, and then the musicians enter the image and play it until the end mark. Whether the music is diegetic or not is ambiguous because the sound starts before the family is ready to perform and the instrumentation on the soundtrack differs from the trio in the image (the audible clarinet is absent from the image while the shamisen in the image is inaudible). However, the father's cue of *chindon* percussion to start the playing is synchronized (as with the strong sound effects discussed above). More than audio realism, director Kimura must have wanted to end the film with a cheerful *chindon-ya* performance as a bright symbol of Shitamachi life. In contrast to *Tokyo ondo*, however, no dancing congregation is represented in the long prologue and the relation of the title song to the narrative is markedly weak. Kimura only exploited the hype to produce a politically inflected melodrama. The important thing is that the title song starts the film and ends it. The prolonged prologue is excessive to the narrative but anticipates the conclusion. Nevertheless, Katsutarō and *chindon-ya* could not live together in the mind of the general public.

Conclusion

Michael Slowik argues that 'a theme song could thus operate both as a narratively related motif and as a commodifiable product'.[20] As for the latter, he analyses the close business relationship between Hollywood and Tin Pan Alley, noting that 'the major studios invested heavily in music publishing companies during this period'.[21] Sound and/or talkie films potentially produce hit songs. However, the Japanese case is the opposite, where a hit song could produce sound and/or talkie films but not inversely: no film studios were affiliated with or bought music publishers. The priority of hit songs – the one-way traffic from phonograph to screen – was almost a rule in the Japanese entertainment business. This might be caused by the failure of the Victor-Nikkatsu collaboration in Mizoguchi Kenji's *Tokyo kōshinkyoku/ Tokyo March* (1929). They tried to sell the talkie film and its theme song as a package, but the film ended up being silent due to the technical failure of the Mina Talkie sound system. The song, by contrast, was a historic hit (it reportedly sold over 300,000 copies), plugging into journalism, theatre, and all the emergent mass media, while the record was played in movie theatres in the same way as with *kouta eiga*. Although the exclusive tie-up

20 Slowik *After the Silents*, p. 48.

21 Ibid. p. 51.

between song and silent film became common afterwards, there are no examples of their bilateral profitability in this period. Mizoguchi's first talkie was *Furusato/Hometown* (1930) featuring the most popular tenor Fujiwara Yoshie, who sang pre-existent songs in the narrative. The title song, 'Furusato', recurs several times as a narrative key yet it was originally a school song published in 1914 (like 'Home, Sweet Home' or 'The Last Rose of Summer'). It was (and continues to be) a 'national' song fitting for Fujiwara's public image rather than a 'popular' song produced by the entertainment industry. The same is true for *The Neighbour's Wife and Mine*, which used all pre-existing songs, except for 'Speed Hoi', written by a studio composer and sung by a jazz 'madam' in the music scene. However, it did not become a hit song, or a number much consumed outside the cinema.

With the all-talkie increasing in the mid- and late 1930s, the tie-up between popular song and film became smoother and commercially more effective. Some top singers participated in the films as actors (even if only in cameos) and some actresses started recording title songs. Many films played the theme song in the romantic scenes or as 'attractions' in which the singer, suspending the narrative time for three minutes, presents a sort of mini show (for example, in the *kayō eiga*, or 'popular song film').[22] In other films, the instrumental version of the title song was underscored repeatedly throughout the film. With close analysis, one might discover the continuity of use of popular song from silent films to talkies. The actors recruited from the Asakusa revue scene and the actresses recruited from Girls' Opera could sing and act to launch new roles in the all-talkie popular song film. They were the central force of early musicals in Japan produced from 1933 onwards. The musicals were mainly oriented to urban audiences and most of the songs were Japanese translations of Western tunes. They had no tie-up with record labels, as did the *kayō eiga*. However, musicals such as Makino Masahiro's *Oshidori Utagassen/Singing Lovebirds* (1939) and *Hanako-san/Miss Hanako* (1943) used newly made theme songs in a more complicated way than the films discussed here. The director and music director of the later films were more sensitive to and familiar with Hollywood musicals than the (music) directors of our trilogy. Katsutarō's trilogy was produced simply to exploit the commercial power of her songs to the maximum, though she herself did not appear in the narratives.[23] It is an

22 See Raine, 'The Musical'.

23 Katsutarō appeared in a cameo in Shinkō Kinema's *Shima no Musume Katsutarō Monogatari/The Island Girl: Katsutarō's Story* (1933), directed by Suzuki Tarokubei (See '*Shima no Musume Katsutarō Monogatari*', p. 86.), and she played a leading role in *Katsutarō Komoriuta/Katsutarō's*

intriguing example of 'commerce and storytelling' in the transitional period, a period before the format and routines of sound-image synchronization and business conventions were fixed.[24]

Bibliography

Marié Abe. *Resonances of Chindon-ya. Sounding Space and Sociality in Contemporary Japan* (Middletown: Wesleyan University Press, 2018).

Hosokawa Shuhei. 'Sketches of Silent Film Sound in Japan: Theatrical Functions of Ballyhoo, Orchestras, and *Kabuki* Ensembles'. In *The Oxford Handbook of Japanese Cinema*, edited by Daisuke Miyao (Oxford: Oxford University Press, 2014), pp. 288-305.

Hosokawa Shuhei. 'Odoru nashonarizumu. *Tokyo Ondo* no wa to yagura'. *ex musica* 0 (February 2000), pp. 6-19.

'*Katsutarō Komoriuta*'. *Kinema junpō* 563 (1 January 1936), p. 102.

Kita. 'Miharayama' *Shin-seinen* (April 1935), p. 305.

Kitagawa Fuyuhiko. '*Shima no musume*' [Shōchiku version]. *Kinema junpō* 466 (1 April 1933), p. 125.

Kitagawa Fuyuhiko. '*Shima no musume*' [Henrī kinema version]. *Kinema junpō* 466 (1 April 1933), p. 125.

Kitagawa Fuyuhiko. 'Tokyo ondo'. *Kinema junpō* 486 (21 October 1933), p. 88.

Kishi Matsuo. 'P·C·L eiga: *Sakura ondo*'. *Kinema junpō* 499 (11 March 1934), p. 65.

Kojima Hiroshi. 'Sakura ondo tomodaore'. *Kinema junpō* 502 (11 April 1934), p. 12.

Q. '*Sakura ondo*'. *Asahi Shimbun*, 12 March 1934, p. 5.

'*Nagisa ni utau: Shima no musume*' [Kawai eiga version], *Kinema junpō* 464 (11 March 1933), p. 58.

Michael Raine. 'The Musical: *Heibon* and the Popular Song Film'. In *The Japanese Cinema Book* (London: BFI, 2020), pp. 335-347.

'*Shima no musume*' [Shōchiku version], *Kinema junpō* 464 (11 March 1933), p. 57.

'*Shima no Musume Katsutarō Monogatari*', *Kinema junpō* 486 (21 October 1933), p. 86.

Michael Slowik. *After the Silents. Hollywood Film Music in the Early Sound Era, 1926-1934* (New York: Columbia University Press, 2014).

Katherine Spring. *Saying It with Songs. Popular Music and the Coming of Sound to Hollywood Cinema* (Oxford: Oxford University Press, 2013).

Takada Tamotsu. 'Tokyo Ondo no Hanran'. *Kaizō* (November 1933), pp. 130-135.

Lullabye (1936), directed by Nagatomi Eijirō (see '*Katsutarō Komoriuta*', p. 102). Both of them were fictive (tear-jerker) biopics of Katsutarō herself, which testifies to her immense popularity.

24 Spring, *Saying it With Songs*, p. 1.

'Tōto eigakan: nigatsuyonshū, sangatsu isshū: bangumi oyobi keikyō chōsa'. *Kinema junpō* 465 (21 March 1933), pp. 25-28.
'Tōto eigakan: sangatsu sanyonshū: bangumi oyobi keikyō chōsa'. *Kinema junpō* 466, (1 April 1933), pp. 31-32.
'Tōto eigakan: nigatsuyonshū, sangatsu isshū: bangumi oyobi keikyō chōsa "Hibiya gekijō"'. *Kinema junpō* 500 (21 March 1934), p. 25-28.
Yoshimoto [Akimitsu]. 'Naze ryūkōka wa sanshinsuru?'. *Shin-seinen* (October 1935), p. 286.

About the Author

Hosokawa Shuhei is Professor Emeritus at the International Research Center for Japanese Studies, Kyoto. He is author of *Sentiment, Language, and the Arts. The Japanese-Brazilian Heritage* (Brill 2020) and coeditor of *Karaoke around the World: Global Technology and Local Singing* (Routledge 1998). He has written widely on the history of popular music in modern Japan, and has published in English on silent film sound and the sound design of *Godzilla*.

3 Japanese Cinema and the Radio

The Sound Space of Unseen Cinema

Niita Chie

Abstract

This chapter analyses two forms of radio drama in the late 1920s and early 1930s to show how the medium was linked to cinema as part of the culture of the sound image. It argues that *eiga monogatari* (film stories) narrated by *benshi* with a musical accompaniment advertised films and produced intermedia entertainment for their listeners. These *eiga monogatari* were displaced by *eigageki* (film dramas) that featured the voices of actors who could not yet be heard in the cinema, performing dialog from the film along with music and a *benshi* narration. The *eigageki* prepared the audience for synchronized Japanese talkies, even as the genre dissolved into regular radio dramas featuring film actors after the transition to sound.

Keywords: radio drama, *benshi*, cinema and radio, *eiga monogatari*, *eigageki*, talkies

On 17 March 1928, the Yomiuri newspaper ran an article called 'A Night of Movies'. This programme consisted of titles such as Chaplin's *The Circus*, Nikkatsu's *jidaigeki* (period film) *Chikemuri Takadanobaba*/*Blood Splattered Takadanobaba*, and a comedy, *Katsudō kyō jidai*/*Movie Crazy Age*, created by the Shōchiku studio. The names of *benshi* and musicians are listed as performers in the details for *The Circus* and *Blood Splattered Takadanobaba*, accompanied by the still photographs from the films. Shimazu Yasujirō is credited as director of *Movie Crazy Age*, along with familiar names of actors from the Shōchiku studio.[1] This article is not a programme for a film screening at a particular movie theatre. It is for a radio broadcast and

1 'Katteteki ni erabareta puro no Eiga no yū', p. 9.

Raine, M. and J. Nordström (eds.), *The Culture of the Sound Image in Prewar Japan*.
Taylor & Francis Group 2020
DOI: 10.5117/9789089647733_CH03

its detailed description is listed in the *Yomiuri* newspaper's radio section. According to this article, 'A Night of Movies' started at 7:30 pm on Tokyo Broadcasting Station, and each title was thirty minutes long. Chaplin's *The Circus* and Nikkatsu's *Blood Splattered Takadanobaba* were offered as *eiga monogatari* (film stories), one of the most popular genres of early Japanese radio, in which the story of each film was narrated by *benshi* with a musical accompaniment. On the other hand, Shōchiku's *Movie Crazy Age* was not exactly an adaptation of a film but based on an original script for radio created by a scriptwriter. Kitamura Komatsu wrote this 'radio comedy', and its feature role was played by Watanabe Atsushi, the screenwriter of and actor in the first Japanese talkie, *Madamu to nyōbō/The Neighbour's Wife and Mine* (1931). The director of this radio comedy was Shimazu Yasujirō, who, in collaboration with Kitamura Komatsu, led the production of Japanese early talkies a few years later, including *Jōriku daiippo/First Steps Ashore* (1932). Instead of still photographs from the film, the newspaper shows a photograph of actors standing in front of the radio microphone.

When we think about cinematic sound culture, we cannot ignore the fact that those working in both film production and exhibition were also involved in creating audible drama on the radio before the coming of the talkies. Since the 1925 start of radio broadcasts in Japan, and especially during the first decade, films were often adapted for the radio and reached audiences through the *benshi*'s narration, music, sound effects and actor's voice. In so doing, the emerging radio established itself as a mass medium, by exploiting the popularity of cinema. It was also a way in which film expanded cinematic space beyond the screen by using the sounds which best represented film at that given moment, from the *benshi*'s charismatic storytelling to film theme songs, or the actor's voice with which audiences were not yet familiar.

This cinematic space outside film was not, of course, constructed only by radio, but also through written media such as newspapers and magazines, along with other elements of sound culture including stage revues and phonograph records. However, Japanese radio broadcasting was not a commercial enterprise but a public one under the strong supervision of the government, which provided an official and legitimate aspect to the film-radio relationship that other industrial tie-ups such as film and phonograph companies lacked. Film-radio tie-ups were common elsewhere, but the most active period of the Japanese film-radio relationship is also different. In the United States, for example, industrial cooperation between the two media, especially radio adaptations of film, became popular from the mid-1930s, i.e. long after the talkies became the norm of film production.

In Japan, however, it was the opposite; we can find greater numbers of radio drama versions of films during the silent film period and in the early stage of talkies, and fewer from the mid-to-late 1930s.

Film and radio interacted in many ways: as radio dramas created by film directors and film actors, comic radio talk shows called *mandan* performed by *benshi*, music performances by movie theatre orchestras, and medleys of film theme songs. This chapter focuses on two genres of radio adaptation of film: *eiga monogatari* performed by *benshi*, and *hōsō eigageki* (broadcast film drama), or just *eigageki* (film drama), performed by film actors. It is worth analysing these two genres because they were particularly popular during the first decade of radio broadcasting, and because they show how the film diegesis was constructed beyond the screen through radio sound. It also makes clear that the shift of popularity from *eiga monogatari* to *eigageki* on radio parallels the transition from silent films to talkies in terms of sound representation and the mode of reception of film.

Media Regulation and Standardization

Japanese radio broadcasting started from the Tokyo Broadcasting Station in March 1925, followed by the Osaka Broadcasting Station in June, and the Nagoya Broadcasting Station in July. Although these three stations initially started as commercial corporations, they were soon incorporated into one public organization under government supervision. In 1926, the three stations were merged into Nippon Hōsō Kyōkai, later known as NHK. NHK went on to establish new stations in other areas of Japan, constructing a nationwide broadcasting network. Listeners would license the NHK broadcasts by paying a monthly 'receiving fee'.[2] On the first broadcasts by NHK there were 5000 license holders. By 1928, they had become half a million, a million in 1931, and two million in 1934. The radio penetration rate in Tokyo was the highest in the country: 22% in 1930, 50% in 1935, 75% in 1940, and 84% in 1942.[3]

One of the crucial aspects that characterized Japanese radio before WWII is that broadcasting was public, supervised by the government, and there was no commercial broadcasting supported by sponsors. Even before the establishment of NHK, the government was strongly aware of the potential of radio's influence on Japanese society, and the Ministry of Communications

2 The radio's receiving fee in 1929 was 75 sen per month, whereas the average ticket price for a movie was 40 to 50 sen. Sasa, *Rajio engeki*, p. 94.

3 Nihon Hōsō Kyōkai, *Nihon hōsō shi* Vol. 1, pp. 847-850.

became the authority over radio broadcasting. Whereas the control over press and film was achieved by post-censorship, radio broadcasting required pre-censorship. Scripts had to be checked in advance, and even when on the air, officials from the Ministry of Communications who monitored the broadcasting had the power to pull the plug if anything changed and became inappropriate.[4] They were eager to incorporate popular entertainment into radio programmes in order to increase the number of license holders, but they also made an effort to provide a public service, offering not necessarily popular programmes such as educational and cultural broadcasting. Throughout the 1920s and 1930s, radio became a major medium to support popular culture, along with motion pictures and magazines. However, the radio's primary character as public broadcasting under the government's control influenced radio programming, as well as the relationship between radio and other popular media.

The Japanese film industry was deeply impacted by 1923 Great Kanto Earthquake, which hit both film studios and movie theatres in the Tokyo area. However, the recovery was fast, and in 1923 the first western style reinforced concrete theatre was built in Osaka, and reconstruction of theatres in the Tokyo area soon followed. Spurred by the nationwide increase in the number of movie theatres, the output of film production almost doubled after the earthquake, which led to a golden age of Japanese cinema from the mid-1920s.[5] As film production and exhibition flourished, its regulation and control also became stronger. Film censorship, which had been conducted by local police forces, became a nationally uniform standard in 1925, governed by the Home Ministry. Along with the radio broadcasting which started in the same year, we can situate both film and radio in the same process of government control and national standardization, in spite of their diversity and popularity as mass culture.

As I will explore in the following section, the cinematic sound space of the 1920s to the early 1930s, which was relatively diverse and non-homogeneous compared to the visual space on the screen, explored another dimension through radio. At the same time, radio sound, whose existence was possible only when the Ministry of Communications authorized it, lent a legitimate, uniform nature to the cinematic sound space. Together with the technology of synchronized sound films, the construction of film diegesis through radio helped to create the homogeneous and uniform sound of talkie cinema.

4 Ibid., pp. 79-80.

5 Tanaka, *Nihon eiga hattatsushi*, p. 12.

Genres of Entertainment Broadcasting

Film-related radio programmes were among many genres of radio broadcasting in the 1920s and 1930s. The major categories of radio programmes of the day were 'culture', 'entertainment', and 'news'. Culture programmes, which include lectures, children's hour, and educational programmes, best represent the nature of Japanese radio as public broadcasting. Because of the immediacy of radio, news programmes were regarded as highly important, especially after the outbreak of the Sino-Japanese War in 1937. Within this news category, sports programmes, which started in 1927 as live broadcasts of high school baseball games, established the importance of that genre through reporting the Olympic Games in 1932 and 1936.

Whereas radio news programmes were established based on collaboration with a prior medium with the same role (i.e. newspapers), radio entertainment programmes were initiated by broadcasting the existing amusements of the day. This category could be divided into 'performing arts' (kabuki theatre, modern theatre, or oral storytelling such as *naniwabushi* and *kōdan*) and 'music' (Japanese music and Western music). There were also programmes that were not adapted from other media, but originated for radio, such as 'radio drama' and 'radio scenery' that used sound effects and sometimes dialog to conjure virtual scenes.

Film adaptations were broadcast on the radio from the very beginning of the medium. In March 1925, the French film *Les Misérables* was broadcast with narration by the *benshi* Kumaoka Tendō, and in April of the same year the cast of the Shōchiku film, *Daichi wa hohoemu/The Earth Smiles* (1925) performed a scene in front of a radio microphone. In the following years, the former style of adaptation with *benshi* came to be known as *eiga monogatari*, and the latter with film actors as *eigageki*. These two genres of radio adaptation of film became popular radio programmes in the first decade of the Shōwa period (1925-1935), as we can see in a popularity poll run by NHK Osaka station in 1932.[6]

Osaka-Rakugo: 10.4%
Naniwabushi: 10.2 %
Comedy: 8.9%
Eigageki: 7.8 %
Kōdan: 7.7%
Eiga monogatari: 7.7 %

6 Nihon Hōsō Kyōkai, *Rajio nenkan*, 1932, p. 297.

Radio Drama: 7.7%
Tokyo-Rakugo: 7.4 %
Manzai: 7.3%
Kabuki: 6.8%
Shinpa: 6.6%
Radio Scenery: 6.4%
Radio Revue: 5.1%

It is easy to imagine that oral storytelling such as *rakugo* or *naniwabushi* were ranked at the top among radio programmes, but why was the adaptation of film, a visual art form, so popular? And how were the actual radio drama versions of films aurally constructed? In order to answer these questions, we need to reconsider the sound practice of the contemporary cinema in relation to radio and other sound media. We will start with the *eiga monogatari* and the role of the *benshi*, which freely crossed the borders between cinema, radio and phonograph.

Eiga monogatari

Eiga monogatari was a genre of radio programme, in which a *benshi* narrates the story of a film with a musical accompaniment. In 1931, at the height of its popularity, 70 *eiga monogatari* were broadcast from the Tokyo Broadcasting Station alone.[7] In most cases, one *benshi* would narrate the radio version of one film. In later years, there were also medleys of *eiga monogatari* with multiple *benshi* performing in the same evening.

All broadcasting was done live; *benshi* and musicians visited a broadcasting station, and after a few rehearsals, they performed live in front of the microphone (see Fig. 3.1). Since it was forbidden to make records of broadcasts to sell commercially, it is hard to find a source that would allow us to know what was actually broadcast on the air.[8] There are a few ways to speculate, however, one of which is the newspaper radio section.[9] In June 1925, the first daily newspaper devoted to radio, *Nikkan Rajio Shinbun* was published. In November of the same year, the *Yomiuri* newspaper initiated its radio section, and other major newspapers such as the *Asahi* and the *Miyako* followed the trend. The articles in these newspapers printed

7 Ibid., p. 303.
8 Kurata, *Nihon rekōdo bunkashi*, p. 149.
9 Also, some of the scripts used for broadcasting can be found in NHK Hōsō Museum in Tokyo.

Figure 3.1 A reconstruction of an *eiga monogatari* broadcast from the film *Rajio no Jyoō/Queen of Radio* (P.C.L., 1935). A *benshi* (Ikoma Raiyū) performs beside the musicians.

not only radio programming and schedules but also detailed descriptions and even some scripts for each programme. The *Yomiuri* newspaper, for example, adopted 'lyrics-first' as a motto ensuring readers that they would always print the lyrics of the songs that were to be broadcast. In other words, newspapers not only provided broadcasting information, but also transcribed what was to be on the air.[10] People were able to understand the lyrics of popular songs or the dialogue of dramas coming from the radio, even when they could not clearly hear the sound (or, could not hear at all if they did not have a radio).

From reading the newspaper reports we can gather that *eiga monogatari* were often adapted from foreign films or Japanese period films, either before their release or while they were shown in movie theatres. The average length of an *eiga monogatari* was thirty to forty minutes; radio adaptations were obviously shorter than the original films. The newspaper radio sections

10 Yoshimoto Akimitsu, who initiated the radio section of the *Yomiuri* newspaper, gave the reason why his readers requested the lyrics of songs on the air: 'Our readers cannot be satisfied with, indeed become nervous about, just listening to the radio. Readers, or human beings in general, require not just listening, but seeing (in this case, reading)'. Nihon Hōsō Kyōkai, *Rajio nenkan*, 1932, p. 75.

provided synopses of films with still photographs. They also featured a portrait of the *benshi* and his professional profile, such as his usual venues and specialty film genres. Therefore, not only the original film, but also the *benshi* who narrated it became visible and reached an extended audience.

Many of the prominent *benshi* of the day appeared on the radio. At the Tokyo Broadcasting Station, Tokugawa Musei, Matsui Suisei, and Yamano Ichirō represented the sophisticated style of the Tokyo Yamanote area, while Ishii Shunpa and Kunii Shika gave energetic performances in the Asakusa style. Ikoma Raiyū and Ōtsuji Shirō who were best known for narrating foreign films were also regularly featured on the radio.[11] It is most likely that the *benshi*'s radio appearances were offered by broadcasting stations, and *benshi* were paid a 'performance fee' for each performance. Ōtsuji Shirō, one of the major *benshi* who performed on radio, recalled the early days of broadcasting. 'Radio was still a rare thing, and when we were asked to perform on radio, we were as excited as if we were "chosen" to be a bride'.[12]

What did radio appearances mean for the *benshi* in the 1920s? As Aaron Gerow suggests, from the 1910s to the 1920s, the *benshi*'s social status as well as their role in cinema changed greatly. Because of the criticism toward the conduct and morals of the early *benshi*, who were generally called *katsuben*, films as well as the *benshi* who narrated them became the target of regulation and censorship by the authorities. Also, because of the influence of the *jun'eigageki undō* (Pure Film Movement) in 1918, which advocated the importance of film text over the *benshi*'s oral storytelling, the *benshi* were gradually subordinated by the film text in movie theatres, just providing a smooth explanation of the film rather than being 'attraction' themselves.[13] In order to escape the negative image associated with the earlier name *katsuben*, the *benshi* began to call themselves *setsumeisha* ('explainers'). In the case of the radio *eiga monogatari*, the *benshi* was usually introduced under this title. Performing on radio along with other notable actors of traditional theatres and prestigious storytelling arts must have contributed to improving the *benshi*'s status. As Ōtsuji Shirō said, being on the radio was a proud achievement.

At the same time, the fact that radio programmes with *benshi* narration were possible indicates that the power of the *benshi* to create film diegesis

11 According to a popularity poll, Matsui Suisei was the most popular *benshi* of the *eiga monogatari*. See 'Nanashū engei to shinjin hōsō no suigyo: kouta no ninki nimanhyō o toppa suru', p. 10.

12 'Maruhadaka no eiga monogatari: Shibaura no karihōsōjō jidai', p. 5.

13 Aaron Gerow, *Visions of Japanese Modernity*, pp. 139-148, 210.

was still strong. While in movie theatres the *benshi* might have become secondary to film texts from the mid-1920s, they became the primary force to create cinematic sound space on the radio. A clear example of this would be the practice of broadcasting *eiga monogatari* before the film's release. The newspaper article that introduced the *eiga monogatari* of Chaplin's *The Circus* also wrote, 'among many benefits of listening to radio, one would be certainly listening to the *eiga monogatari* with music and sound effects before it is released in theatres'.[14] Broadcasting *eiga monogatari* before the release of the original film was sometimes criticized as advertisement for a particular company or theatre chain, when public broadcasting was supposed to forbid any commercials. Still, this practice indicates that it was possible to construct the film diegesis through the *benshi*'s narration.[15]

An even more extreme example would be the *eiga monogatari* of Chaplin's *City Lights*, which was broadcast by Yamano Ichirō on 15 July 1931. At that time, it was uncertain whether the film would ever be released in Japan. *Asahi* newspaper reported 'Chaplin's *City Lights*. Looks like it's not coming, for financial reasons. Suck it up, Japanese, and listen to the *eiga monogatari* on the radio'.[16] It was eventually released in 1934, but at the time of broadcasting of *City Lights*, even Yamano, who narrated it on the radio, had not seen the film. He created the *eiga monogatari* based on the information he heard from a reporter from *Kinema junpō* film magazine who had actually watched the film in the United States.[17] In this case, the broadcasting of the *eiga monogatari* cannot be said to have worked as an advertisement since no distribution company or theatre was expected to show the film. It was broadcast for Chaplin's fans in Japan, who were eager to see his latest film, offering an original sound space to the Japanese audience, independent from the film text.

The Phonograph and Music

The popularity of the *eiga monogatari* on radio was also paralleled by the popularity of *benshi* narration on phonograph records. Since 1925, many

14 'Katteteki ni erabareta puro no Eiga no yū', p. 9.

15 'Eiga monogatari no hōsō ni shūwai no jijitsu bakurosu benshi ni mo taigūsa no jōjitsu', p. 7. Here, a member of the staff at the Tokyo Broadcasting Station who was responsible for casting *benshi* in *film stories* was suspected of receiving bribes from film companies and *benshi*.

16 'Mā eiga monogatari de Nihonjin wa gaman shiro', p. 9.

17 'Minai eiga monogatari sore wa Chappurin no "Machi no hi"', *Miyako Shinbun*, 15 June 1931, p. 6.

records labelled as *eiga setsumei* ('film explanation') were released by several recording companies in Japan. Records of Western films and Japanese films, and especially those of *jidaigeki* were popular, usually accompanied by music. *Benshi* who often made phonograph records such as Kumaoka Tendō also appeared on the radio.[18] By establishing the popularity of *eiga setsumei* records, Watanabe Hiroshi pointed out the importance of voice narrative forms on Japanese records, contrary to the general expectation that the phonograph is a medium for pure music. Watanabe further argues that even after the coming of talkies, when the popularity shifted away from film explanation, the records of popular songs and music followed the pattern of records of storytelling, as we can see in *kouta setsumei* (popular song explanation), which featured a song with a *benshi*'s introduction, or offered a new narrative inspired by a song. Watanabe also suggests that this storytelling format offered a way to introduce western music to Japanese audience in a more familiar way.[19]

The integration of western music and storytelling was a common feature of the broadcasting of foreign films as well. For example, Fritz Lang's *Die Nibelungen: Siegfried* (1924) was released in Tokyo at the Teikoku Theatre on 20 March 1925, with narration by Tokugawa Musei, and Japanese Symphony Orchestra conducted by Yamada Kōsaku. They played the original score for the film composed by Gottfried Huppertz. The sound that accompanied this film was broadcast via radio the same year on 16 August.[20] Tokugawa Musei, who performed both in the cinema and the radio, recalls that when in the theatre the sound of the orchestra was so loud that he could not make his voice carry over it, therefore he was relieved to find that in the broadcasting station a microphone was placed in front of him.[21]

Typically, an orchestra of ten to twenty musicians offered musical accompaniment in major urban movie theatres in the 1920s. The music they played in the movie theatre could also be heard via radio. The Shōchiku orchestra, conducted by Shimada Harutaka, and the Nikkatsu orchestra conducted by Tanaka Tomiaki regularly performed for *eiga monogatari* on the radio. Because public broadcasting had the goal of cultural enlightenment, broadcasting opera or symphony music was favoured over popular music, despite the general disinterest towards western music.[22] Yamada

18 Kurata, *Nihon rekōdo bunkashi*, pp. 159-160.

19 Watanabe, *Saundo to media no bunka shigengaku*, p. 362.

20 Satō, '1925-1926 nen ni kakete no JOAK ni okeru opera kanren bangumi', p. 146.

21 Tokugawa, *Iroha kōyū roku*, pp. 109-110.

22 Nihon Hōsō Kyōkai, *Nihon hōsō shi*, p. 237.

Kōsaku's orchestra, for example, became the major source for western music programmes on radio, and many of the musicians of that orchestra were recruited from those in movie theatres.[23] Radio musical programmes contributed to the popularization of western music in Japan, which was in a close relationship with the sound practice of cinema.

Eiga monogatari and Sports Broadcasting

We can also find similarities between *eiga monogatari* and sports programmes. Sports broadcasting started in 1927, when the Osaka Broadcasting Station broadcast live coverage of high school baseball games. Since then, radio announcers regularly performed live commentary of sports events, especially baseball. Yamaguchi Makoto points out that radio created a new kind of participation, 'hearing' sports, which is different from 'playing' sports, or 'watching' sports.[24] Among radio announcers, Matsuuchi Norizō, for example, became well known to listeners by his sports coverage style inspired by *kōdan* storytelling. His commentary was so popular that the recordings of his play-by-play coverage of baseball matches between the Waseda and Keiō universities were released as phonograph records in 1930 and 1931 (although these recordings were not the coverage of actual games, but those of imaginary ones recorded in a studio). Sports broadcasting helped to increase the number of baseball fans and established an original space of participation in which 'a game is boring when it is seen, but exciting when it is heard'.[25] This kind of virtual liveness and audience participation was also seen during broadcasting of the Los Angeles Olympics in 1932. Since the Japanese broadcaster was not allowed to broadcast from the stadium, what they did instead was *jikkan chūkei* ('virtual coverage'); after they attended each event, they went to the studio where they could broadcast, and reported the event as if they were speaking live from the stadium.

Sports broadcasting and radio's *eiga monogatari* are similar in a sense that they both offer audible representation of something essentially visual (the player/actor's body movement) through sound effects and music (in the case of baseball games, they would be cheers, applause and songs by supporting groups) and, most of all, through oral description by interpreters (the announcer/*benshi*). Just as sports broadcasting could make a boring

23 Ibid., p. 240.
24 Yamaguchi, 'Kiku spōtsu no ririku', p. 110.
25 Takeyama, *Rajio no jidai*, p. 186.

game exciting, *benshi* narration did sometimes 'make a bad movie good'.[26] As radio sports coverage created a new space of participation based on a game at a stadium, *eiga monogatari* on radio produced cinematic space through sound outside of the movie theatre.

Shimizu Hiroshi's *Daigaku no wakadanna*/*Young Master at University* (1933) portrays the captain of a college rugby team, who struggles to choose between his love life and the team's victory in a game. This film was made as a 'sound version', which was a common format during the transitional period from silent to talkies in Japan. It has synchronized sound effects and music, but no dialogue. The only time that we hear the human voice in this film is in the final scene of the rugby match, when we can hear the voice of a radio announcer reporting the game. This voice has been synchronized as diegetic sound (the captain's father is listening to radio at home). However, the sound could have been offered by a *benshi*, or could have been interchangeable with the *benshi*'s voice during the screening in a movie theatre. This film incorporated the human voice usually offered by a *benshi* into the diegetic sound of the film text. The film has everything that constitutes the diegetic sound of the film: music, sound effect, cheers, songs, and applause, except one thing: dialogue by characters.

Eigageki

The issues concerning the transition to talkies in Japan are usually demonstrated by the displacement of *benshi*, and, unlike in the United States, the fact that few actors were replaced because of their 'good' or 'bad' voice. Before the talkies, however, the voices of the film actors were already put on trial, in a sense, through their exposure on the radio. Since the beginning of Japanese broadcasting, radio stations were eager to present notable actors from kabuki, *shinkokugeki* (the new theatre for drama with historical subjects), *shinpa* (the new theatre for drama with contemporary subjects), and s*hingeki* (modern western-style theatre) on their programmes. Film actors also appeared on radio from the early days; the cast of Shōchiku's *The Earth Smiles* acted a scene from the film for radio in April 1925. Since then, radio adaptations of film with screen actors were broadcast as *eigageki*. On 16 January 1926, for example, Mizoguchi Kenji's *Kami ningyō haru no sasayaki*/*A Paper Doll's Whisper of Spring* was broadcast with the same cast as the film, featuring

26 Anderson, 'Spoken Silents in the Japanese Cinema', p.287.

Umemura Yōko.[27] It is not certain whether Mizoguchi himself directed this radio adaption. However, the programme was not well received.[28] Based on what we can glean from the newspaper column, which cited only the actors' names, we can speculate that their dialogue alone could not constitute a radio drama well enough to be understood by the audience.

The first newspaper article which discussed *eigageki* as a genre, was an article on *Kami no sugata/The Form of God*, which was aired on 15 December 1926.[29] Iwatō Shisetsu directed the film, which was released in the following year 1927. This radio drama was called 'the first *broadcast eigageki*', and Iwatō explain this genre as 'the mixture of *eiga monogatari* and broadcast theatre drama'. There is an excerpt from the script in the newspaper article, from which we can understand that Iwatō (the director and a former *benshi*) provided the narration, and the climax of the story was portrayed through the actors' dialogue. Iwatō also notes that there are too many sound effects in ordinary radio dramas, so he decided to use music instead to portray actions and dramatic emotions. These descriptions indicate that broadcast *eigageki* took over the format of *eiga monogatari* with *benshi* and musicians and added the actors' dialogue as a kind of attraction.

Eigageki and Talkies

Although there are a few *eigageki* in 1925 to 1928, it was after 1929 that *eigageki* became a prominent genre along with the popularity of *kouta eiga* (ballad films) and talkies. Although previous attempts had been made at launching sound film in Japan, the first successful exhibition of synchronized sound films in Japan is usually recognized as 9 May 1929, when the Fox Movietone films, *Marching On* and *Songs of the South Seas* were released. On 26 May, the sound of *Alibi*, another early talkie was broadcast live from the Musashinokan in Tokyo. 'It was brief and some lines of dialogue were cut, but the scenes with sound effects were clearly broadcast and became a good introduction to the talkies'.[30] It was also reported that although they could broadcast directly from the Movietone projector, in order to present the theatrical presentation, they picked up the sound from the speakers in

27 'Hōsō eiga geki: *Kami ningyō (Haru no sasayaki)*', p. 9.
28 Komagome, 'Hōsō eiga geki', p. 10.
29 'Hōsō eiga geki: *Kami no sugata*', p. 10.
30 *Rajio no nihon*, July 1929, quoted in Nihon Hōsō Kyōkai, *Nihon hōsō shi* Vol. 1, pp. 268-269.

the theatre, with the narration of the *benshi* Tokugawa Musei. A Japanese radio magazine noted:

> First we heard the pleasant overture indicating that an incident happened, followed by the second reel of film with Jazz and chorus in the National Theatre, and the sound of an automobile explosion, whistle by the police, gunshots, a knock on a door and a scream. Those sounds were broadcast vividly and realistically [...]. This is the handshake of talkie and radio. This is the revolution of the 'machine art'.[31]

On 27 May, the day after this live broadcast from the Musashinokan, *Tokyo kōshinkyoku/Tokyo March* (1929) was broadcast as an *eigageki* from the Osaka Broadcasting Station. *Tokyo March* was the first example of a film that exploited the theme song through a tie-up between a film studio and a phonograph company. The film was originally planned as a talkie, but because of technical difficulties, ended up as a silent film.[32] While the film itself was silent when it was shown in a movie theatre, the sound it was supposed to have (i.e. the actors' voices and the theme song) was broadcast via radio under the direction of the film director, Mizoguchi Kenji. Tanaka Masasumi has argued that 'the ideal form of *Tokyo March* as a talkie was realized by dividing image and sound, silent film and radio drama'.[33] Tanaka sees the significance of *eigageki* on the radio in the late silent era as follows:

> *Eigageki* served as virtual talkies before the actual coming of talkies. Silent films without sound and radio without image came together and simulated talkies. As a precedent form, we can say that the *eigageki* was 'another trailer for the talkie'.[34]

Eigageki as virtual talkies were popular until the mid-1930s, i.e. until the talkies became the norm of film production. *Madamu to nyōbō/The Neighbour's Wife and Mine*, the first successful Japanese all-talking film, was released in August 1931. If we look more closely at the *eigageki* that were released during this period, we can understand the changes in sound practice of both cinema and radio. The following table gives the titles of *eigageki* adapted from silent or part-talkie films in the 1931-1932 season.

31 Ibid.
32 Nagato, *Eiga onkyō ron*, pp. 67-68.
33 Tanaka, *Ozu Yasujirō no hō e*, pp.151-152.
34 Ibid.

Table 3.1 Titles of *eigageki* adapted from silent or part-talkie films in the 1931-1932 season

1931-10-12	BK	*Dokusō*	Shinkō Kinema	silent
1931-11-1	AK	*The Brothers Karamazov*	German film	talkie
1931-11-1	AK	*Seishun zue*	Shōchiku	silent
1931-11-1	AK	*Shinshaku benten kozō*	Nikkatsu	silent
1931-12-8	BK	*Uwasa no onna*	Shinkō Kinema	silent
1931-12-12	AK	*Nanatsu no umi*	Shōchiku	silent
1932-1-3	AK	*Adauchi senshu*	Nikkatsu	silent
1932-1-12	AK	*Konjiki yasha*	Shōchiku	silent
1932-2-1	BK	*Tetsu no hanawa*	Shinkō Kinema	silent
1932-2-19	AK	*Manshū kōshinkyoku*	Shōchiku	part-talkie
1932-2-20	BK	*Ogasawara ikinokami*	Shinkō Kinema	silent
1932-2-26	BK	*Hatobue o fuku onna*	Nikkatsu	silent
1932-4-2	BK	*Daichi ni tatsu*	Nikkatsu	silent
1932-4-20	AK	*Ginza no yanagi*	Kawai Film	silent
1932-4-26	BK	*Saikun kaihōki*	Nikkatsu	silent
1932-5-20	BK	*Tsukishiro*	Shinkō Kinema	silent
1932-5-25	AK	*Eikan namida ari*	Fuji Film	silent
1932-6-10	AK	*Taiyō wa higashi yori*	Shōchiku	sound
1932-8-10	BK	*Shin gion kouta*	Shinkō Kinema	silent
1932-9-4	AK	*Hototogisu*	Shōchiku	silent

AK=Tokyo Broadcasting Station; BK=Osaka Broadcasting Station. Source: Nihon Hōsō Kyōkai, Rajio nenkan, 1933, p. 454.

As we can see from this list, the original films adapted into radio drama were those from Nikkatsu, Shōchiku, Shinkō Kinema and some minor studios, and included P.C.L. after 1933. *Eigageki* were broadcast either from the Tokyo station (AK) or the Osaka station (BK), two major areas of film production and film talent. Among the titles, *The Brothers Karamazov* is the only foreign film; the original German talkie was adapted into a radio drama, performed by Maruyama Sadao and other *shingeki* actors.[35]
The original cast performed in each radio adaptation, which was usually broadcast before the release of the film (see Fig. 3.2). Since Japanese radio was not a commercial organization, there was no industrial tie-up between film

35 Most *eigageki* were based on Japanese films, but there are a few adaptations of foreign films as well. These were performed by Japanese actors; the resulting radio drama could be seen as a trial of dubbing foreign talkies. A notable example is the adaptation of *Dishonored* (Paramount, 1931); the role of Marlene Dietrich was played by Okada Yoshiko, the role of Victor McLaglen was played by Tokugawa Musei, narration by Yamano Ichirō, and direction and staging by Furukawa Roppa. It was introduced as a 'radio talkie'. *Asahi Shimbun*, 19 July 1931, p. 5.

Figure 3.2 Cast of the *eigageki* adaptation of *Taiyō wa higashi yori/The Sun Rises in the East* (Shōchiku, 1932). First published in Sasa Kenji. *Rajio engeki*. Tokyo: Dōbunsha, 1934, p.271.

and radio as we see between Nikkatsu and Victor Records with *Tokyo March*, or between P.C.L. and Dai Nihon Bīru Kabushiki Kaisha, later restructured post war into Asahi Beer, with the film *Ongaku kigeki: Horoyoi jinsei/A Tipsy Life* (1933). However, we can surely imagine that studios took advantage of their films appearing on radio before the film release for advertisement purposes.[36]

Some Features of *Eigageki*

Sasa Kenji, a writer at NHK, analysed the radio adaptation of Shōchiku's *Ai yo jinrui to tomo ni are/Love, Be with Humanity* in his book, *Rajio engeki*.[37] His analysis gives us an understanding of the main features of the *eigageki*. The radio drama version was broadcast on 12 April 1931, and the original

36 There was no direct contract between radio stations and film studios or actors, nor any regular programmes hosted by film actors. However, Shōchiku once requested that radio stations should first ask the company before they offered a radio appearance to their contract players. 'Haiyū no mudan hōsō makarinarane: kongo, kōshō wa chokusetsu Shōchiku e to JOAK e mo mōshiire', p. 7.

37 Sasa, *Rajio engeki*, pp. 273-282.

film was released a week later. The film featured Kamiyama Sōjin, who had worked in Hollywood and made a big comeback with this film. The *eigageki* on the radio also featured Kamiyama, and the other original cast, including Suzuki Denmei and Tanaka Kinuyo. The 'explainer' of the drama was *benshi* Shizuta Kinpa, the 'broadcast conductor' was the film director, Shimazu Yasujirō, and the 'musical conductor' was Shimada Harutaka conducting the Shōchiku orchestra. The *eigageki* starts with the announcement of the cast by a radio announcer, followed by musical accompaniment and the theme song by Satō Hachirō. After Shizuta explained the characters and their relationships, the audience heard the actors' dialogue. The *benshi*'s explanation and the actors' dialogue were integrated throughout the play, until Shizuta wrapped up the story and the programme ended with the theme song.

This example shows that all the various forms of sound that cinema exhibited during the transitional period from silent to talkies, such as the actors' dialogue, the *benshi*'s explanation, theme song, and music, were brought together in the radio *eigageki*. For *eigageki* of Shōchiku films, Shizuta Kinpa usually provided the narration. The writer of the article argues regarding the role of *benshi* in *eigageki*:

> Most of *eigageki* are broadcast on a date close to the original film release. Casting a *benshi* such as Shizuta Kinpa, who is famous for his Asakusa style emotional narration, is not purely to create a dramatic narrative, but rather to evoke the atmosphere of a movie theatre, and consequently the popularity of cinema.[38]

The writer further notes that this rendering of the atmosphere of cinema is one of the unique aspects of *eigageki*, which cannot be seen in ordinary radio dramas. The *eigageki* also provides music more continuously than ordinary radio dramas. In *Love, Be with Humanity*, every scene -- romance, forest fire, wedding, quarrel, reconciliation between father and son -- is accompanied by music. In those scenes, the role of the music was to evoke the atmosphere of the cinema.

These practices of *eigageki* are reminiscent of those of silent film exhibition or *eiga monogatari* on the radio, but *eigageki* is also accompanied by a theme song. This is surely related to the popularity of *kouta eiga* such as *Tokyo March*. On the other hand, the *benshi* narrated *eiga monogatari* gradually lost its popularity. Some contemporary critics argued that this was

38 Ibid., pp. 271-272.

due to the change of sound that represented the cinema, from the *benshi*'s narration to the theme song.

> The reason behind the decline of *eiga monogatari* is the development of talkies. First, since the *benshi* narration was eliminated from typical film exhibition, it became more and more a form of storytelling, and not associated with film. Second, the sound associated with film is no longer a *benshi* narration but a theme song. So, along with the development of talkies, we need to popularize theme songs.[39]

Newspapers' radio sections listed the titles of theme songs and their lyrics. Singers who sang theme songs would be credited as 'solo artist', acquiring a status equal to that of which the *benshi* previously had. Among those popular singers, Hagoromo Utako and Mano Kikuyo often appeared in *eigageki* on the radio.

Lastly, the most important feature of the *eigageki* was the actors' voice. I could not find any sources that discussed how audiences reacted when they first heard the voice of famous screen actors.[40] Whether the initial audience response was positive or not, the fact that those actors who appeared on radio continued their career after cinema's conversion to sound indicates that their voices had indeed been accepted by the audience. We can even speculate that one of the reasons there was little replacement of actors during the transition from silent to talkies in Japan was that screen actors had already confronted the microphone on the radio before the coming of talkies. In the United States, where motion picture and radio were both commercial enterprises, it was not until 1932 that the severe competition between the two industries turned into cooperation. Radio adaptations of films performed by Hollywood screen actors only became regular programmes on the air after the mid-1930s.[41] In Japan, radio broadcasts by film actors became prominent during the late silent period and the early years of talkies. Once talkies became the norm of film production and exhibition, the number of radio dramas adapted from film decreased.

It was not only film actors but also directors that made their microphone debut on the radio before they made talkies. Whereas in the United States,

39 Nakagomi, 'Ian Hōsō to Rōmushasō', p. 24.

40 According to NHK *Hōsō* magazine, rather than being impressed the audience was likely disappointed by the actors' poor delivery of dialogue. Ibid., p. 20.

41 For details on the Hollywood film industry and radio, or screen actors on radio drama, see: Jewell, 'Hollywood and Radio' and Hilmes, *Hollywood and Broadcasting*.

the director of radio drama usually came from the radio field, most *eigageki* on Japanese radio were directed by the director of the original film. Tanaka Masasumi pointed out Shimazu Yasujirō and Mizoguchi Kenji as two major film directors who were most active working on radio.[42] Shimazu, for example, made his radio debut when he directed the radio adaption of his own film *Obotchan/The Young Master* in 1926. In the same year, he wrote and directed an original radio drama called *Tetsuro no tsubuyaki/Whisper of the Metro Line*, in which he made experimental use of the microphone by adapting cinematic techniques into radio such as using voice close-ups and voice overlapping between scenes. He directed another original radio drama, *Katsudō kyō jidai/Movie Crazy Age* written by Kitamura Komatsu in 1928. After he directed a few radio adaptations of his own films including *May Love Be with Humanity* in 1931, he directed his first talkies, *Shōhai/Win or Lose* and *Jōriku daiippo/First Steps Ashore*, both in 1932.

In the case of Mizoguchi, before he directed his first sound film, the part-talkie *Furusato/Hometown*, in 1930, three of his films had already been adapted into radio. He came to direct radio adaptations of his films *Tokyo March* in 1929, and *Taki no shiraito/The Water Magician*, *Aizō Tōge/The Mountain Pass of Love and Hate*, and *Maria no Oyuki/Oyuki the Virgin* in 1933. He also directed radio adaptations of his talkies, including *Naniwa erejī/Osaka Elegy* and *Gion no kyōdai/Sisters of the Gion* in 1936. As Tanaka Masasumi has shown, Mizoguchi directed the radio drama of *Tsuchi/Earth*, based on Nagatsuka Takashi's novel, with *shinpa* actors in 1937. This acclaimed radio drama led to the film adaptation of the novel, which was directed by Uchida Tomu in 1939.

Conclusion

As *benshi* gradually disappeared from movie theatres, the *eiga monogatari* as a radio genre also faded out. By 1932 when the *benshi* strikes against the talkies reached their peak, some *benshi* such as Tokugawa Musei, Ōtsuji Shirō, and Matsui Suisei had already established themselves as radio personalities, and worked actively on *mandan*, a new radio genre of comic storytelling. They continued making *eigageki* after the arrival of the talkies for several years, but by 1940, they were categorized as general radio drama, not specifically as adaptation of film. As for the broadcasting of foreign films, *talkie chūkei* (live broadcasting of talkies) became popular from 1935

42 Tanaka, *Ozu Yasujirō no hō e*, pp. 149-153.

to 1939. It broadcast musical scenes of foreign films from the screening room of distribution companies. Notable examples of broadcast films are *Leise flehen meine Lieder, Top Hat, Silly Symphonies, One Hundred Men and a Girl, Moonlight Sonata*, and *The Big Broadcast of 1938*. These live broadcasts of musical scenes from films were categorized as music programmes on the radio rather than radio dramas.

This chapter has focused on radio adaptations of film as a primary example to show the intermedia relationship between film and radio. If we broaden our focus on actors' appearance on the radio, there are many more examples. For example, Natsume Sōseki's *Sanshirō* was adapted into a radio drama performed by actors from the P.C.L. studio and directed by Yamamoto Kajirō in September 1936. In April the same year, P.C.L. had produced the film adaptation of Natsume Sōseki's *Wagahai wa neko de aru/I Am a Cat* with the same cast and director. We can see the subsequent radio adaptation as a kind of sequel to the film adaption of a novel by the same author. In other instances, some film directors directed radio comedies, for example Shimazu Yasujirō's *Movie Crazy Age*, and Shimizu Hiroshi's *Fūsendama to pajama to koi/Balloon, Pyjama and Love,* which was broadcast on 20 September 1931. These radio comedies were advertised with the name of the studio and must have constituted an aspect of Shōchiku's modernism at the same time that they helped define the style of each director.

The relationship between film and radio in the late 1930s was foregrounded by an *eigageki* event featuring the major studios on 2 October 1939.[43] On this programme, actors from the five major studios (Nikkatsu, Shōchiku, Daito, Tōhō, Shinkō) were all gathered at the Tokyo Broadcasting station, where they performed radio drama versions of their films. At the beginning of the *eigageki*, there was an announcement by the government of the *Eigahō* (motion picture law), which became effective a day before the broadcast. Government control over the film industry was manifested via a medium that was from its start under the supervision of the government. Radio, which diversified the cinematic sound space starting in the mid-1920s, now served to bind the film industry into one homogeneous voice.

The *eiga monogatari* and the *eigageki* constituted a cinematic sound space beyond the movie theatre. The *eiga monogatari*, integrated with newspaper radio sections and phonograph records of storytelling, expanded the diegesis of films through the *benshi*'s narration. Like contemporary radio sports broadcasting, it helped to create a new form of audience participation, even as it was sometimes completely independent of the diegesis presented on

43 'Gosha kyōen no eiga geki', p. 6.

screen. In *eigageki*, which also had *benshi* narration and music, the voice of the actors served as the main attraction. Along with the coming of talkies and the popularity of the *kouta* films, the creative force of sound changed from the *benshi*'s voice to theme songs and the actors' voice. In the midst of the technical difficulties of the early talkies, radio sound complemented the lack of synchronized film sound by providing new alternatives or possibilities of cinematic sound. The coming of the talkies changed a great deal of cinematic sound from the diversity of the *benshi*'s live performance to the uniformity of the synchronized sound of the actors' voices. It was between this diversity and uniformity of cinematic sound that the inter-media relationship of Japanese film and the radio was created.

Bibliography

J. L. Anderson. 'Spoken Silents in the Japanese Cinema; or, Talking to Pictures: Essaying the *Katsuben*, Contextualizing the Texts'. In *Reframing Japanese Cinema: Authorship Genre, History*, edited by Arthur Nolletti, Jr. and David Desser (Bloomington: Indiana University Press, 1992), pp. 259-311.

'Eiga monogatari no hōsō ni shūwai no jijitsu bakurosu benshi ni mo taigūsa no jōjitsu'. *Yomiuri Shimbun*, 13 January 1929, p. 7.

Aaron Gerow. *Visions of Japanese Modernity: Articulations of Cinema, Nation, and Spectatorship, 1895-1925* (Berkeley: University of California Press, 2010).

'Gosha kyōen no eiga geki'. *Yomiuri Shimbun*, 2 October 1939, p. 6.

Michele Hilmes. *Hollywood and Broadcasting: From Radio to Cable* (Urbana: University of Illinois Press, 1990).

'Haiyū no mudan hōsō makarinarane: kongo, kōshō wa chokusetsu Shōchiku e to JOAK e mo mōshiire' *Yomiuri Shimbun*, 19 August 1930, p. 7.

'Hōsō eiga geki: *Kami ningyō (Haru no sasayaki)*'. *Yomiuri Shimbun*, 16 January 1926, p. 9.

'Hōsō eiga geki: *Kami no sugata*'. *Yomiuri Shimbun*, 15 December 1926, p. 10.

Richard B. Jewell. 'Hollywood and Radio: Competition and Partnership in the 1930s'. *Historical Journal of Film, Radio and Television* 4:2 (1984), pp. 125-141.

'Katteteki ni erabareta puro no eiga no yū'. *Yomiuri Shimbun*, 17 March 1928, p. 9.

Komagome Junsei. 'Hōsō eiga geki'. *Yomiuri Shimbun*, 22 January 1926, p. 10.

Kurata Yoshihiro. *Nihon rekōdo bunkashi*. (Tokyo: Iwanami Bunko, 1960).

'Mā eiga monogatari de nihonjin wa gaman shiro'. *Asahi Shimbun*, 15 June 1931, p. 9.

'Maruhadaka no eiga monogatari: Shibaura no karihōsōjō jidai'. *Asahi Shimbun*, 1 June 1931, p. 5.

'Minai eiga monogatari sore wa Chappurin no "Machi no hi"'. *Miyako Shinbun*, 15 June 1931, p. 6.
Nagato Yohei. *Eiga onkyō ron: Mizoguchi Kenji eiga o kiku* (Tokyo: Misuzu Shobō, 2014).
Nakagomi Motojirō. 'Ian Hōsō to Rōmushasō'. *Hōsō* 5.10 (1935), pp. 22-25.
'Nanashū engei to shinjin hōsō no suigyo: kouta no ninki nimanhyō o toppa suru'. *Yomiuri Shimbun*, 29 October 1929, p. 10.
Nihon Hōsō Kyōkai. *Nihon hōsō shi* (Tokyo: Nihon Hōsō Kyōkai, 1951).
Nihon Hōsō Kyōkai. *Nihon hōsō shi* Vol. 1 (Tokyo: Nihon Hōsō Kyōkai, 1965).
Nihon Hōsō Kyōkai. *Rajio nenkan* (Tokyo: Nihon Hōsō Kyōkai, 1932).
Nihon Hōsō Kyōkai. *Rajio nenkan* (Tokyo: Nihon Hōsō Kyōkai, 1933).
Sasa Kenji. *Rajio engeki* (Tokyo: Dōbunsha, 1934).
Satō Suguru. '1925-1926 nen ni kakete no JOAK ni okeru opera kanren bangumi'. *Ōmon Ronsō* 85 (2013), pp. 135-157.
Takeyama Akiko. *Rajio no jidai: Rajio wa chanoma no shuyaku datta* (Kyoto: Sekai Shisōsha, 2002).
Tanaka Jun'ichirō. *Nihon eiga hattatsushi* Vol. 2 (Tokyo: Chūōkōronsha, 1980).
Tanaka Masasumi. *Ozu Yasujirō no hō e: modanizumu eigashi ron* (Tokyo: Misuzu Shobō, 2002).
Tokugawa Musei. *Iroha kōyū roku* (Tokyo: Masu Shobō, 1953).
Watanabe Hiroshi. *Saundo to media no bunka shigengaku* (Tokyo: Shunjū-sha, 2013).
Yamaguchi Makoto. 'Kiku spōtsu no ririku'. In *Taishū bunka to media*, edited by Yoshimi Shunya and Tsuchiya Reiko (Kyoto: Mineruba Shobō, 2010).

About the Author

Niita Chie is Associate Professor in the Graduate School of Human and Environmental Studies, Kyoto University. She has written on the presence of radio in American film history, comparative histories of the variety stage in Japan and the USA, and is currently engaged in a study of performance in American audiovisual media.

4 Architecture of Sound

The Modernization of Cinematic Space in Japan

Ueda Manabu

Abstract
This chapter shows how cinema architecture responded to the demands and affordances of the film medium during the silent period and the transition to sound. It traces a series of developments in the orientation, size, and distribution of cinemas in Japan and argues that they contributed to the tendency toward a unified and synchronized presentation of films. Purpose-built cinemas changed their layout from the wide and shallow theatre format to box-like spaces oriented around a long axis that focused audience attention on the screen. With the introduction of amplification and recorded sound, cinemas also increased in size and spread around the country, enabling a standardized cinema experience through the creation of uniform seating and the production of sound films.

Keywords: cinema architecture, theatre architecture, cultural geography of cinema, film exhibition, uniform seating

Introduction

This chapter argues that the cinema, as an apparatus of film reception, changed its exhibition space as sound film spread in Japan. The introduction of the talkie not only affected the representational form of Japanese films: the very space for receiving those films was also reshaped. Existing research on Japanese film history has discussed the spread of the sound film in Japan as a problem relating to the form of representation. Aside from some discussion of the disappearance of the *benshi* (the silent film narrator), an investigation into the way that the talkies changed the exhibition space of the cinema itself

Raine, M. and J. Nordström (eds.), *The Culture of the Sound Image in Prewar Japan*.
Taylor & Francis Group 2020
DOI: 10.5117/9789089647733_CH04

has been lacking.[1] In this chapter, I argue that once the exhibition of sound film became practical, the cinematic space of exhibition was expanded in two ways: first, the urban cinemas grew in size; and second, the number of theatres in the rural provinces increased. In other words, the continuing development of cinema's sound technology promoted an architectural and geographical expansion of the physical space of Japanese film exhibition.

In order to analyse the expansion of the exhibition spaces associated with sound film I will first consider the way in which films were presented in cinemas during the 1910s, before the exhibition of sound film became practical.

Cinema Architecture During the Pre-Talkie Era

The transition to feature film talkies was not the first time that the exhibition space of the cinema was transformed due to changes in film representation. For example, during the pre-talkie era in Japan during the 1920s, Japanese film style gradually transformed into the continuity editing system. Such transitions came to alter even cinema architecture.

Most cinema architecture in the 1910s imitated contemporary Japanese theatres, which meant that some seats provided poor lines of sight to the screen. In particular, that form of theatre architecture was unable to provide adequate sightlines from the balcony seats on the upper floor. For example, a Tokyo cinema, the Chiyodakan, opened in 1911, had to have a part of the balcony seats removed because audience sightlines in that section were blocked.[2] In another case, the balcony seats on the second floor of the Fukuhōkan cinema in Tokyo were arranged in a curve, as in an opera house. This provided a poor line of sight to the screen from the back row of seats.[3] These examples are typical of cinema architecture of the 1910s.

It seems that the use of this style of cinema architecture, imitating theatres for live performance, was related to the preference in Japanese film style for long shots and long takes in the 1910s, which was contemporaneously intended to refer to Japanese forms of drama such as kabuki. For example, Komatsu Hiroshi argues that 'Japanese films during the 1910s could be understood as governed by the universal law of theatrical performance that

1 Recent studies include Gerow, '*Benshi* ni tsuite', pp. 117-159; Fujiki, *Zōshoku suru perusona*; Dym, *Benshi*.

2 Katō, 'Waga kuni ni okeru katsudō shashin kan no kenchiku enkaku (4)', pp. 116-117.

3 *Ibid.*, p. 122.

disappeared and remained only in the memory of the audience after the performance was over'.[4] In other words, the relatively cheap cinema of the 1910s was an alternative apparatus, a substitute for kabuki and contemporary high culture drama theatres. As Iwasaki Akira, a famous film critic, recalled from his childhood in the 1910s, 'generally speaking, cinemas were considered to be a cheaper substitute for theatres'.[5] In addition, cinemas in rural areas had to have a theatrical architecture because traveling theatre companies often played in the same space.

However, this form of architecture was not popular with cinephile intellectuals. For instance, in the 1910s the pioneering Japanese film director, film theorist, and film critic Kaeriyama Norimasa criticized the imitative style of cinema architecture:

> Because a screen is a plane, it is unreasonable that we look aside, up and down at it. Therefore, broad and shallow buildings with three floors are no good. The new style of purpose-built cinemas in the West have a single floor and are oriented around the long axis.[6]

Kaeriyama's opinion on cinema architecture was complementary with the films that he later came to direct, which aimed to incorporate the continuity editing style of Classical Hollywood Cinema.

In the 1920s, the exhibition space of the cinema began to change to accommodate that different form of spectatorship. Spectatorship as a mode of reception shifted from one that enjoyed the attractive performance of the *benshi*'s verbal narration to one that tended to immerse itself in that mode of film representation characterized as the continuity system. The reception of films in the new exhibition spaces worked against the disturbance of spectatorial immersion by the *benshi*'s excessive performances of verbal narration: now, the film screen was central to film exhibition, in place of the performance of the *benshi*. In other words, those changes in architecture seem to prepare the space of exhibition for the appearance of the talkie.

For example, the Bunmeikan, a small cinema located in Kagurazaka, which was on the outskirts of Tokyo in the 1910s, was praised by intellectuals such as Kaeriyama for adopting the style of 'one floor oriented around the long axis'. The seating did not obstruct the visibility of the screen because

4 See Komatsu, 'Eigashi no aratana chihei', p. 44.
5 Iwasaki, *Eiga ga wakakatta* toki, p.115.
6 Kaeriyama, 'Jōsetsukan no kenchiku mata setsubi', p. 17.

there were no balconies and the seats were arranged around a long axis perpendicular to the screen, unlike the cinemas that were imitations of theatres in Tokyo. The Musashinokan, equipped with seats with good sight lines, was built in 1920 and became a cinema representative of Shinjuku, a new theatre district in Tokyo that developed during the 1920s. Katō Shū, who designed the cinema, said the reason he avoided copying the architecture of live theatre was that Japanese and Western films were shown there together.[7] The Western films screened with Japanese films were characterized by the continuity system, and so required an absorption in the image that was facilitated by direct sightlines.

The division between the style of Japanese and foreign feature films screened in cinemas become more fluid with a shift in Japanese film style around 1920. This also came to affect cinema architecture. It seems symbolic that Kaeriyama's films, *Sei no kagayaku/The Glory of Life* and *Miyama no otome/Maid of the Deep Mountains*, both directed in 1919, were released in the Tokyo cinemas Azabukan and Toyotamakan, which mainly screened foreign films. Japanese filmmakers, especially from the Shōchiku Kinema company that was founded in 1920, were exploring the mode of representation of international cinema, incorporating the style of Classical Hollywood Cinema into their films. Although Japanese film had been received by audiences as an alternative to theatre in the 1910s, the newly constructed Musashinokan changed cinema architecture by giving priority to good sightlines, coinciding with a shift in Japanese film style. These changes in film style caused mainstream audiences to give greater importance to the mode of representation, characterized by continuity editing, of the film on the screen.

Audiences came to desire not a substitute for theatrical plays but a cinematic form of representation. The background to those changes was a shift in popularity from the verbal narration of the *benshi* to the visual narration of films on the screen. The theatrical representation of Japanese films in the 1910s was due to not only primitive camerawork but also the popularity of the *benshi*. Their performance of verbal narration was foregrounded when juxtaposed with films containing fewer shots. For example, Shibata Masaru, an early cameraman, said '*benshi* never favoured close-up shots. They complained that the close-up shot made them feel terribly let down'.[8] In that sense, it seems symbolic that the head *benshi* of the Musashinokan was Tokugawa Musei, who eliminated

7 Katō, 'Waga kuni ni okeru katsudō shashin kan no kenchiku enkaku (7)', p. 74.

8 Shibata, 'Jun eiga geki to kouta eiga', p. 26.

excessive performance from his film narration.[9] In place of showy verbal flourishes, his performance was intended to explain the contents of the film clearly and concisely.

Architectural Expansion of Cinemas in the 1930s

Although changes in cinema architecture had been prepared during the pre-talkie era, the appearance of talkies influenced film exhibition in Japan in several ways. The introduction of the talkie inevitably brought with it unemployment for the *benshi* and the musicians that had belonged to cinemas, while opinions regretting the disappearance of the silent cinema space were also voiced, although actual silent exhibition had hardly existed in Japan.[10] We should recognize that such a space for silence may have existed in Japanese cinemas, though we are likely to imagine them more accurately as noisy spaces filled by the *benshi*'s narration and a fusion of Japanese and Western music.[11]

We can trace the spatial expansion of talkie film exhibition from the perspective of cinema architecture. The flagship cinemas that had been newly built in the transitional period to the talkie, such as the Nihon Gekijō, greatly exceeded the size of the cinemas built during silent film era. The spread of the talkie in these exhibition spaces meant that the oral arts of narration and the fusion of Japanese and Western music by live performers was replaced by the sound of the speaker system. The new space displaced the bodies of the *benshi* and the band players, extinguishing the sense of distance between the actual sound and the image source, creating a homogeneous space for the sound. That shared and homogenous space for sound created by the new architecture and the new technology was also supported by new business practices, such as the Tōhō studio's policy of uniform seat pricing. On this point, the management plan for a new cinema

9 One of the major *benshi*, Tokugawa Musei, developed a style of narration that integrated his voice into the screen images, prepared the way for the popularization of sound films during the pre-talkie era. See Kitada Akihiro, 'Yūwaku suru koe', pp. 130-131.

10 Katō, '"Tōkī" no shutsugen', p. 24.

11 Of course, the completely silent moment in the exhibition space was exceptional and not common at that time but we should recognize that such a space for silence may have existed in Japanese cinemas, as Rick Altman shows that in American cinemas 'silent films were in fact sometimes silent, it seemed, and what's more, it did not appear to bother audiences a bit'. See Rick Altman, 'The Silence of the Silents', p. 649. On the 'soundscape' of cinemas in Japan during the silent era, see Hosokawa, 'Sketches of Silent Film Sound in Japan', pp. 288-305.

built by Tōhō, the Hibiya Eiga Gekijō, that was printed for readers of the *Kinema junpō* magazine, the most widely read film magazine in Japan, was revolutionary. The plan announced that all seats would be the same price and that audiences would be completely changed between programmes, instead of being allowed to enter at any point.[12]

The Tōhō studio played a major role in the changes in film architecture during the transition to sound in Japan. Tōhō originated as an exhibition company in 1932 under the name Tokyo Takarazuka Theatre Co. Ltd., and later in 1937 merged with the early sound film production companies P.C.L. and J.O. Studio, thereafter producing films for the first time. Tōhō was closely linked with the appearance of talkies and its founder, Kobayashi Ichizō, insisted that the management of cinemas was the basis for film industry growth:

> If local movie theatres do not profit, distribution agencies cannot be profitable. Without distribution agencies being profitable, it is not logical that production companies are profitable. If we hope to completely change the Japanese film industry into a profitable business, we must first reform local movie theatres into a profitable business.[13]

Based on Kobayashi's management policy emphasizing the exhibition space of the cinema, we might consider that this shift to the homogenous space of the talkie was the reason for the shift to uniform seat pricing in cinemas. After the Hibiya Eiga Gekijō, which was opened in 1934 (Fig. 4.1) by Tōhō and boasted a capacity of about 1,500 people, launched the unusual policy of fifty *sen* uniform seats, other cinemas followed.[14]

Noël Burch has argued of Japanese silent cinema that, '*benshi* removed the narrative burden from the images and eradicated even the possibility of the images producing a univalent, homogeneous diegetic effect'.[15] However, in contrast to Burch's understanding, the homogeneous space created by the sound system was supported by the spread of uniform seats in the cinemas, dissolving the sense of distance from the source of live sounds that was always present in the silent cinema.

The homogeneous reception space for sound was created by the installation of loudspeakers in cinemas. This also led to the expansion of the

12 Suzuki, 'Marunouchi kaiwai manpo', p. 20.
13 Kobayashi, *Tōyō keizai panfuretto 21*, pp. 15-16.
14 Tanaka, *Nihon kyōiku eiga hattatsu shi*, p. 243
15 Burch, *To the Distant Observer*, p. 79.

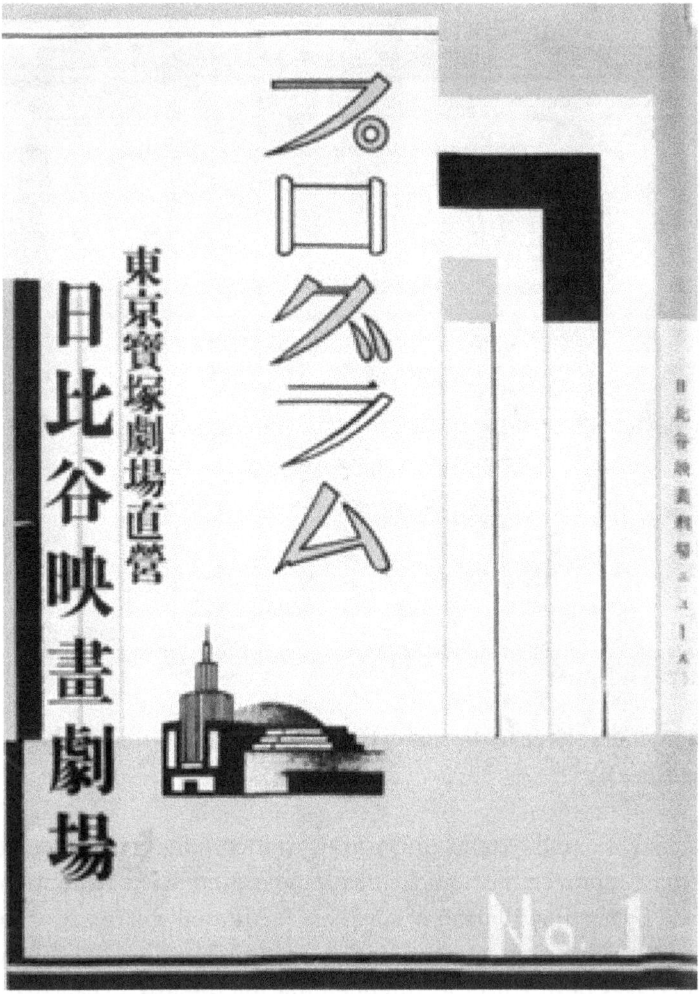

Fig. 4.1: The opening brochure of the Hibiya Eiga Gekijō (1934). From the collection of the Theatre Museum at Waseda University.

architectural space since, as Katō Shū, a major Japanese cinema architect, explained:

> The volume of the oral art of the narrator and the sounds of musical instruments are certainly limited, and especially in case that the size of a hall is large we can hardly expect the acoustic effect [of the narrator and musicians] to be satisfactory. However, in the case of talkies, it is extremely advantageous that the reproduction of sounds depends on using loudspeakers that are louder than the live sound source and able to

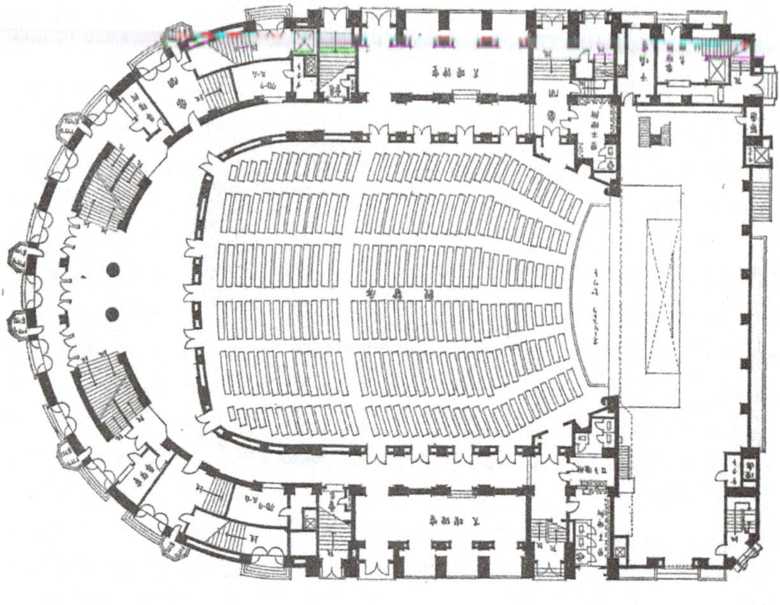

Figure 4.2 The first floor plan of the Nihon Gekijō, in *Nihon eiga jigyō sōran: Shōwa go nen ban* (Tokyo: Kokusai Eiga Tsūshinsha, 1930).

> adjust the sound volume to the size of the hall, by adding to the number of the loudspeakers.[16]

Katō indicated that sound systems, unlike live narration, homogenized sound in the cinema. Moreover, the homogenization of sound in the exhibition space caused by the installation of speakers facilitated the increase in size and capacity of the cinema building. It is significant that the Nihon Gekijō, which was built with the aim of emulating the Roxy Theatre in New York and could accommodate about 4,000 people, was completed in 1933. Given that the Osaka Shōchikuza, which was completed in 1923 and was a representative picture palace in Japan during the silent era, had a seating capacity of only about 1,000, we can recognize that the scale of the Nihon Gekijō was revolutionary among Japanese cinemas designed for film screenings. The Nihon Gekijō was acquired by Tōhō in 1935 as one of the main theatres of the Tōhō bloc, located in the centre of Yūrakuchō, a

16 Katō, *Eigakan no kenchiku sekkei*, p. 165. However, Katō also indicated that 'talkie sound is electrically reproduced sound and the sound is much more powerful than the human voice or musical instruments, so it increases reverberation' (p. 174). In the strict sense of the word, the sound space of exhibition could not be homogenized.

new theatre district in Tokyo from the 1930s (Fig. 4.2). The architectural expansion of cinemas was one of the phenomena that the development of the talkie brought forth.

The Geographical Expansion of Cinemas in the 1930s

The spread of cinema sound systems influenced not only the expansion of the architectural space of cinemas but also the geographical expansion of film exhibition. With the introduction of the talkie, cinemas spread in the provinces. In that sense, the geographical expansion of cinemas was influenced by the development of sound systems in Japan. Although the narration of the *benshi* was an essential element to complete film representation during the silent era, the best *benshi* were gathered in the cinemas of metropolitan areas such as Tokyo and Osaka. For example, in 'The Great Ranking of National Moving-Picture Narrators' (published by Yoshizawa Kunijirō, 1919) that ranks the famous narrators belonging to cinemas in Eastern Japan (east of Nagoya), narrators of the Tokyo-Yokohama area accounted for fifty of ninety-three people granted higher ranks such as *genrō* (elder statesman). Considering that most of the famous *benshi*, such as Tokugawa Musei, were active in Tokyo cinemas, it is clear that the spectator's affect in the reception of silent films, even of the same film, would be different between urban and provincial areas.

I argue that the disparity of skills between *benshi* in the cities and provinces acted to prevent the expansion of film exhibition into the provinces during the silent period. In general, the top of the hierarchy in all performing arts was occupied by entertainers of Tokyo in the east of Japan and of Kamigata (Osaka and Kyoto) in the west. As one indication of that state of affairs, it is clear that the salary of *benshi* differed between urban and rural areas. For example, Umemura Shisei's monthly salary at the Teikokukan in Tokyo was 130 yen while Ii Goro's monthly salary at the Teikokuza in the Chūbu region west of Tokyo was only 85 yen.[17]

The talkie was intended to eliminate such disparities. Specifically, we can see this tendency in the change in the number of cinemas from 1930 to 1940. Comparing the urban areas of Tokyo, Kanagawa (including Yokohama), Aichi (including Nagoya), Kyoto, Osaka and Hyogo (including Kobe), which were the six major cities in the pre-WWII period, with other provincial areas

17 See Ueda ed., *Nikkatsu Mukōjima to shinpa eiga no jidai ten*, p. 44, and Mizuno, *Nagoya katsuben ichidai*, p.85.

in the 1930s, the rate of increase in the number of cinemas in the provincial areas, with the exception of the Tohoku region, exceeded the rate in all cities except Hyogo (Table 1). The different trends in those two exceptional areas can also be explained: Hyogo covers a large administrative area, including rural areas, and the Tohoku region was economically destitute, hit particularly hard by the Great Depression and the great famine in the first half of the 1930s.[18] The rate of increase in Tokyo and Kyoto, the main cities of the Japanese film industry during the silent era, was around 50%, less than the 86% national average, since many cinemas had already been built in those cities during the silent era.

In the expansion of cinema into the provinces, a secondary factor in addition to the spread of talkies was the establishment of the railway transportation network in the 1930s. In the silent period, there were physical limitations to the transportation of prints duplicated in Tokyo and Kyoto to provincial cinemas. For example, Kushima Katsutarō, the manager of a Hokkaido-based exhibition company, stated that 'The exhibitors in the Hokkaido region felt the inconvenience of the distance from Tokyo at that time'.[19]

In any case, it is clear that the introduction of talkies coincided with an increase in the number of cinemas. During the 1930s, cinemas that were wired for sound increased rapidly, in the provinces as well in the cities. The penetration rate of sound systems, of varying levels of quality, in cinemas changed from 10% or less in 1931 into 70-100% in 1939 (Table 2). In order to consider the relationship between the increasing number of cinemas and the penetration rate of sound systems in those cinemas, it should be noted that the penetration rates of talkie sound systems in the Hokkaido region, the Chubu region and the Chugoku region, which were the regions of especially high rates of increase in the number of cinemas, exceeded 95 percent in 1939. Of course, it must be acknowledged that this proportion is only the penetration rate of sound systems and does not take into account the difference in size of rural and urban cinemas, nor the difference in quality between different talkie exhibition systems.

The increase in the number of cinemas in the provinces meant that the space for receiving films in Japan had changed geographically. As a film

18 See Table 4 for detailed figures. The Great Depression that began in 1929 greatly influenced the Japanese economy, producing a deflationary recession and in particular a collapse in the agricultural market. The agricultural economy of the Tohoku region, which had been flourishing, suffered an especially serious blow. See *Gendai nihon keizai shi*, p. 3-6.

19 See 'Musei eiga katsudo dai shashin (2)', p.13.

market, the provinces began to occupy an important position. The ratio of the number of cinemas in the six major cities in Japan to the number of cinemas in other areas was 37:63 in 1930, the same ratio as in 1926 before the introduction of talkies. However, the ratio in 1940 was 33:67. These ratios refer to the number of cinemas, and not the number of tickets sold, so they do not reflect the relative size of the audiences in these different areas. Nevertheless, we can at least say that the number of cinemas in the provinces had increased more than in the cities.[20] In addition, over the 1930s some provinces replaced cities in the ranking of areas with the highest number of cinemas (Table 3). It is especially interesting to note that Hokkaido and Shizuoka, Niigata and Nagano, which were sparsely populated in spite of having large populations within their huge administrative zones, occupied higher positions in the ranking of the number of cinemas in 1940. On the other hand, Kyoto, which had a small population but with a densely populated city centre, fell to number eleven. In other words, the number of cinemas came to be approximately proportional to the population of the administrative zone, regardless of whether the zone was predominantly urban or rural, densely or sparsely populated (Tables 4 and 5). It is worth considering whether those changes were caused through the abolition of regional disparities in sound representation caused by the differing quality of live performers. In other words, the growth of cinema in Japan depended on an expansion of the geographical space for exhibiting Japanese films and on an expansion of the homogeneous space for receiving film sound that was realized by recorded sounds reproduced through loudspeakers. Talkies made it possible to produce a homogenous cinematic space not only in the city but also in all Japanese-speaking areas, subordinating the varied live sound aspect of film exhibition to the audio duplication technology of the talkie.

Conclusion

The talkies effected the architectural and geographical expansion of cinemas in Japan, entailing the homogenization of exhibition spaces. From an architectural point of view, the homogenization of cinema spaces was caused by the spread of sound systems and uniform seating, losing the advantage of a sense of distance from the source of live sounds such as narration and musical accompaniment. The difficulties of the distance between the

20 Based on *Shōwa jūnana nen eiga nenkan*, the number of cinemas in Tokyo, Kanagawa, Aichi, Kyoto, Osaka and Hyogo was 397 and the number of others was 665.

Table 4.1 Regional changes in the number of cinemas in the 1930s

Region	1930	1936	1940	Increase in cinemas from 1930 to 1940 (%)
Tokyo	209	254	316	51
Kanagawa	53	72	86	62
Aichi	50	61	84	68
Kyoto	45	65	67	49
Osaka	115	151	207	80
Hyogo	53	61	105	98
Hokkaido region	51	60	182	257
Kanto region	106	125	193	82
Kinki region	56	95	103	83
Chubu region	92	110	230	150
Tohoku region	101	131	149	48
Hokuriku region	66	69	124	88
Chugoku region	84	117	167	99
Shikoku region	48	65	89	85
Kyushu region and Okinawa	138	196	260	88
National total and average	1267	1632	2362	86

Compiled from data in Shōwa jūnana nen eiga nenkan *(Tokyo: Nihon Eiga Zasshi Kyōkai, 1942).*

Table 4.2 The regional proportion of sound equipment in cinemas of the 1930s

Region	Proportion of sound equipment in 1931 (%)	Proportion of sound equipment in 1939 (%)
Tokyo	11	100
Kanagawa	1	95
Aichi	10	100
Kyoto	3	88
Osaka	6	100
Hyogo	4	99
Hokkaido region	9	100
Kanto region	2	92
Kinki region	3	74
Chubu region	6	98
Tohoku region	8	80
Hokuriku region	8	92
Chugoku region	5	96
Shikoku region	6	70
Kyushu region and Okinawa	9	93

Compiled from data in Shōwa kyū nen ban kokusai eiga nenkan *(Tokyo: Kokusai Eiga Tsūshinsha, 1934) and* Shōwa jūroku nendo ban Nihon eiga nenkan *(Tokyo: Daidōsha, 1941).*

Table 4.3 The top ten ranking of regional cinema by number, 1930 and 1940

top ten in 1930	number of cinemas	top ten in 1940	number of cinemas
Tokyo	209	Tokyo	316
Osaka	115	Osaka	207
Fukuoka	64	Hokkaido	182
Kanagawa	53	Fukuoka	116
Hyogo	53	Shizuoka	111
Hokkaido	51	Hyogo	105
Aichi	50	Kanagawa	86
Kyoto	45	Aichi	84
Shizuoka	40	Niigata	73
Hiroshima	26	Nagano	70

Compiled from the data of Shōwa jūnana nen eiga nenkan *(Tokyo: Nihon Eiga Zasshi Kyōkai, 1942).*

Table 4.4 The top thirteen ranking of the administrative populations in 1930

Administrative division	Population (Unit: Thousands of people)	Area (Unit: km^2)	Population density (Unit: People/km^2)	Cinema density (Unit: People/Cinema)
Tokyo	5409	2145	2522	25880
Osaka	3540	1813	1953	30783
Hokkaido	2812	88775	32	55137
Hyogo	2646	8322	318	49925
Aichi	2567	5081	505	51340
Fukuoka	2527	4940	512	39328
Niigata	1933	12579	154	55229
Shizuoka	1798	7770	231	44950
Nagano	1717	13604	126	61321
Hiroshima	1692	8437	201	65077
Kanagawa	1620	2353	688	30566
Kagoshima	1557	9081	171	222428
Kyoto	1553	4623	336	23179

Compiled from data in Shōwa go nen kokusei chōsa saishū hōkoku sho *(Tokyo: Tokyo Tōkei Kyoku, 1938).*

sound source and the audience was also solved in the talkie era, enabling an increase in the size of the cinema auditorium. For example, Mizuno Eizaburō, a *benshi*, said that in order to increase the volume of his voice, 'I put jars into the ground under the stage to reverberate in the cinema'.[21] In addition, from a geographical point of view, cinemas, which had been concentrated in the city due to the exhibition constraints of the silent era, advanced into

21 Mizuno, *Nagoya katsuben ichidai*, p. 104.

the provinces in the 1930s. That process expedited the homogenization of the distribution of the cinemas in Japan. Thus, talkies not only changed the mode of representation and the production of Japanese films, but also transformed the cinematic spaces of their reception.

Table 4.5 The top thirteen ranking of the administrative populations in 1940

Administrative division	Population (Unit: Thousands of people)	Area (Unit: km²)	Population density (Unit: People/km2)	Cinema density (Unit: People/Cinema)
Tokyo	7284	2145	3429	23051
Osaka	4737	1814	2643	22884
Hokkaido	3229	88775	37	17748
Hyogo	3174	8323	387	30229
Aichi	3120	5081	623	37143
Fukuoka	3041	4940	626	26216
Kanagawa	2158	2353	930	25093
Niigata	2022	12578	164	27699
Shizuoka	1983	7770	260	17864
Hiroshima	1823	8437	222	37204
Kyoto	1705	4621	374	25448
Nagano	1683	13626	126	24042
Fukushima	1595	13782	118	39875

Compiled from data in Kokusei chōsa shūtaisei jinkō tōkei sōran *(Tokyo: Tōyō Keizai Shinpōsha, 1985).*

Bibliography

Rick Altman. 'The Silence of the Silents'. *The Musical Quarterly* 80.4 (Winter, 1996), pp. 648-718.

Noël Burch. *To the Distant Observer: Form and Meaning in the Japanese cinema* (Berkeley and Los Angeles: University of California Press, 1979).

Jeffrey A. Dym. *Benshi, Japanese Silent Film Narrators, and Their Forgotten Narrative Art of Setsumei: A History of Japanese Silent Film Narration* (Lewiston: the Edwin Mellen Press, 2003).

Fujiki Hideaki. *Zōshoku suru perusona: eiga sutādamu no kakuritsu to Nihon kindai* (Nagoya: University of Nagoya Press, 2007).

Aaron Gerow. *Visions of Japanese Modernity: Articulations of Cinema, Nation, and Spectatorship, 1895-1925* (Berkeley: University of California Press, 2010).

Aaron Gerow. '*Benshi* ni tsuite: juyō kisei to eigateki shutai'. In *Nihon eiga wa ikiteiru 2: Eigashi o yominaosu* (Tokyo: Iwanami Shoten, 2010), pp. 117-159.

Kaeriyama Norimasa. 'Jōsetsukan no kenchiku mata setsubi'. *Kinema rekōdo* 28 (1915), pp. 17-20.

Hosokawa Shuhei. 'Sketches of Silent Film Sound in Japan: Theatrical Functions of Ballyhoo, Orchestras and *Kabuki* Ensembles'. In *The Oxford Handbook of Japanese Cinema*, edited by Daisuke Miyao (Oxford: Oxford University Press, 2014), pp. 288-305.

Iwasaki Akira, *Eiga ga wakakatta toki: Meiji Taishō Shōwa sandai no kioku* (Tokyo: Heibonsha, 1980).

Katō Shū, 'Waga kuni ni okeru katsudō shashin kan no kenchiku enkaku (1)', *Kenchiku shinchō* 6.1 (1925), pp. 14-18.

Katō Shū, 'Waga kuni ni okeru katsudō shashin kan no kenchiku enkaku (2)', *Kenchiku shinchō* 6.2 (1925), pp. 8-12.

Katō Shū, 'Waga kuni ni okeru katsudō shashin kan no kenchiku enkaku (3)', *Kenchiku shinchō* 6.3 (1925), pp. 24-28.

Katō Shū, 'Waga kuni ni okeru katsudō shashin kan no kenchiku enkaku (4)', *Kenchiku shinchō* 6.4 (1925), pp. 20-26.

Katō Shū, 'Waga kuni ni okeru katsudō shashin kan no kenchiku enkaku (5)', *Kenchiku shinchō* 6.6 (1925), pp. 5-9.

Katō Shū, 'Waga kuni ni okeru katsudō shashin kan no kenchiku enkaku (6)', *Kenchiku shinchō* 6.7 (1925), pp. 7-11.

Katō Shū, 'Waga kuni ni okeru katsudō shashin kan no kenchiku enkaku (7)', *Kenchiku shinchō* 6.9 (1925), pp. 10-14.

Katō Shū. '"Tōkī" no shutsugen to eigakan kenchiku'. *Kokusai eiga shinbun* 41 (1930), pp. 24-25.

Katō Shū. *Eigakan no kenchiku sekkei* (Tokyo: Kōyōsha, 1932).

Kitada Akihiro. 'Yūwaku suru koe/eiga(kan) no yūwaku: Senzenki Nihon eiga ni okeru koe no hensei'. In *Iwanami kōza Nihon kindai no bunka 6: kakudai suru modānitei* (Tokyo: Iwanami Shoten, 2002), pp. 115-146.

Kobayashi Ichizō. *Tōyō keizai panfuretto 21: Eiga jigyō keiei no hanashi* (Tokyo: Tōyō Keizai Shuppanbu, 1937).

Kokusei chōsa shūtaisei jinkō tōkei sōran (Tokyo: Tōyō Keizai Shinpōsha, 1985).

Komatsu Hiroshi. 'Eigashi no aratana chihei'. *Nihon eiga wa ikiteiru 2: Eigashi o yominaosu* (Tokyo: Iwanami Shoten, 2010), pp. 1-20.

Mizuno Eisaburō. *Nagoya katsuben ichidai* (Nagoya: Fubaisha, 1995).

'Musei katsudō dai shashin (2)' in *Eiga shiryō*, Vol. 11, 1964, p. 13.

Shibata Masaru. 'Jun'eigageki to kouta eiga'. In *Kikigaki kinema no seishun*, edited by Iwamoto Kenji and Saiki Tomonori (Tokyo: Riburopōto, 1988), pp. 7-46.

Shōwa kyū nen ban kokusai eiga nenkan (Tokyo: Kokusai Eiga Tsūshinsha, 1934).

Shōwa jūroku nendo ban Nihon eiga nenkan (Tokyo: Daidosha, 1941).

Shōwa jūnana nen eiga nenkan (Tokyo: Nihon Eiga Zasshi Kyōkai, 1942).

Shōwa go nen kokusei chōsa saishū hōkoku sho (Tokyo: Tokyo Tōkei Kyoku, 1938).
Tanaka Jun'ichiro. *Nihon kyōiku eiga hattatsu shi* (Tokyo: Katatsumuri sha, 1979).
Ueda Manabu, ed. *Nikkatsu Mukōjima to shinpa eiga no jidai ten* (Tokyo: Theatre Museum at Waseda University, 2011).

About the Author

Ueda Manabu is Associate Professor in the Department of Humanities, Kobe Gakuin University. He researches early cinema and pre-cinema from the perspective of visual culture and is the author of a book on early Japanese cinemas and their audiences, *Nihon eiga sōsōki no kōgyō to kankyaku* (Tokyo: Waseda Daigaku Shuppanbu, 2012).

5 No Interpreter, Full Volume

The *benshi* and the sound transition in 1930s Japan

Michael Raine

Abstract
This chapter traces how the growth of electronically mediated sound in the middle of an economic crisis disrupted the soundscape of cinemas, and their labour relations. The introduction of talkies displaced the musicians and then the *benshi* from cinemas showing western films. Even before Japanese studios were equipped for talkie production, cinemas showing Japanese films displaced the musicians with recorded sound and 'sound versions'. The *benshi*, who had been the main attraction of Japanese film exhibition, were also threatened by that development. They became the central figures in industrial actions that were billed as a struggle against machine civilization, a struggle that played out in the cinemas and in the press against a background of economic and political instability.

Keywords: sound culture, recorded music, record accompaniment, talkies, labour, *benshi* strikes

Silent cinema was seldom silent. In most countries, film played with musical accompaniment and, in its earliest forms, often with a live narrator. Cinema in Japan (and its colonies) was almost unique in preserving that interpreter (the *setsumeisha, katsuben,* or *benshi*; in Taiwan the *piansu*; and in Korea the *pyŏnsa*) until the introduction of talkies – films with dialogue recorded, synchronized, and played back by electronic sound apparatuses. The delayed transition to synchronized sound film exhibition in Japan has often been explained as due to a cultural preference for the *benshi*, based on a long history of oral narrative entertainment. Audiences were indeed familiar with storytellers and narrators standing apart from dramatic performers, but this chapter traces the introduction of new recorded sound technologies

Raine, M. and J. Nordström (eds.), *The Culture of the Sound Image in Prewar Japan*.
Taylor & Francis Group 2020
DOI: 10.5117/9789089647733_CH05

into studios and cinemas, and the industrial unrest that it caused in the midst of an economic crisis, to argue that economic factors were at least as important as cultural factors in Japan's delayed transition to sound. Even in the midst of a rising tide of cultural nationalism, cinema in Japan was an emblem of modernity and audiences responded positively to Japanese sound films when they were available. Although Japanese film culture is usually described as 'resistant' to sound cinema that is only half of the equation: even as the *benshi* and musicians protested their redundancy, a close reading of contemporary documents shows that technologies of sound reproduction proliferated and were celebrated by critics, audiences, and cinema managers.

Much has been made of the *benshi*'s unique performance, resistant to technical reproducibility, but even before they (along with cinema musicians) were displaced by talking pictures they had been absorbed into a manually synchronized sonic performance. That 'manually synchronized sonic performance' included the synchronization of a live musical soundtrack under the direction of the cinema orchestra conductor with the vocal performance of the *benshi*, which followed a script that gives voice to and describes the actions of stars playing characters on the screen. Although some commentators have made much of the *benshi*'s freedom of interpretation, even before the introduction of the talkie that was not typically the case.[1] As the commentary in the 1933 *Japanese Cinema Labour Yearbook* had it, ten years earlier male and female *benshi* were the main attraction, but the form and content of Japanese cinema had changed and now the *benshi* survived as a sober 'explainer' or 'interpreter' (*setsumeisha*).[2] Although it varied by region, genre, and audience demographics, the *benshi* was increasingly part of a '*dispositif*' that conformed to the expectations of audiences more interested in stars than 'local idols'.[3]

1 See for example Standish, 'Mediators of Modernity' for the argument that even mid-1930s films were subordinate to the '*benshi* cadenza'. However, as we will see, research by Aaron Gerow in *Visions of Japanese Modernity* and Hideaki Fujiki in '*Benshi* as Stars' contradicts that argument.

2 *Nihon eiga rōdō nenpō*, p. 89.

3 See Takeyama, quoting *benshi* Matsui Suisei, on the *benshi* as a 'local idol' in Tanaka et. al., 'Hōbun taitoru mondai', p. 30. See Foucault, *Power/Knowledge*, p. 194 for a discussion of the dispositif as an apparatus that links discursive and non-discursive structures in ways that discipline human behaviour. Foucault was interested in more powerful institutions than the cinema but the pattern of norm and exclusion, of technical and architectural materiality affecting consciousness, and of effects produced without definite subjective intention, is similar.

The introduction of recorded sound playback systems into cinemas and the creation of 'sound versions' – *saundo-ban* or *saundo-shiki*, an intermediary form of cinema in which music and sound effects, but not dialogue, were played from the film soundtrack – provoked labour struggles known as '*benshi* strikes' that roiled Japanese cinemas in the early 1930s. The strikes took place in the context of an ongoing economic crisis made worse by the global Depression and were used as proxies for the political struggles between leftist activists and an authoritarian state during the 'red decade' of 1925-1935.[4] Urban unemployment in the early 1930s topped 20% and industrial disputes turned violent. Strikers in several industries fought with police and company guards, demanding reinstatement or months of wages as severance pay, instead of the officially mandated two weeks. One common tactic was to occupy the workplace, or to cause public disorder so that the police would force the employers to compromise in order to restore calm.[5] All these tactics were employed by striking studio and cinema workers too. The strike tactics of sensory interventions into the space of the cinema highlighted the contrast between humans and machines, dramatizing a melodrama of human uselessness that played out across multiple industries in an increasingly mechanized civilization. The introduction of electronic sound apparatuses into cinemas was part of a general drive for the 'automatization' of the film text that had both economic and aesthetic justifications in the film industry. Although talkies did not predominate until the major studios built new sound stages between 1934 and 1936, after the strikes of 1932 few questioned that the conversion would occur. Rather than characterize Japanese film culture as 'resistant' to the introduction of recorded sound perhaps it is better understood as 'constrained' – by some audience preferences and the power of the benshi, but also by import taxes, economic weakness, and technological lag.

The *benshi*

As Jeffrey Dym has shown, the *benshi*'s autonomous art of *setsumei* dominated early cinema in Japan. The *benshi* were stars with their own fandoms, lecturing audiences on films and foreign customs, a constant narrating

4 Bowen-Struyk, 'Japanese Proletarian Literature'.

5 For an extended discussion of this period see Gordon, *A Modern History of Japan*, Chapter 11.

presence beside and apart from the films.[6] The performance of single or multiple *benshi* at film screenings influenced the form of Japanese cinema, which did not at first internalize a 'narrator system' nor 'classical' norms of *découpage*.[7] Even around 1930, many cinemas in Japan seem to have been more brightly lit than in Europe and America: cinemas accommodated a more dispersed gaze, not only on the film but on the programmes that were given out in every cinema, and even on the *benshi* standing at the side of the screen.[8] For many western commentators, the split address of the *benshi*, inherited from a long history of 'commingled media', made Japanese cinema in general a (political) modernist form *avant la lettre*, or at least an alternative to western modes of film narration.[9] However, that description of the aesthetically avant-garde, potentially subversive popularity of the *benshi* is drawn from the first two decades of the twentieth century, before the emergence of cinema as the dominant form of mass culture. In the late 1910s, a group of filmmakers and critics tried to 'modernize' Japanese cinema by purging it of its ties to premodern forms of theatre and vocal storytelling. That *jun'eigageki undō* (Pure Film Movement) called for visual forms of narration, including closer shot scales and more dynamic editing, and for more intertitles that would control the *benshi*'s grandstanding. As Aaron Gerow argues, the *benshi* has been understood in three main ways: as creating an intimacy between audience and interpreter that makes the film image an illustration of oral storytelling; as enhancing the illusionism of the visual narration by providing the audience with access to narrative understanding and character interiority; and as a split, anti-illusionist form of narration homologous to western modernism. The Pure Film Movement exemplified that second understanding, which also aligned with the interests of cultural bureaucrats in creating a national censorship system to shape

6 Dym, *Benshi*. See also Misono, *Katsuben jidai*.

7 Komatsu, 'Some Characteristics of Japanese Cinema before WWI'. For the narrator system, see Gunning, *D. W. Griffith*. For the classical description of 'classical' film form, see Bordwell, Staiger, and Thompson, *The Classical Hollywood Cinema*.

8 'Report of the (Japanese) Secretariat Committee', pp. 380-409. Illumination in the auditorium during screenings varied between 0.6 lux and 1.7 lux, with the recommended range of 1.5-2 lux seen as sufficient to read 8-point type in the film programme. See also Kondo, *Ofu-sukuriin no media-shi*, p. 95 for contemporary accounts of illumination in cinema auditoria.

9 Burch, *To the Distant Observer* makes the classic case for this position. Anderson, 'Spoken Silents in the Japanese Cinema' makes a more culturally informed argument for commingled media in Japan.

an autonomous national cinema that could educate Japanese citizens and face up to western films.[10]

The Japanese studios, modelled on Hollywood studios, that replaced artisanal production around 1920 also had an interest in rationalizing and controlling production, distribution, and exhibition through the use of planning departments and scripts, contract cinemas organized into chains, and *benshi* performances standardized by training, licensing, and censored scripts. Those forces moved 1920s Japanese cinema away from the performative culture it shared with *kōdan*, *rakugo*, and other forms of verbal narration, and toward a 'modern' technologically reproducible art more like western cinema. Many Japanese filmmakers had long objected to the *benshi*'s intervention, attempting to control the narration by inserting frequent intertitles, often written in a complex style.[11] By the 1920s, many Japanese films used more intertitles than the Hollywood films they had surpassed at the box office and *benshi* often performed alone, constrained by scripts and intertitles, as well as by audiences that expected to see adaptations of popular literature performed by their favourite stars. As Fujiki Hideaki has shown, the *benshi* was part of a celebrity system, privileged but also subject to narrational norms and technological replacement.[12] Of course, those changes were uneven and incomplete: *benshi* for western films tended to be more sedate than *benshi* for Japanese films; those for period films (*jidaigeki*) more florid than for films set in modern times (*gendaigeki*); *benshi* were more popular in rural areas than in the cities; and everywhere *benshi* spoke with regional accents that gave the films a local rather than universal flavour.[13]

Although some Phonofilm programmes played earlier, it was the introduction of western talkies (*hassei eiga*) at major cinemas in 1929 that created the category of non-talkie (*muhassei eiga, musei eiga*) in Japan.[14] Despite the pre-existing presence of the *benshi*'s voice in the cinemas, that technological development rendered existing Japanese films potentially obsolete. It was imperative that Japanese cinema, which had only surpassed foreign films at the box office a few years earlier, find ways to emulate the foreign sound image. From the perspective of producers and exhibitors, live performers restricted the unencumbered circulation and self-sufficiency of the film text and thereby its

10 See Gerow, *Visions of Japanese Modernity*, especially Chapter 4. See also Laura Lee, *Japanese Cinema Between Frames*, Chapter 2.

11 See for example Kinoshita, *Mise-en-scène of Desire*, p. 248-252 for a discussion of the intertitle as narrational technique (*wajutsu*).

12 Fujiki, '*Benshi* as Stars'. See also Fujiki, *Making Personas*.

13 See Dym. *Benshi* and Fukuchi Gorō. 'Musei no deshi to shite' for descriptions of these differences.

14 See for example 'Tōkī wa doko e (9)', p. 4.

potential for closer tie-ups with other media such as recorded popular music that constituted cultural modernity after the start of radio broadcasting in 1925 and electronic sound recording of popular songs in 1927.[15] Hollywood studios had already announced upcoming slates of all talking features by mid-1929, so the writing was on the wall. After RCA bought the Victor record company in the USA, a critic in *Kinema junpō*, noting that technology tended to flow from the USA to Japan, hoped that since Victor Japan already had a contract with Shōchiku and was negotiating one with Nikkatsu, 'soon we will be able to hear the sound of Kurishima Sumiko and Bandō Tsumasaburō's live voices'.[16]

However, the economic instability of 1920s Japan and the global depression that hit in 1930 introduced a hiatus between inevitability and actuality. Japanese studios could neither afford the new recording technology nor build the sound stages to use it. In addition, the cinemas, initially the fifty or so large urban cinemas that showed exclusively western films, struggled to install talkie projectors – Cinephone at Shōchiku-related cinemas and Movietone, Western Electric, RCA, or Tobis systems at most of the others – and amplifiers wired to exponential horn and moving-coil loudspeakers, behind or in front of the screen. Once the infrastructure of sound amplification was in place, cinemas used it in any way they could to avoid the stigma of showing silent films and to embrace the modernity of the technological sound image. For example, cinemas installed record players, typically in the projection booth, that were used for interval music (*kyūkei ongaku*) and record accompaniment (*rekōdo bansō*) in the cinema. This provided the audience with a sonic experience for the remaining silent films that was similar to the dialog-free sound versions that preceded 'all talkies' in the USA as well as Japan. Once exhibitors had committed to those investments, the cinemas had to face the question of what to do with their highly paid *benshi* and expensive orchestras. Conflict was inevitable.

Record accompaniment

Cinemas already played records in their lobbies to attract audiences, but historian of Japanese popular culture Kurata Yoshihiro dates the most significant intensification of the relationship between the two media to February 1929,

15 See the introduction to this volume for more information on the intermedial context of Japanese cinema in this period.

16 'Nihon no tōkī ni Beikoku ga tōshi ka', p. 7. Kurishima and Bandō were of course major movie stars.

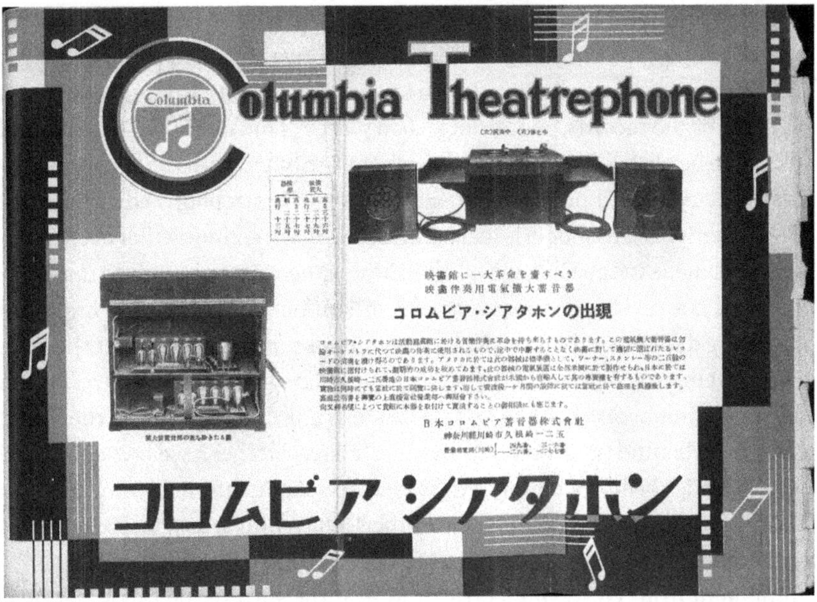

Figure 5.1 Columbia Theatrephone advertisement, *Kokusai eiga shinbun* 32 (10 October 1929), unpaginated front matter.

when the Denkikan, a first-run cinema for western films in the Asakusa district of Tokyo, installed an electronic record playback system.[17] The Denkikan used a Victor Electrola connected to amplified speakers, with a volume control behind the *benshi*. The record player allowed the Denkikan to replace the musical accompaniment to films and the interval music played by a live orchestra between films with records of classical music and popular songs. According to an article in *Kinema junpō*, the system cost 1700-1800 yen and the cinema contracted with Victor records to supply classical music and popular songs for only 10 yen per week. It could be run by just one 'music-picking pilot' (*senkyoku sōjūsha*) and could replace the piano and all the expensive musicians.[18] Even before the introduction of synchronized sound films, such interval music programmes would become a staple of all cinemas that were wired for sound. Cinema programmes listed a selection of popular or classical records, with their catalogue numbers from the major record companies, and sometimes with a 'music explanation' that paralleled the *benshi*'s explanation of the film.[19]

17 Kurata, *Nihon rekodo bunkashi*, p. 153.

18 Takada, '"Seiga" ichinen (2)', p. 10. See also Misono. *Katsuben jidai*, p. 116.

19 See for example the programme for Shōchiku's Shinbashi Kinema, 6 June 1930, or the 12 March 1931 programme for the Hongōza, which specialized in second-runs of Western films for the nearby University of Tokyo students.

At the relatively high end, such systems included the Columbia Theatrephone. In 1929 the elite Musashinokan and Hōgakuza cinemas fired their musicians and seem to have installed this system, which came equipped with a library of 500 records, containing 2,000 pieces of music and assorted sound effects, to be played according to cue sheets distributed with the films or freely chosen by the music-picking pilot, like a DJ. The Theatrephone advertisement (Fig. 5.1) emphasizes modern science and electricity, claiming that every component is made in the USA, where the Theatrephone is the standard machine. It promises a 'revolution in musical accompaniment', replacing the orchestra and using dual turntables to produce continuous music throughout the film. As a contemporary article said, the Hōgakuza had a system with 500 records in the projection booth, hooked up to a Western Electric projector so the sound came from behind the screen just like in a talkie, whether it was synchronized [i.e. with cue sheets] or simply used as record accompaniment.[20] In fact, film historian Douglas Gomery identifies the Theatrephone as a talkie-adjacent technology installed by cinemas in the US that could not afford to lease talkie equipment from Western Electric or RCA at the start of the talkie period.[21] The Theatrephone displaced the manual synchronization of sound and image in the silent cinema with a hybrid, quasi-automatic synchronization that still depended on the human agency of the 'engineer' (*gishi*) in the projection booth even before talkie projectors were installed in Japanese cinemas.

The published arguments for using recorded sound included both authenticity and austerity. Recorded sound provided access to the cultural uplift of western music recorded in the West and could replace expensive musicians with machinic alternatives. Ironically, the recorded music had more 'authenticity' than live musicians for at least some Japanese audiences because it contained the performances of European musicians, with their presumed cultural proximity to classical music. The *Kinema junpō* article that listed the costs of the Denkikan record accompaniment system claimed it was popular because you could hear the 'world class music' of Efrem Zimbalist's violin, much preferable to the 'uncontrolled musicians' of a typical movie orchestra.[22] It was also better and cheaper: the electronic amplifier produced greater volume than mechanical systems and allowed the cinema to fire musicians who cost 600-700 yen per month.[23] After the successful installation at the Denkikan, film journals and newspapers

20 'Hōgakuza no rekōdo bansō', p. 10

21 Gomery, *Shared Pleasures*, p. 222-223.

22 Takada, '"Seiga" ichinen (2)', p. 10.

23 'Gakushi junan jidai ni men shite domei kikan o sakuseisu', p. 2.

reported that in the 'fast-paced modern age' musicians were being displaced by Japanese-made versions of the Victor Electrola record player at the Shibuya Kinema, Ushigomekan, and other cinemas.[24]

Cinemas that showed Japanese films also began to use record accompaniment, borrowing the trappings of science and modernity granted to the sound image without requiring a synchronization of sound and image that was not yet feasible. The Kanda Gekijō, which specialized in Shinkō films, was an early adopter in May 1929. Nikkatsu cinemas, too, invested in electronic sound. *Samurai Nippon* (Itō Daisuke, 1931) had a popular theme song that was printed in the programmes distributed by the cinema along with the Victor Records catalogue number. The advertisement also announced that the song's composer, aristocrat Matsudaira Nobuhiro, was a leading light in period film accompaniment and has chosen a series of records to accompany the rest of the film.[25]

It is not clear how much the Theatrephone system cost for the entire package, but soon there were Japanese and part-Japanese alternatives that allowed for the rapid dissemination of record accompaniment. The Victon (sic) Electric Symphonila was produced by Chiyoda Shōkai in various versions that seem to have matched the Theatrephone setups. The advertisement in Fig. 5.2 lists prices for Victon Electric Symphonila sound equipment that ranged from 800 to 1500 yen, including imported amplifiers and domestic-made speakers. The selling points for this 'Wonder of film accompaniment' were electronic, scientific, and national: according to the advertisement, the apparatus is a 'most scientific production' of superior engineers and researchers, a 'leap forward in scientific management' of the cinema that can be used with talkie projectors to prepare for the day when all Japanese films are talkies. The advertisement goes on to claim that costs for electricity and record rental are only about 20 yen per week, sound can easily be adjusted to accommodate *benshi* explanation, *and* that orders are flooding in (*mōshikomi zattō*)! By the end of 1931, prices were lower since, as an advertisement for the Kohno Electric Phonodio put it, manufacturers were importing only the most high-tech components from the USA and making the rest cheaper in Japan (see Fig. 5.3). Used with the accompanying library of records, the

24 See Takada, '"Seiga" ichinen (2)', p. 10 and 'Nihon eiga tōkī-ka ni Beikoku Bikutā-sha tōshi ka', *Niroku shinpō*, 2 June 1929, p. 4 for reports of record accompaniment at these cinemas; see 'Hōgakuza wa tsui ni gakujin o kaikosu', *Asahi Shimbun*, 11 June 1929, p. 7 for the 'fast-paced modern age' phrase.

25 Programme for the Kanda Tōyō Kinema, 25 February 1931, reprinted in Nihon Eiga Terebi Producer Kyōkai. *Puroguramu eigashi*, p. 196.

Figure 5.2 Advertisement for the Victon Electric Symphonila, *Kinema junpō* 333 (11 June 1929), p. 10.

Figure 5.3 Advertisement for the Kohno Electric Phonodio, *Kokusai eiga shinbun* 62 (20 September 1931), unpaginated front matter.

advertisement promises the complete automation of music accompaniment by means of this 'wonder of modern science'.

According to reports and assumptions in the film journals of the time, even smaller and non-urban cinemas were tempted to invest in the new sound technology. *Kinema junpō*, the biggest film publication in Japan that was both a critical journal and a trade magazine, ran regular reports from provincial cinemas, which often discuss the prevalence of record accompaniment and snipe at the *benshi* for not speaking loud enough to be heard over the record player. Even in the far northern city of Morioka where, as one writer put it, 'they have no idea what a talkie is', and the prints were so scratched it looked like it's raining all the time, a cinema manager said that record accompaniment should be used to play interval music as well as the film's theme song and accompaniment. After all, said that manager, 'rather than a few fake musicians playing live and covering up their mistakes, music from an electric record player, with its perfect tone and wide choice of pieces, is a more stable and forward-looking choice'.[26] There were relatively few purpose-built cinemas (*jōsetsukan*) in the provinces – only 22 in Yamagata prefecture in 1933, for example. Films were also shown in alternative venues and company workplaces, as well as by itinerant exhibitors. For the latter market the Sekai company advertised a lightweight 'Super Sekaiphone' that promised to attach to lightweight projectors such as the DeVry projector in order to play music from the soundtrack (with another attachment) or from records, or even from the radio for silent films.[27]

In Japan during the economic crisis cinema admission prices dropped by one third.[28] The country underwent a painful deflationary adjustment, causing cinemas to try to cut costs and/or raise attendance. On the cost side, newspapers reported that record accompaniment would spread across the country and all musicians would lose their jobs.[29] In June 1929, the musicians at Tokyo cinemas showing western films, such as composer Yamada Kōsaku at the Hōgakuza, followed their counterparts in the USA in claiming that music is alive and record accompaniment kills living films. They set up an office in Yoyogi to agitate among cinema musicians and *benshi*, with the slogan, 'don't use talkies or Victrolas'.[30] At the same time musicians and *benshi* in western Japan formed a struggle committee against the use of the Victrola for record accompaniment or 'record dubbing' (*rekōdo fukikomi*) of soundtracks, as well as the production of talkies. However, the attitude of both journalists and protestors seems quite fatalistic: few proposed that live sound had a future.[31] Total attendance fell between 1930 and 1931, the first downturn in the history of Japanese cinema. Wages and employment also sagged, and cinemas turned to records and sound films to save on the costs of musicians and the star *benshi*. Columbia and other record companies put out records of the classical standards previously played by live cinema orchestras, and the credit for 'music department' in many film programmes

26 See Hijikata, 'Nihon zenkoku isshū eigakai shijō angya daishichihō', p. 109 for the description of audience ignorance and scratched film prints; Fujisawa, 'Rekōdo bansō no rigai', p. 18 for a discussion of record accompaniment.

27 Advertisement in *Kinema shūhō* 175 (20 October 1933), p. 16.

28 Fujioka, 'Nihon eiga kōgyōshi kenkyū'.

29 'Nihon eiga tōkī-ka ni Beikoku Bikutā-sha tōshi ka', p. 4.

30 Kurata, *Nihon rekōdo bunkashi,* p. 154. See also Wurtzler, *Electric Sounds* for the US context.

31 See 'Setsumeisha to gakushi aida ni tōkī hantai undō okoru', *Kobe yūshin shinbun*, 30 June 1929, p. 5, for anti-talkie; 'Gakukai tōkī fūji', *Niroku shinpō* 22 July 1929 for record dubbing.

disappeared between 1929 and 1931. The Asahi Film Year Book for 1929-1930 blames the rise of record accompaniment for job losses among musicians at cinemas specializing in western films.[32]

	1928	1929	1930	1931	1933
Purpose-built cinemas	1,259	1,270	1,288	1,488	1,667
Audience (millions)	181.3	192.5	198.2	194.7	
Benshi (male)	5,975	6,731			5,300
Benshi (female)	81	56			
Musicians (male)		4,000			6,500
Musicians (female)		1,500			
Benshi per cinema	4.8	5.3			3.2
Musicans per cinema		4.3			3.9

Figure 5.4 Japanese cinemas, audience, *benshi*, and musicians, 1928-1933. Source: *Nihon eiga rōdō nenpō dai ikki* (Tokyo: Rōdō Keizai Chōsasho, 1933), pp. 11-12, 37-38.

Kurata Yoshihiro argues that if we include the musicians' families, 200,000 people were affected by the waves of redundancies that followed the introduction of talkie technology.[33] However, even as replacing the musicians with machines was commonplace, it was also complicated. On the attendance side of the exhibition calculus, live music took on a new value when it was no longer part of the 'invisible' infrastructure of film exhibition. In the search for audiences, many of the larger first-run cinemas hired back or absorbed the fired musicians and put on stage shows to attract audiences.[34] For example, despite its investment in record accompaniment, the Denkikan still had a live orchestra in May 1929, when it staged a revue of Kikuchi Kan's *Tokyo Kōshinkyoku/Tokyo March* that coincided with Mizoguchi Kenji's film adaptation at the neighbouring Fujikan cinema.[35] By 1931, although cinemas that specialized in western films such as the Musashinokan and the Hōgakuza showed pure film programmes, other cinemas used live performances to draw in audiences. The four-hour programmes of Nikkatsu films at the Ueno Nikkatsukan included 40 minutes of live music.[36] Individual cinema policies differed but figures from the *Japanese Cinema Labour Yearbook* show that between 1929 and 1933 the number of *benshi*

32 *Eiga nenkan* (1929), p. 55.

33 Kurata, *Nihon rekodo bunkashi*, p. 154. It is not easy to see how Kurata arrived at this number.

34 Misono, *Katsuben jidai*, p. 122.

35 See the programme for the Denkikan cinema, 30 May 1929.

36 'Report of the (Japanese) Secretariat Committee', p. 398.

decreased but the number of projectionists and musicians in Japanese cinemas actually increased. While there were 6,787 *benshi* in 1929 and 5,300 in 1933, there were 3,117 projectionists and 5,500 musicians in 1929 and 4,200 and 6,500 respectively in 1933. The number of cinemas also increased, from 1,270 in 1929 to 1,667 in 1933, so the number of projectionists simply tracked the number of cinemas, remaining stable at 2.5 per cinema. On the other hand, the number of musicians declined from 4.3 per cinema to 3.9, and the number of *benshi* declined more rapidly, from 5.3 per cinema to 3.2, although the only cinemas that had switched to all-talkies by that point were the relatively small number of cinemas that specialized in western films. Perhaps that decline, and in particular the decline in the number of female *benshi*, was due more to a shift from multiple *benshi* performing live lip-syncing (*kowairo*) to the more sedate 'single *benshi* taking turns' (*kōtai dokuen*) that was advertised in film programmes and not yet to the replacement of *benshi* by the talkies.

Western talkies and the *benshi*

If the fate of the musicians after the introduction of sound playback devices is still somewhat cloudy, the rationalization of the *benshi* system is clearer. First, the *benshi* were fired from the cinemas that specialized in western films and then they lost their power during a series of strikes in the spring of 1932 that preceded their gradual disappearance, even from cinemas that showed Japanese films. Japanese speech had always been part of film exhibition so the *benshi* were indispensable until they could be replaced by Japanese talkies and by some means to translate foreign talkies. *Benshi* resisted the challenge of the new technology. For example, in July 1930 the *Niroku shinpō* newspaper reported that famous interpreter of western films Tokugawa Musei had turned off the sound at the Musashinokan to allow him to translate important dialogue for the crime melodrama *Alibi* (Roland West, 1929).[37] However, cinephiles resisted the *benshi*'s control: the author of the newspaper article on *Alibi* complained that this 'new experiment' demonstrated 'the tyranny of the *benshi*' (*setsumeisha ōbō*), an attempt to 'muzzle the voice' (*koe fūji*). In a later round-table on the talkie, Musashinokan publicist Nakata Takeo said that the experiment lasted for only two days before reverting to playing

37 'Setsumeisha ōbō? Kyūyo no issaku=Koe fūji: Tokugawa, Yamano no atarashii kokoromi', *Niroku shinpō*, 7 July 1929, p. 4.

the soundtrack in full.[38] Musei recalled that he had been forced to shout between the lines of English dialogue in *Alibi* and wished he had a fader to control the sound volume while he was performing his explanation.[39] With the spread of recorded music and sound films the *benshi* lost power over the cinema soundscape as their direct connection to the orchestra conductor was superseded by the sound apparatus, with the volume control in the projection booth.

No one did more than scriptwriter and film critic (and later studio executive) Mori Iwao to promote subtitles as a replacement for the *benshi*. He made the case in his 'Kabin to hanataba' column in *Kinema shūhō* from the beginning of 1931 and discussed the prospects for mediating foreign cinema in a series of round-tables with exhibitors, *benshi*, academics, and other journalists in the same journal. Mori reviewed experiments such as 'X-versions' that inserted silent English intertitles, which the *benshi* would translate, after passages of dialogue. Also, 'side titles' projected onto a screen beside the screen that could lose synchronization and 'made your neck hurt'.[40] He debated *benshi* Tokugawa Musei on the necessity of the *benshi*, acknowledging that *benshi* silent cinema was an authentic art of which Japan could be proud at the same time that the talkie rendered it obsolete. Musei responded by trying to quarantine the subtitle as something for intellectuals, claiming that audiences in the working-class film district of Asakusa would miss the intimacy of the *benshi*'s voice and never accept reading films in order to understand them.[41] However, although audiences in July 1930 had voted against *benshi*-interpreted western talkies at the Shōchikuza cinemas in Asakusa and Shinjuku, preferring western silent films instead, in February 1931 the 'audience voice' column in *Kinema shūhō* quoted the reaction to a screening of *Morocco* (Joseph von Sternberg, 1930) with subtitles and no interpreter at the Asakusa Denkikan. Of the twelve respondents, ranging in age from about 16 to 35, one preferred a *benshi* and one felt strange watching a film without the *benshi*'s voice but the rest preferred subtitles superimposed on the image.[42]

38 See Nakata's comment in Iida Shinbi et. al., 'Tōkī kenkyū zadankai', p. 108.

39 Tokugawa Musei recalls the screening in Tokugawa, Yamano, and Matsui, 'Tōkī to setsumei-sha', p. 299. Like many artists, Musei was popularly known by his pseudonymous personal name.

40 Mori, 'Kabin to hanataba 8', p. 8.

41 Tanaka et. al., 'Hōbun taitoru mondai', p. 28-32.

42 'Musei eiga yunyūsha no katsuyō', p. 5 and 'Kankyaku no koe', p. 33. For a dense historical and theoretical account of *Morocco* and the introduction of subtitling to Japan see Nornes. *Cinema Babel*, especially Chapter 4.

Some of Mori's interlocutors continued to object to foreign language talkies on purist and practical grounds: the subtitles destroyed the beauty and composition of the visual image, and the films insulted Japanese audiences by making them listen to a language they could not understand, or confused them by mixing that language with the *benshi*'s necessary explanation.[43] Even after the successful screening of *Morocco* with subtitles had convinced Hollywood studios to subtitle their prints in Japan, western films played with and without the *benshi*: for example, in July 1931 *Honor Among Lovers* (Dorothy Arzner, 1931) played in the Shōchiku chain cinemas with a *benshi* at the Taishōkan and subtitled with no interpreter at the Hōgakuza and Musashinokan.[44] Those two cinemas, along with the Teikoku Gekijō, were the elite exhibition spaces for foreign films, with the latest projectors, sound systems, and perforated screens. In those spaces cinema became a unified experience, contained within a single print and projected through a system that no longer required live performers. The *benshi* were dislodged from the cinemas that specialized in western film and forced to work freelance, or in other professions that depended on a trained and mellifluous voice, such as radio announcing, master of ceremonies, and the new genre of solo comic talk called *mandan*.[45] Cinephiles, at least, were not sympathetic to the *benshi*'s plight. The *Kinema shūhō* specialist magazine argued that 'more ten than years ago the *benshi* had the power to determine the size of the audience, but sadly with the passage of time and the mechanization of modern civilization, it's inevitable that they will be left behind and oppressed'. Famous *benshi* such as Ikoma Raiyū found himself narrating cheap Shinkō period films at the Kanda Gekijō, and formed a group to tour rural areas, where the *benshi* was still popular.[46]

From late 1931 programmes given out by the Teikoku Gekijō, Shōchiku's flagship cinema that specialized in western films, carried the English slogan 'No Interpreter, Full Volume', advertising the absence of the explanatory and emotive *benshi* and the presence of the high quality Western Electric sound system. At the Teikoku Gekijō, you could experience authentic recorded music, and dialog spoken by the stars, as opposed to a paltry local imitation. That animus against the 'interpreter' was part of a longer-term process of

43 Adachi, 'Hōbun jimaku mondai', p. 30; Iida, 'Tōkī to setsumei no mondai', p. 34.

44 SP programme, 1 July 1931.

45 See 'Setsumeisha kyōkai asu de hakkaishiki', *Asahi Shimbun*, 3 March 1931, p. 2 for a reference to Tokugawa Musei's *mandan* activities. Niita Chie points out in this volume that the elite *benshi* had prepared the way for working in radio by their participation in *eiga monogatari* (film stories) and *eigageki* (film dramas) on the radio.

46 'Setsumeisha no junan jidai', p. 26.

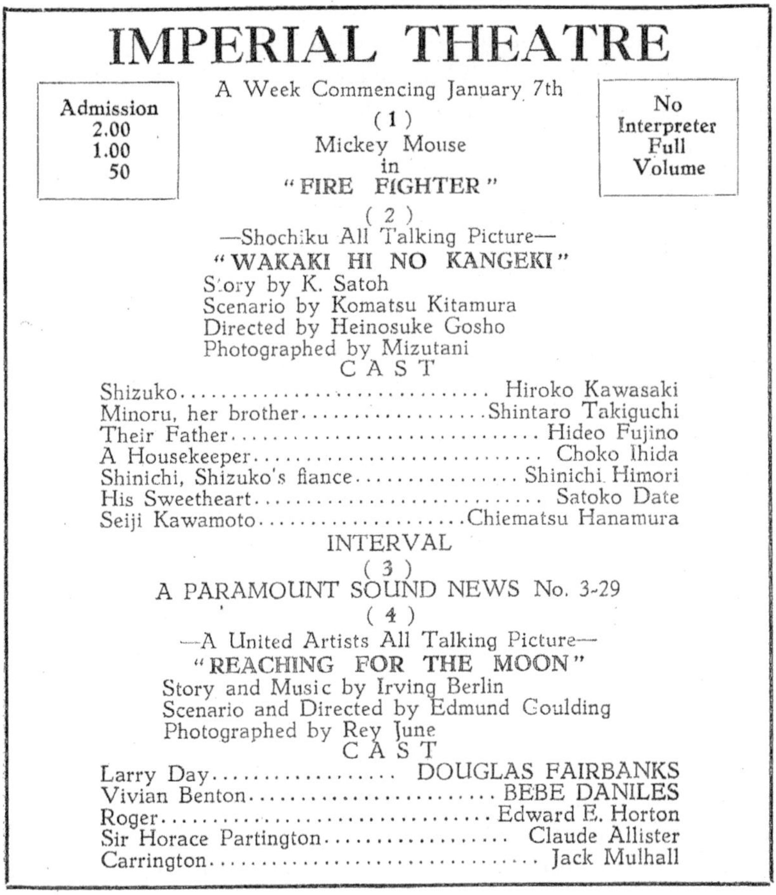

IMPERIAL THEATRE

Admission
2.00
1.00
50

A Week Commencing January 7th

(1)
Mickey Mouse
in
"FIRE FIGHTER"

No
Interpreter
Full
Volume

(2)
—Shochiku All Talking Picture—
"WAKAKI HI NO KANGEKI"
Story by K. Satoh
Scenario by Komatsu Kitamura
Directed by Heinosuke Gosho
Photographed by Mizutani

CAST

Shizuko	Hiroko Kawasaki
Minoru, her brother	Shintaro Takiguchi
Their Father	Hideo Fujino
A Housekeeper	Choko Ihida
Shinichi, Shizuko's fiance	Shinichi Himori
His Sweetheart	Satoko Date
Seiji Kawamoto	Chiematsu Hanamura

INTERVAL

(3)
A PARAMOUNT SOUND NEWS No. 3-29

(4)
—A United Artists All Talking Picture—
"REACHING FOR THE MOON"
Story and Music by Irving Berlin
Scenario and Directed by Edmund Goulding
Photographed by Rey June

CAST

Larry Day	DOUGLAS FAIRBANKS
Vivian Benton	BEBE DANILES
Roger	Edward E. Horton
Sir Horace Partington	Claude Allister
Carrington	Jack Mulhall

Figure 5.5 From the front page of the programme for the Teikoku Gekijō (7 January 1932). *Wakaki hi no kangeki* was Shōchiku's second talking picture.

'automatization' of sound in Japanese cinema, beginning with cue sheets and *benshi* scripts and accelerating with the development of record accompaniment and the sound version, culminating in the commercial exhibition of talkies, first of western films and then of Japanese.

Although the Teikoku Gekijō specialized in western films, it also released Shōchiku's first talkies. The programme in Fig. 5.5 announces the screening of *Wakaki hi no kangeki/Excitement of Youth*, the studio's second talkie after *Madamu to nyōbō/The Neighbour's Wife and Mine*, both directed by Gosho Heinosuke in 1931. Shōchiku's Tsuchihashi Shōchikuphone was the first successful Japanese sound recording system, invented by the Tsuchihashi brothers, Takeo and Haruo. It was the production of these films, and the use of the system to make sound version films from 1932 that precipitated the *benshi* strikes and led to the demise of the *benshi* as an institution. Tsuchihashi Takeo's lively account, given in his eighties, of the development of the system shows how the brothers were embedded in an intermedial culture of the sound image in the Kansai region of western Japan, where they were born.[47] They studied violin and cello with a White Russian refugee from the Soviet revolution at a music school in Kobe and started playing symphonic accompaniment, first to ballet and then in a cinema orchestra at Shōchiku's main cinema in Osaka, the Shōchikuza. The Tsuchihashi brothers would play in the cinema during the day and in jazz clubs at night, as well as recording records and performing on radio broadcasts on the side. They were both radio geeks, with their own crystal radio set, and became more interested in electronics than music. They also contributed to the electrification of commercial ballyhoo that was part of the urban Japanese soundscape. Instead of using street musicians, a store in Osaka gained notice by importing an amplifier from the USA and playing music to attract customers, so the Shōchikuza cinema commissioned the brothers to make an even bigger system. Takeo reports that the finished system, playing records and advertising the programme at the Shōchikuza, was so loud that nearby theatres complained it was interrupting their performances.[48]

The Tsuchihashi brothers were musicians at the Shōchikuza when the cinema took delivery of its first sound projectors – an American Powers Cinephone system that was a rather illicit development of de Forest's Phonofilm. Takeo quit the orchestra to work as an assistant to the engineer sent with the system and quickly learned to take it apart.[49] Although they initially planned their sound system to make newsreels for the Asahi newspaper company, a falling-out led to the Takeo being snatched up by Kido Shirō, head of production at Shōchiku. Having seen sound cinema demonstrations in the USA, Kido knew he needed a domestic sound system even as he publicly protested that it was uneconomical and unnecessary.[50] In 1930, Kido built the brothers a laboratory on the grounds of the Kamata studio, where they perfected their technology. Tsuchihashi Haruo had studied English in college and was a member of the Society of Motion Picture Engineers. He would translate articles they received from Hollywood as they worked on

47 Tsuchihashi, 'Eiga ga koe o hasshita toki'.

48 Ibid., p. 296-297.

49 Kawaguchi Matsutaro in Mori, et. al., '*Madamu to nyōbō* o meguru', p. 9.

50 See for example Kido Shirō interviewed in 'Tōkī wa doko e (6)', p. 4.

their machine. It is not clear how much of the technology was borrowed, but in an early survey of the development of sound cinema in Japan Tanaka Jun'ichirō claims that the brothers gleaned hints from the Powers Cinephone projector and the Fox Movietone system.[51] An article on Japanese cinema in the *Journal of the Society of Motion Picture Engineers* noted, 'While little detail is available concerning this apparatus, it is said to be built on lines very similar to RCA recorders'.[52] Technical details aside, the *benshi* and studio musicians were aware of, and opposed to, the development of an indigenous talkie system. Takeo recalls that he bought a Winchester 401 rifle to defend his laboratory. He built a palisade of floorboards to hide behind, and even fired into the Kamata studio pond to warn off a group of yakuza who had been hired by the *benshi* and musicians to smash his equipment.[53] Tensions were so high that the musicians the studio gathered to record the soundtrack of *The Neighbour's Wife and Mine* were threatened with reprisals. They carried weapons along with their musical instruments and even wore bulletproof vests.[54] That tense situation at the studio in 1931 presaged the strikes that would hit Shōchiku as well as Nikkatsu cinemas the following year, part of a series of strikes that roiled the entire industry.

The '*benshi* strikes'

Most contemporary writing in Japan on the introduction of recorded sound assumed that the 'talkie age' was inevitable, an outgrowth of technology and Japan's subordinate relation to the USA. Ikeda Hisao, new University of Tokyo graduate and Secretary General of the National Cinema Workers Alliance (Zenkoku Eiga Jūgyōin Dōmei) fought against that attitude during the transition to sound. Part of a new generation of leftist intellectuals, Ikeda lamented the lack of class-consciousness in single-occupation unions, criticizing the well-paid *benshi* and projectionists for not striking in solidarity when the musicians were fired.[55] He also blamed the Musicians Union for not fighting harder when the layoffs at the Hōgakuza and the Musashinokan came: they 'just fell into a panic and let their members cry

51 Tanaka, 'Nihon ni okeru tōkī jigyō', p. 18.

52 Ruot, 'The Motion Picture Industry in Japan', p. 636. Tsuchihashi Haruo is listed as a member in *Journal of the Society of Motion Picture Engineers*, April 1931, p. 489.

53 Tsuchihashi, 'Eiga ga koe o hasshita toki', p. 287, 304.

54 Tsuchihashi, 'Eiga ga koe o hasshita toki', p.303.

55 Ikeda, 'Eigakan sōgi no jissai'. Ikeda was a leftist later known for his support of Proletarian literature.

themselves to sleep'.[56] Ikeda analysed the transition to sound in the USA as bringing Hollywood under the domination of electric and finance capital, and argued that the introduction of the same technology to Japan threatened the livelihood of *benshi* and musicians, and increased the workload for the 'projection engineer' (*eisha gishi*). He hoped to radicalize the industry on the model of his National Cinema Workers Alliance, which was founded by musicians and front-of-house staff (*omotekata*) in 1925. However, Ikeda's bark seems to have been bigger than his bite, considering that his union had only about 100 members, split between Tokyo, Yokohama, and Kyoto.[57]

It was only when they lost their own jobs that the *benshi*, those most privileged (because indispensable) members of the cinema workforce, made common cause with other cinema workers. And only when they joined the struggle was a strike even possible. Other workers could easily be replaced; female ushers, for example, were employed by the day. As labour economist Nakamura Masaaki has shown, ushers and ticket sellers made between 15 and 50 yen per month. Projectionists made about 70 yen, as much as the highest rate for musicians playing Japanese music. The best-paid musicians playing western music could get as high as 150 yen per month, exceeded only by the most famous *benshi*, who could make up to 200 yen per month.[58] In the face of falling receipts and mass layoffs, as well as their apparent superfluity, the *benshi*'s high pay was resented by cinema management. Taking the opposite position to Ikeda, Tōge Norihito, a cinema manager in Kobe, complained that the *benshi* and the musicians' pay constituted half the cost of running a cinema.[59] Tōge asked why the *benshi* did not offer to reduce their wages when so many musicians had been fired and the ushers and other workers' jobs were now on the block. In a common refrain, he argued that the commercial value of the *benshi* had been reduced: you could no longer just post the *benshi*'s name and attract a crowd. Although they were not yet dispensable, according to Tōge the *benshi*'s high wages were a 'cancer' on the film world.[60]

The film industry came to the forefront of labour militancy during the transition to sound. Categorized by the Home Ministry as middle class (*chūkan kaikyū*) rather than industrial workers, cinema workers were some of the most bellicose in Japan during this period. Sources do not agree on

56 Ikeda, 'Warera wa ikaga ni tatakatta ka!', p. 10.

57 Ikeda, 'Nihon eiga jūgyōin undō jikki 2', p. 20.

58 Nakamura, 'Senzenki Nihon no eiga rōdō kumiai no hensen', p. 58. Nakamura's article is a helpful guide to the jigsaw puzzle of unions and their affiliations in this period.

59 Tōge, 'Eiga *Morocco* kara', p. 35.

60 Ibid.

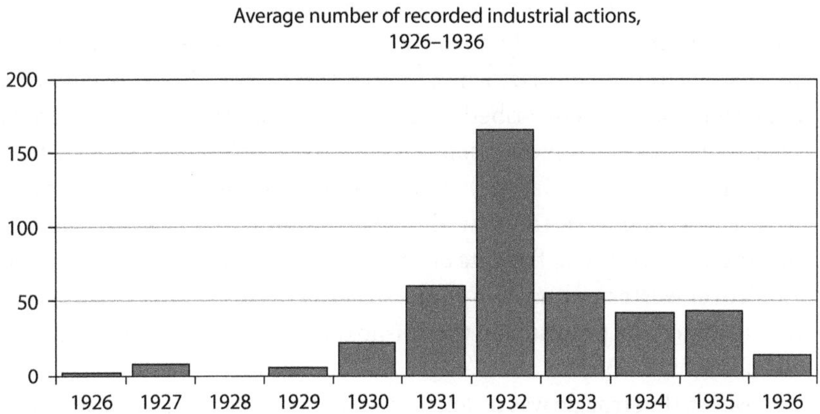

Figure 5.6 Average number of recorded industrial actions in the film industry, 1926-1936. Source: Nakamura Masaaki. 'Senzenki Nihon no eiga rōdō kumiai no hensen', *Ohara shakai mondai kenkyujo zasshi* #700 (February 2017).

the number or type of industrial actions (strike or go-slow; studio worker, *benshi*, or other cinema worker) in the film industry, nor the number of participants, but Fig. 5.6 shows the average number of incidents each year from various sources as tabulated by Nakamura Masaaki. The Home Ministry referred to the protests as non-factory 'special struggles' (*tokushu sōgi*) that increased every year from 1929 to 1932, when they constituted 72% of non-industrial strike actions in Japan. Most of the actions occurred in the cinemas, though there was a strike at one or more studios every year during the period, including one at Shinkō that was concurrent with the 1932 '*benshi* strikes' and the big Nikkatsu strike of the same year.[61] Labour organizers supported disputes at the cinemas since they were highly public spaces, less isolated and protected from public view than the spinning factories and other manufactures that were also centres of unrest. They used the strikes to advertise the labour movement as well as put pressure on the cinema chains.

There was a small strike in September 1930, the first since the big Nikkatsu strike of 1913, after *benshi* at the Asakusa Tokyokan and Yūrakukan did not receive their full pay. Another strike at the Musashinokan in May 1931 spread to other cinemas.[62] Yet another strike erupted at the Nihonkan in August 1931, after wages were cut 20-50%. The *benshi*'s privilege shows even during this deflationary adjustment: their wages were cut the least

61 Nakamura, 'Senzenki Nihon no eiga rōdō kumiai no hensen', p. 68.

62 'Setsumei chū no *benshi* kanshū e bira de utau', p. 2.

and the lowest-paid employees (ushers, ticket sellers, and 'boys') were cut the most.[63] After these early skirmishes, the major strikes occurred in the spring and summer of 1932, when foreign films were almost exclusively talkies with subtitles inscribed onto the image and the Japanese studios began to increase their production of talkies and synchronized sound films, even before they had finished their purpose-built sound stages. On 18 April the Taishōkan, part of the new Shōchiku-Paramount chain of cinemas showing western films, fired its *benshi* instead of having them stand idle or talk over western films. Two-hundred *benshi* from forty cinemas across the city joined the protest, and the Taishōkan briefly became the centre of anti-talkie agitation.[64]

However, the struggle was no longer confined to cinemas showing western films. Even before Nikkatsu and Shōchiku could produce a full slate of talking pictures, they found ways to incorporate sound in their films as an 'added value'. Shōchiku used its Tsuchihashi sound recording system to produce not only full talkies but also stopgap films that were given many different labels. 'Part-talkie' designated films that, for financial or technical reasons, were released with both silent and talkie sequences. From April 1932, Shōchiku also made 'sound version' (*onkyō-ban* or *saundo-ban*) films with only music and sound effects that would be accompanied in the cinemas by a *benshi*, speaking over the music or in the periods of silence. There were also '*benshi* sound versions' in which the *benshi* narration was dubbed onto the sound track, or 'neo film sans silence' when films mixed several of the above strategies.[65] As this polylingual label indicates, what was important was for the studios to associate these not-fully-synchronized films with the modern West, and disavow their relation to the newly 'silent' cinema of the *benshi*.

Nikkatsu, too, was moving deeper into the talkie. Desperate to compete with western sound films and the new Shōchiku system, in January 1932

63 Misono, *Katsuben jidai*, p. 118; 'Nihonkan-in kakushu ni tan o hasshita misō no jūgyōin sōgi', p. 18.

64 'Tōkī ga tsukuru eigakan jūgyōin sōgi Asakusa Taishōkan o honbu ni', p. 14.

65 For the appellation 'neo film sans silence' see the programme for the Marunouchi Shōchiku gekijo for June 1934. Perhaps the first discussion of the 'sound version' in English was Freiberg, 'The Transition to Sound in Japan', pp. 76-80. However, Freiberg misreads the label as 'sound band' and does not recognize the continued presence of the *benshi* in the cinema for all but the '*benshi* sound version'. The sound version replaced the musicians and threatened the *benshi* by virtue of its status as a sound image: a sign of the ability of studios to record, inscribe, and produce sound in the cinema. As Shōchiku production chief Kido Shirō later said, although the consequences were not immediate the sound version was a 'fatal blow' to the musicians and the *benshi*. See Kido, *Nihon eigaden*, p. 87.

Nikkatsu announced that it would use the new talkie system from P.C.L. to film synchronized talkies and to add music, dialogue, and sound effects to its films, the first of which was released in March of that year. The studio also used the P.C.L. system to produce a talkie, *Toki no ujigami/The Man of the Right Moment* directed by Mizoguchi Kenji in April. In response, workers at the Nikkatsu chain cinemas in Tokyo went on strike and the unrest spread to the cinemas showing Japanese films in the main working-class screening district of Asakusa. These events marked the climax of the industrial disputes: in April 1932, cinemas showing both Japanese and western films, to middle class and working class audiences, at cinemas owned by the two biggest film studios, were on strike at the same time.

The emotive language of the newspaper articles reporting the strikes, borrowed from the emotional intensification of a *benshi* performance, wrote the story of the strikes as a melodrama of human uselessness, a metaphor for all the other workers who were being laid off during the economic crisis. Headlines referred to the *benshi* and their allies as 'victims of the flourishing of the talkie', predicting that 'the age of *benshi* lamentation is at hand'.[66] They positioned the *benshi* as a residual group, 'chased out by machine civilization'.[67] The *benshi* was the most public face of humans in modern Japan facing their own uselessness in comparison with machines. When the strikes spread to cinemas showing Japanese films in Asakusa, newspapers reported that the *benshi* and musicians had gone on an all-out strike. For the first time, Japanese silent films would really be silent. Articles report that customers grumbled and asked for a discount when the films were shown silent (or at least, without *benshi*) but almost all of them stayed to watch the films.[68] The strikers demanded better conditions for ushers and other cinema workers, but despite their agitation they were in a weak position and resisted only long enough to gain compensation according to seniority when the inevitable layoffs came.

The '*benshi* strikes' were spectacular, characterized by a sensory intervention into the screening space. The *benshi* did not simply parade in the street or hold strike meetings. They used their bully pulpit to intervene directly in the cinema, disrupting screenings by stopping in the middle of a film and voicing their demands, or throwing leaflets from the balcony, or releasing noxious fumes and firecrackers into the auditorium during a show.[69] The

66 'Tōkī zenpan no gisei', p.11.

67 'Kikai bunmei ni owaruru mure', p.11.

68 Ibid.

69 For a description see 'Eisha chū ni hanabi', p. 11.

studios used strikebreaking unemployed *benshi*, amateur *benshi*, and the talkie apparatus itself to resist the strikers – driving individual reels of two sound prints between cinemas to show in as many places as possible. As the headline put it, the studios 'fight anti-talkie forces with the talkies: machines don't resist'.[70] In response, the strikers occupied the space of the cinema: on the night before May Day strikers, led by *benshi* with musicians and members of the Kanto Workers' Union, occupied the Nikkatsu studio's flagship Kanda Nikkatsukan and took three guards hostage. When the police were called to regain control of the space, the occupiers threw chairs, ash, and 160 spittoons at them from the second floor.[71] Ten policemen were hurt, the auditorium was trashed, and the strike committee was threatened with arrest. As the newspapers reported, 'Nikkatsu strikers and the police [...] Just like street fighting. Riot at Kanda Nikkatsu worse than fighting in a sword film'.[72]

The failure of the 'occupy' strategy at the Nikkatsukan led to a twist in the last major strike: occupy the projection booth and take the machines hostage. The Western Electric setup at the prestigious Shinjuku Musashinokan was worth 45,000 yen, whereas a simple domestic system cost only 2,000. On 11 June, seven workers from the Musashinokan (only one was a *benshi*) occupied the 5.4m x 2.7m x 2.7m booth in a 'packed like sardines' strategy to prevent Shōchiku from absorbing the cinema into its SP chain. Newspapers followed the story all week, giving it an extraordinarily varied political valence: the strikers were described as singing the Internationale but also as 'suicide troops' (*kesshitai*), the word used to describe the ultranationalist naval officers who had assassinated Prime Minister Inukai the previous month.[73] The reports were also surprisingly sentimental, describing the harmonica serenades the strikers were treated to by sympathetic policemen, as well as their suffering when the authorities stopped up the ventilation to the booth, how they survived on three buns a day, and had to use the sand buckets in the projection booth for more than putting out nitrate fires (Fig. 5.7).[74]

In other words, the reports highlighted the aspects of *voice* and *embodiment* that were the figurative if not literal significance of the '*benshi* strikes'. But even this gesture just proved the priority of the machinic over the

70 'Han-tōkī ni tōkī de taikō', p. 7.

71 Hikone, 'Nikkatsu sōgi kaiketsu suru made', p. 14.

72 'Nikkatsu eigakan no sōhigyō', p.1.

73 'Eishashitsu o senryo shite', p. 11.

74 Cited in Watanabe and Watanabe, 'Senzen no rōdō sōgi 6', p. 74-79.

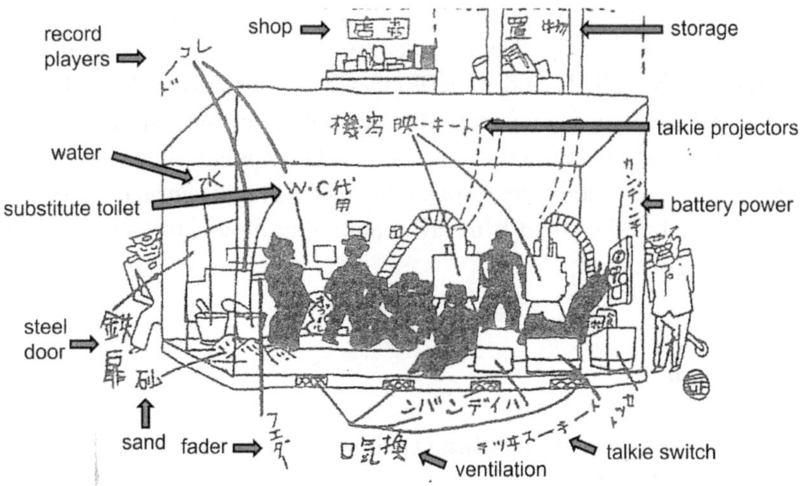

Figure 5.7 Occupying the Musashinokan projection booth, 11-17 June 1932. *Yomiuri Shimbun*, 16 June 1932. My translations.

human. As the first reports on the occupation of the projection booth put it, 'the expensive machines are a cause for anxiety'.[75] The projection booth was a protected space, fitted with steel doors because of the danger of nitrate fires. The strikers tied the doors to the talkie projectors and announced that the authorities could not get them out without 'damaging their precious machines' unlike at the Kanda Nikkatsukan, the police kept their distance. Even so, the protest ended after a week, and although the Musashinokan agreed to the strikers' immediate demands the cinema was still folded into Shōchiku's chain and the *benshi* and musicians eventually lost their jobs. In March 1932 the SP programme that was handed out in the Shōchiku-Paramount chain cinemas advertised the Ufa musical comedy *Die Drei von die Tankstelle* (1930), narrated by a *benshi* at the Taishōkan even as it played 'no interpreter' at other cinemas in the chain. After the strikes, there is no more mention of the *benshi* in the advertisements for films at any of the SP cinemas.

The first demand of the strikers at Shōchiku cinemas showing Japanese films was to oppose the production of domestic talkies and sound versions. Yet when the strike ended, although the company agreed to some of the conditions, it absolutely refused to negotiate over the production of sound films. As one article concluded, Shōchiku successfully resisted the strikers' 'agitation and propaganda' (*aji pro*) and wrangled a resolution without

75 'Eishashitsu o senryo shite', p.11.

making any concessions: 'you could say it was a victory for the company'.[76] The '*benshi* strikes' of 1932 do not mark the end of *benshi* in Japanese cinemas, but they surely mark the end of *benshi* cinema as a cultural dominant. Even in 1935, *benshi* remained in Japanese cinemas and some hired yakuza to invade Shōchiku Head of Production Kido Shirō's home when they were finally fired.[77] However, Kido soon resolved the problem and *benshi* disappeared with the last of the silent films after Shōchiku moved to its new Ōfuna studio in 1936.

Conclusion

By 1934, cinemas were installing their second-generation systems, differentiating themselves by upgrading to superior Western Electric sound systems as part of their cultural modernity along with air conditioning and international modern architecture. New theatres were larger, to better amortize the expensive talkie systems, and designed with a view to acoustics, or at least to volume.[78] Film screenings of sound films were tied-in with records that played during the interval between films and were advertised in the cinema programme. As more and more cinemas converted to sound, the local *benshi* and musicians were left unemployed. Japanese film presentations were almost never silent or voiceless but, with the introduction of the sound image, films without recorded soundtracks came to be called 'voiceless films' (*musei eiga*). Through this phrase, and its corollary the voiced film (*hassei eiga*), the labour of the *benshi* was rendered invisible by its technological supercession. In May 1936, the Kanda Cinema Palace held its first "week of silent film masterpieces", advertising the films as a last chance to experience famous *benshi* accompaniment to silent films that were losing their censorship clearance. The *benshi*, once the epitome of a modern dandy, was now an object of nostalgia.

The battle over the *benshi*'s voice, part of a longer struggle for control of the modern cinema soundscape, was real and quite violent: a sensory intervention in the space of film exhibition. The strikers put their bodies on

76 Hikone, 'Musashinokan sōgi no keiken', p. 16. This long article on the strikes at the Musashinokan and Shōchiku cinemas showing Japanese films lists the demands that the strike committees made, and the studio's response.

77 See 'Ori mo ori battō de chinnyū', p. 2 for a description of the incident, also recounted in Kido. *Nihon eigaden*, p. 131-36.

78 For an account of the acoustic design of new cinemas, such as the Nihon Gekijō see Satō, 'Eiga gekijō no onkyō', p. 24-26.

the line – they introduced noxious gas and fireworks into crowded cinemas, fought pitched battles with the police and, most memorably, occupied the projection booth at the premier Musashinokan cinema for a week. As James Lastra has argued, automatic speech and music produces anxieties about the capacities of the human in the face of the machine: machine-based simulation threatens to render humans obsolete even in their most human aspects (voice and embodiment).[79] Newspapers reported the cinema labour struggles in Japan as '*benshi* strikes' in the midst of an economic crisis with unemployment at record highs. Focusing on the most popular and most 'live' aspect of cinema exhibition, the reports figured broader anxieties about the precarious relation between humans and a modern culture of automation, even as that same drama also played out on Japanese cinema screens, in films such as *Metropolis, A Nous la Liberté, I Was Born, But...*, and *Modern Times*.

Bibliography

Adachi Tadashi. 'Eiga jihyō: hōbun jimaku mondai'. *Kinema shūhō* 50 (27 February 1931), p. 30.

Joseph Anderson. 'Spoken Silents in the Japanese Cinema; or, Talking to Pictures: Essaying the Katsuben, Contexturalizing the Texts'. *Reframing Japanese Cinema* (Bloomington: Indiana University Press, 1992), pp. 259-311.

David Bordwell, Janet Staiger, and Kristin Thompson. *The Classical Hollywood Cinema: Film Style and Mode of Production to 1960* (New York: Columbia University Press, 1985).

Heather Bowen-Struyk. 'Japanese Proletarian Literature during the Red Decade, 1925–1935'. *Oxford Research Encyclopedia* of *Literature* (Oxford: Oxford University Press, 2017). DOI: 10.1093/acrefore/9780190201098.013.196. (Accessed 20 April 2020).

Noël Burch. *To the Distant Observer: Form and Meaning in the Japanese Cinema* (Oakland: University of California Press, 1979).

Jeffrey Dym. *Benshi, Japanese Silent Film Narrators, and their Forgotten Narrative Art of Setsumei* (Mellen Press, 2003).

'Eisha chū ni hanabi. Setsumeisha sōgi'. *Asahi Shimbun*, 11 April 1932, p. 11.

79 Lastra. *Sound Technology and the American Cinema*, in particular Chapter 1. Lastra's larger argument is in favour of the aesthetic and cultural potential of the iteration of a sound and its recording, like the separation between speech and writing, but he also shows how the automatic registration of sound was imagined as a perfect replacement.

'Eishashitsu o senryo shite, kanzume senjutsu o kaishisu, Musashinokan jūgyōin no shichimei ka, shokuba shishu no shinshudan', *Asahi Shimbun* 12 June 1932, p. 11.

Michel Foucault. *Power/Knowledge: Selected Interviews and Other Writings, 1972-1977* (New York: Pantheon, 1980).

Freda Freiberg. 'The Transition to Sound in Japan'. In *History on/and/in Film: Selected Papers Form the 3rd Australian History and Film Conference*, edited by Tom O'Regan and Brian Shoesmith (Perth: History & Film Association of Australia, 1987), pp. 76-80.

Hideaki Fujiki. '*Benshi* as Stars: The Irony of the Popularity and Respectability of Voice Performers in Japanese Cinema'. *Cinema Journal* 45.2 (2006), pp. 68-84.

Hideaki Fujiki. *Making Personas: Transnational Film Stardom in Modern Japan* (Cambridge, MA: Harvard University Asia Center, 2013).

Fujioka Atsuhiro. 'Nihon eiga kōgyōshi kenkyū: 1930 nendai ni okeru gijutsu kakushin oyobi kindaika to purezentēshon'. *CineMagaziNet!* 6 (2002). http://www.cmn.hs.h.kyoto-u.ac.jp/CMN6/fujioka.html (Accessed 20 April 2020).

Fujisawa Keinosuke. 'Rekōdo bansō no rigai'. *Kinema junpō* 387 (1 December 1931), p. 18.

Fukuchi Gorō. 'Musei no deshi to shite'. *Koza Nihon eiga 1: Nihon eiga no tanjō* (Tokyo: Iwanami Shoten, 1985), pp. 310-319.

'Gakushi junan jidai ni men shite domei kikan o sakuseisu'. *Niroku shinpō* (9 July 1929), p. 2.

Aaron Gerow. *Visions of Japanese Modernity: Articulations of Cinema, Nation, and Spectatorship, 1895-1925* (University of California Press, 2010).

Douglas Gomery. *Shared Pleasures: A History of Movie Presentation in the United States* (Madison: University of Wisconsin Press, 1992).

Andrew Gordon. *A Modern History of Japan: From Tokugawa Times to the Present, 4th Edition* (Oxford: Oxford University Press, 2019).

Tom Gunning. *D. W. Griffith and the Origins of American Narrative Film: The Early Years at Biograph* (Champaign: University of Illinois Press, 1994).

'Han-tōkī ni tōkī de taikō. Nikkatsu, Nikkō 23-kan no sōgidan tsui ni zene suto e', *Asahi Shimbun*, 3 May 1932, p. 7.

Hijikata Eiji. 'Nihon zenkoku isshū eigakai shijō angya daishichihō: Morioka eiga sensen ijō nashi'. *Kinema junpō* 397 (11 April 1931), p. 109.

Hikone Tōkichirō. 'Nikkatsu sōgi kaiketsu suru made. Horobiyuku shokugyōsha no tame ni'. *Kinema shūhō* 109 (13 May 1932), pp. 14-18.

Hikone Tōkichirō. 'Musashinokan sōgi no keiken'. *Kinema shūhō* 115 (24 June 1932), pp. 14-16.

'Hōgakuza no rekōdo bansō'. *Kinema junpō* 338 (1 August 1929), p. 10

Iida Saneharu. 'Tōkī to setsumei no mondai de Mori Iwao-shi ni sasagu'. *Kinema shūhō* 50 (27 February 1931), pp. 34-35.

Iida Shinbi et. al. 'Tōkī kenkyū zadankai sokkiroku (1)'. *Kinema junpō* 341 (1 September 1929), pp. 105-108.

Ikeda Hisao. 'Eigakan sōgi no jissai'. *Kinema junpō* 384 (21 November 1930), p. 41.

Ikeda Hisao. 'Warera wa ikaga ni tatakatta ka! Soshite ikagani tatakaitsutsuaru ka! Nihon eiga jūgyōin undō jikki (1)'. *Kinema shūhō* 67 (3 July 1931), pp. 8-10.

Ikeda Hisao. 'Nihon eiga jūgyōin undō jikki (2)'. *Kinema shūhō* 68 (10 July 1931), pp. 18-20.

'Kankyaku no koe', *Kinema shūhō* 48 (13 February 1931), p. 33.

Kido Shirō. *Nihon eigaden: Eiga seisakusha no kiroku* (Tokyo: Bungei shunjū shinsha, 1956).

'Kikai bunmei ni owaruru mure. Setsumeisha to gakushi nado, tsui ni sōhigyō. Asakusa kara shinaigai e hakyū', *Asahi Shimbun*, 19 April 1932, p.11.

Hiroshi Komatsu. 'Some Characteristics of Japanese Cinema before WWI'. In *Reframing Japanese Cinema: Authorship Genre, History*, edited by Arthur Nolletti, Jr. and David Desser (Bloomington: Indiana University Press, 1992), pp. 229-258.

Kondo Kazuto. *Ofu-sukurīn no media-shi: Senzenki no Nihon no eigakan puroguramu o meguru 'yomu koto', 'kaku koto', 'miru koto'* (PhD dissertation, University of Tokyo, 2018).

Kurata Yoshihiro. *Nihon rekōdo bunkashi* (Tokyo: Iwanami Shoten, 2006).

James Lastra. *Sound Technology and the American Cinema: Perception, Representation, Modernity* (New York: Columbia University Press, 2000).

Laura Lee. *Japanese Cinema Between Frames* (Cham, Switzerland: Palgrave Macmillan, 2017).

Misono Kyōhei. *Katsuben jidai* (Tokyo: Iwanami Shoten, 1990).

Mori Iwao, 'Kabin to hanataba 8', *Kinema shūhō* 50 (27 February 1931), p. 8.

'Musei eiga yunyūsha no katsuyō', *Kinema shūhō* 23 (25 July 1930), p. 5.

Nihon eiga terebi producer kyōkai. *Puroguramu eigashi: taishō kara senchū made natsukashi no fukkokuban* (Tokyo: Nihon Hōsō Shuppan Kyōkai, 1978).

'Nihonkan-in kakushu ni tan o hasshita misō no jūgyōin sōgi'. *Kinema shūhō* 73 (7 August 1931), p. 18.

'Nikkatsu eigakan no sōhigyō. Keikan jūmei jūkeishō'. *Miyako shinbun*, 2 May 1932, p.1.

Mark Nornes. *Cinema Babel: Translating Global Cinema* (Minneapolis: University of Minnesota Press, 2007).

Nakamura Masaaki. 'Senzenki Nihon no eiga rōdō kumiai no hensen'. *Ohara Shakai Mondai Kenkyujo zasshi* 700 (February 2017), pp. 56-72.

Nihon eiga rōdō nenpō dai ikki (Tokyo: Rōdō keizai chōsasho, 1933).

'Nihon eiga tōkī-ka ni Beikoku Bikutā-sha tōshi ka'. *Niroku shinpō* (2 June 1929), p. 4.

'Nihon no tōkī ni Beikoku ga tōshi ka'. *Kinema junpō* 333 (11 June 1929), p. 7.

'Ori mo ori battō de chinnyū. Kesa Kido Shōchiku jinmutei e. Shōchiku sōgidan ōen no futari'. *Asahi Shimbun*, 28 March 1935, p. 2.

'Report of the (Japanese) Secretariat Committee'. In *Proceedings of the International Committee on Illumination, Eighth session, September 1931* (Cambridge: Cambridge University Press, 1932), pp. 380-409.
Satō Takeo. 'Eiga gekijō no onkyō'. *Eiga kagaku kenkyū* 7 (25 December 1930), pp. 21-33.
'Setsumei chū no *benshi* kanshū e bira de utau'. *Asahi Shimbun*, 7 May 1931, p. 2.
'Setsumeisha kyōkai asu de hakkaishiki', *Asahi Shimbun*, 3 March 1931, p. 2.
'Setsumeisha no junan jidai ni nanori o ageta furī ransā ichiryū doko ga zenji sanka shitara senzoku setsumeisha no ichi wa abunai'. *Kinema shūhō* 62 (22 May 1931), p. 26.
Isolde Standish. 'Mediators of Modernity: "Photo-interpreters" in Japanese Silent Cinema'. *Oral Tradition* 20.1 (2005), pp. 93-110.
Takada Masaru. '"Seiga" ichinen (2)'. *Kinema junpō* 331 (11 May 1929), pp. 38-40.
Tanaka Jun'ichirō et. al. 'Hōbun taitoru mondai zadankai sokki'. *Kinema shūhō* 48 (13 February 1931), pp. 28-32.
Tōge Norihito. 'Eiga *Morokko* kara Mori-shi no setsumeisha ron sono ta'. *Kinema shūhō* 50 (27 February 1931), p. 35.
'Tōkī ga tsukuru eigakan jūgyōin sōgi Asakusa Taishōkan o honbu ni'. *Kinema shūhō* 105 (15 April 1932), p. 14
'Tōkī wa doko e (6)'. *Niroku shinpō*, 18 May 1929, p. 4.
'Tōkī wa doko e (9): Muhassei eiga no kairyō ni tsutome yo. Kamata Gosho, Miuru ryoshi komogomo kataru'. *Niroku shinpō*, 22 May 1929, p. 4.
'Tōkī zenpan no gisei. *Benshi* himei jidai kuru. Iguchi Shizunami nado jūmei totsujo kaiko sare kessoku, sōgi ni hairu'. *Asahi Shimbun*, 9 April 1932, p.11.
Tokugawa Musei, Yamano Ichirō, and Matsui Suisei. 'Tōkī to setsumeisha'. *Kinema junpō* 352 (1 January 1930), pp. 299-300.
Watanabe Sōzō and Watanabe Etsuji. 'Senzen no rōdō sōgi 6: Watanabe Sōzō-san ni kiku – Eishashitsu o senkyo, shōri shita Shinjuku Musashinokan sōgi – 1932-nen han tōkī-ka dai sōgi no arashi no naka de'. *Gekkan Sōhyō* (April 1978), pp. 74-79.
Steven Wurtzler, *Electric Sounds: Technological Change and the Rise of Corporate Mass Media* (New York: Columbia University Press, 2008).

About the Author

Michael Raine is Associate Professor of Film Studies at Western University, Canada. He has written widely on Japanese cinema, with an emphasis on the transition to sound, wartime image culture, and the 'cinema of high economic growth' around 1960. He has published most recently on the Japanese musical, wartime cinema in Occupied Shanghai, and the Cold War media environment of 1960s Japan.

6 The Image of the Modern Talkie Film Studio

Aesthetics and Technology at P.C.L.

Johan Nordström

Abstract

This chapter examines how studio P.C.L., during its first years, circa 1933-1935, utilized its modern facilities and sound recording equipment as well as the studio's unique labour composition to create both a distinctive self-image for the studio and an often bright and upbeat audio-visual aesthetic for their films. These factors together gave birth to a new Japanese genre of light entertainment, infused with music and song, utilizing aesthetic traits of musical style, staging, and pacing from the urban revue and variety stages, as well as injecting a sense of temporal liveness into the recorded sound and cinematic experience.

Keywords: P.C.L., Tōhō, Enomoto Ken'ichi (Enoken), Asakusa revue, Japanese musical films

Introduction

The importance of song and musicality for the early Japanese sound cinema cannot be overestimated. Starting with the release of Kimura Sotoji's *Ongaku kigeki: Horoyoi jinsei/A Tipsy Life* (1933) the newly founded all sound film studio P.C.L. came to utilize its modern facilities and sound recording equipment to create a bright and upbeat audio-visual aesthetic for its films and a distinctly modern self-image for the studio. As the bricolage of technological prerequisites necessary to facilitate the widespread establishment of an electrically mediated Japanese sound cinema converged, P.C.L., more than any other studio, came to be seen as emblematic of this development.

Raine, M. and J. Nordström (eds.), *The Culture of the Sound Image in Prewar Japan*.
Taylor & Francis Group 2020
DOI: 10.5117/9789089647733_CH06

P.C.L.'s utilization of the potential of the sound film; infusing its films with music and song, and appropriating aesthetic traits of musical style, staging, and pacing with that of the urban revue and variety stages, gave birth to a new genre of Japanese light entertainment, while at the same time infusing these films with a sense of temporal liveness, indirectly addressing the problem of the 'lack of liveness' in the recorded sound and cinematic experience. Catering to the needs of the modern city audience of salarymen, city people and university students for light upbeat entertainment, the narratives of P.C.L.'s films were frequently centred around the new salaried middle class, and came to incorporate elements of urban modernism and musicality.

The slow spread of sound in rural areas meant that the vast majority of P.C.L.'s audiences would by necessity be urban, a phenomenon commented on by studio head Uemura Taiji. He remarked that 'from now on film has to be geared towards the big cities' and that as the majority of cinema goers are located in the cities 'from a commercial point of view, in order to be successful film has to be principally urban centred'.[1] As noted by Satō Toshiaki, the early P.C.L. films were distributed by the Tōwa corporation, which specialized in importing and distributing foreign cinema, with the result that P.C.L.'s films were initially screened in high-end cinemas otherwise dedicated to western sound cinema, for an audience consisting predominantly of students and office workers who were used to foreign cinema.[2] All of the above contributed to P.C.L.'s image as a film production company geared towards city people with a distinctly modern image, and aligned the studio and its creative output squarely with western mass culture, the new and the modern. This chapter will examine the creation of the modern, bright and up-beat, P.C.L. image, the studio's approaches and strategies to song and musicality and the intermedial relation between early Japanese musicals and the variety stage, where many of the P.C.L. actors had their background. This study of early Japanese musical and revue films will illuminate the aesthetic modes through which Japanese cinema incorporated and utilized the new sound film technology, as it sought to maximize its commercial appeal.

Birth of the Modern Japanese Film Studio

P.C.L. appeared at the specific point in time when cinema in Japan was beginning to make its transition in earnest from silent to sound film. By

1 K.O.T., 'Kenkyushitsu haikingu (1) P.C.L. hōmon', p 111.

2 Satō, 'Eiga no naka no Enoken - Yamamoto Kajirō to no koraborēshon', p. 43.

1933, slightly more than a third of the country's cinemas had been wired for sound; this was near-universally the case for cinemas showing western films. According to Michael Raine's research, in Tokyo 85% of seats in cinemas showing Shōchiku films, and 75% of seats in cinemas showing Nikkatsu films were wired for sound.[3]

P.C.L. has often been described as the most modern of film studios, whether by employing the word '*kindaiteki*' or the word '*modan*'. This raises the question of wherein P.C.L.'s modernity is to be found. Certainly, one aspect of P.C.L.'s modernity must be located in its corporate structure and industrial origins, which came to influence its business practices, pushing it towards a rationalist model heavily influenced by the production system of Hollywood. Another aspect may be located in their progressive labour polices, which gave birth to what perhaps can be called the first, albeit short-lived, labour union within a major Japanese film company, the P.C.L.C., short for P.C.L. Club, and to close to equal treatment of film staff and studio workers, regardless of their hierarchical position within the corporate structure.[4] Yet another aspect might be, as Yomota Inuhiko points out, the relative youth of everyone working at the studio, and how it became a safe haven, an asylum, for left leaning intellectuals, former proletarian movement members, artists, and, later in the 1930s, draft dodgers.[5]

The first film studio incarnation of P.C.L., the Kabushiki Kaisha Shashin Kagaku Kenkyūjo (lit. Photo Chemical Laboratory Stock Company) was established on 1 June 1932, with Uemura Taiji as executive chairman. It was formed through the amalgamation of two research laboratories, the Shashin Kagaku Kenkyūjo and the Kokusan Tōkī Sha (lit. the Japanese Talkie Company), both structured under the same parent company, the Orientaru Shashin Kōgyō Kabushiki Kaisha (lit. Oriental Photo Industry Stock Company), a prominent joint-stock company that specialized in photographic exposure material, of which Uemura's father, the influential businessman Uemura Chōsaburō, was executive chairman. In June 1932, the theoretical aspects of P.C.L's sound film technology P.C.L shiki (lit. the P.C.L. System) were deemed a success and the two laboratories were merged into one corporate entity, mainly with the aim of offering simultaneous sound film recording as well as so called *afureko* (post-sound recording technology) services. Unlike most western film studios, in Japan it was still the case that most of the major studios, excepting Shōchiku with their Tsuchihashi-sound

3 See the introduction to this volume.

4 For a detailed account see Nordström, '*Tōkī wa P.C.L*'.

5 Yomota, *Nihoneigashi 100 nen*, p. 91.

system, did not have their own sound stages and recording equipment but instead rented these from secondary companies on a contractual basis.[6]

Many of those who initially came to work at P.C.L. had either previous experience in the Japanese film industry, as for instance Masutani Rin, previously the general manager of technicians/engineering at Shōchiku Kamata studios, or Mineo Yoshio, previously at Minagawa Yoshizō's Phonofilm/Mina Talkie film production company. Others had worked in Hollywood, such as Hayakawa Kōji who had served as a sound technician for three years at the MGM studio, and Ichikawa Tsunaji who had worked at Paramount's Hollywood studio. The very earliest work the studio acquired was to produce newsreels for the Asahi news corporation, and it was these newsreels that caught the eye of Nikkatsu, who after their failed attempt at producing full sound cinema in collaboration with Mina Talkie, utilizing Lee de Forest's Phonofilm sound system, had abstained from further attempts. However, with the success of Shōchiku's *Madamu to nyōbō/The Neighbour's Wife and Mine* (Gosho Heinosuke, 1931), and the steadily increasing presence of various forms of cinema utilizing recorded sound to various degrees within the Japanese movie industry, Nikkatsu decided to once again attempt production, and this time in collaboration with P.C.L.

The first results of this collaboration was Mizoguchi Kenji's *Toki no ujigami/The Man of the Right Moment* and *Onna Kunisada* by Kiyose Eijirō, starring Fushimi Naoe, both of which premiered in April 1932, the same month that Shōchiku's big sound cinema production *Jōriku daiippo/First Steps Ashore* (Shimazu Yasujirō, 1932) was released. Due to this collaboration with Nikkatsu, P.C.L. started to see the limitations of their relatively small sound stage, and when Nikkatsu requested better sound stages that could accommodate live sound recordings, P.C.L. agreed to make the necessary investments into new studio facilities.

P.C.L. accepted Nikkatsu's request and on 30 May 1933 restructured their two research laboratories into a 120.000 yen strong joint stock company by the name of Kabushiki Kaisha Shashin Kagaku Kenkyūjo. The main stock owners were all representatives from the Japanese world of industrial finance: necessary funds came from investors such as Uemura Chōsaburō, company director of the wealthy Dai Nippon Bīru firm (the precursor of the current Asahi and Sapporo beer companies), Sōma Hanji, founder and head of the sugar and sweets manufacturing company Meiji Seito, and Ōhashi Shintarō, co-founder and head of the Tokyo based publishing house

6 As in the case of for instance the Mina Talkie-Nikkatsu collaboration, and the Eastphone-Shinkō Kinema collaboration.

Hakubunkan, with Uemura Taiji as company director, and an economically strong advisory board featuring Uemura's father Chōsaburō, Sōma Hanji, and Kobayashi Ichizō, founder and president of Hanshin Kyūkō Dentetsu (later Hankyū Corporation) and owner of the Takarazuka Revue company.

This was a first for the Japanese movie industry, and considering the fragility of the Japanese economy in 1932, due to the lingering effects of the Depression and Japan's recent abandonment of the gold standard in 1931, the very fact that P.C.L. could acquire the necessary funds for this kind of large scale investment demonstrates one of the characteristics that set it apart from other contemporary film companies. According to early P.C.L. film producer and political activist Ōmura Einosuke, the kind of industrial capitalists backing P.C.L. was of a completely different character from that of, for instance, Shōchiku's Ōtani Takejirō or Nikkatsu's Yokota Einosuke, and their modern and rationalist business practices would come to infuse the new studio. That P.C.L. came to enjoy this kind of corporate backing is also indicative of the clout that both Uemura Chōsaburō and Kobayashi Ichizō wielded, and their influence on P.C.L.'s development, and indirectly the Japanese movie industry as a whole, came to be substantial.

The construction of P.C.L.'s two new sound stages was finalized in November 1932. However, even though Nikkatsu had set up an office branch on P.C.L.'s premises, they rescinded their contract with P.C.L., not having utilized the new facilities even once. According to Tanaka Jun'ichirō, even before P.C.L. finished their enormous new modern sound studio, Nikkatsu had decided that they had no intention of ever using it. Instead, Nikkatsu built their own sound film studio at Tamagawa and started to produce sound film in house in the hope to turn around their fiscal deficit, while simultaneously investing in the Western Electric sound technology as it offered both recording and playback technology.[7]

P.C.L., now with a new modern sound-film studio and no partner, immediately started looking for new customers to whom they could rent their facilities. Ironically, in the aftermath of the Great Nikkatsu Strike of 1932, a group of seven distinguished filmmakers, the so called 'Shichiningumi', formed a short-lived production company, Shin'eigasha, which came to produce two films utilizing P.C.L.'s new facilities; *Showa shinsengumi* (Itō Daisuke, 1932) and *Sakebu Ajia/Asia Screams* (Uchida Tomu, 1933).[8] It was

7 See Ōmura, 'Ōmura Einosuke shikikisho (2)', p. 7-9, for the deficit plans and Mori, *Watakushi no geikai henreki*, p. 157, for the investment.

8 The early 1930s was a period of economical and structural turmoil for Nikkatsu that reached its zenith in a series of strikes and lay-offs in 1932. Much of this turmoil was connected to the

also through this production group that Mori Iwao, later head producer at the studio, became officially connected to P.C.L.

Parallel to Shin'eigasha, a production group called Onga Geijutsu Kenkyūjo, which was connected to Japan's proletarian film movement (Prokino), utilized the sound facilities at P.C.L. to make the tendency film *Kawa mukō no seishun/Youth Across the River* (Kimura Sotoji, 1933). As production was finishing, the Japanese authorities cracked down on Prokino, raiding its main office and arresting those members they managed to catch. However, the production staff of Onga Geijutsu Kenkyūjo, in spite of their political affiliations, came to stay on at P.C.L. This was due to the influence of Uemura Taiji's cousin Ōmura Einosuke, a former Marxist student activist, who described his time at P.C.L. as 'film during the day, political struggle during the night'. He famously is purported to have told the studio executives that 'as long as they can film, it doesn't matter if they are red or not'.[9]

As P.C.L.'s statutes explicitly forbade the company to engage in film production of its own, a new production unit was set up, the P.C.L. (Photo Chemical Laboratory, or Shashin Kagaku Kenkyūjo Kabushiki Kaisha), which existed for two years. When the studio executives saw that the film productions were handled with a strict budget control and according to modern business practices, the company statutes were changed to allow for in-house film production.

Bright and Upbeat – Manufacturing the P.C.L. Image

Just as P.C.L. within the film industry from the very outset became equated with a modern image and Hollywood-style production and business model, so did they also become stylistically associated with a form of light and upbeat entertainment film, infused with song and dance and the spectacle of the modern urban capital.

coming of sound cinema, as for instance the *benshi* and musicians anti-talkie strikes, or as one of the main reasons for Nikkatsu's massive layoffs and attempts to cut staff salaries in order to afford expensive sound film technology for their cinemas. The Great Nikkatsu Strike occurred in August 1932, and involved more or less the whole studio. It resulted in 180 production staff lay-offs, and studio head Ikenaga Kōkyū retiring from his post. In its aftermath, the so-called Shichiningumi incident occurred on 20 September, when seven of Nikkatsu's most famous remaining staff and directors decided to leave the studio to form the Shin'eigasha.

9 Ōmura, 'Ōmura Einosuke shikikisho (2)', p. 6.

At the beginning of the 1930s, industry dominant Shōchiku had embraced much of the Hollywood filmmaking modes into their distinctive 'Kamata' style, however, as shown by Daisuke Miyao, this did not extend to an emphasis on Hollywood-style expressive lighting.[10] Under its slogan 'The Talkie is PCL'/'Tōkī wa PCL' and 'Bright and Fun'/'Akarukute tanoshikute', P.C.L. came to spearhead the move to transfer the visual style of Hollywood to the Japanese cinema. The resulting visual image came to, quite literally, outshine the other studios with its brightness and clarity. From a total budget of 300,000 yen devoted to equipping its newly constructed studio with the latest machinery and furnishing, P.C.L. invested nearly 65,000 yen into lighting equipment, and furthermore, according to P.C.L. cinematographer Miyajima Yoshio, the studio was equipped with 650 kW electricity, unlike other studios that only went up to circa 500 kW.[11]

However, the distinct bright visual style of the early P.C.L. films were not a mere consequence of the studio fixtures, as, according to Kimura Sotoji, there also existed a conscious effort at the studio to produce films with a bright visual style so as to differentiate P.C.L.'s films from those of other studios:

> What was surprising and funny was that there was a goal to create bright films. The other film companies kept making only very dark films. To make a bright film, you not only brighten the tone of the photography, but the whole set, all the way down to the brown pillars of Japanese architecture. You make the walls bright as well, you leave nothing lying around, and you simplify everything.
> Those film directors [working] at other studios couldn't understand why P.C.L.'s films were so bright (laughter). Naturally, neither did the audience.[12]

The bright visual image that was cultivated by P.C.L. came to reach its fullest potential with the arrival in 1934 at the studio of, firstly, cinematographer Mimura Akira, and secondly, two Mitchell NC/BNC cameras, the first of their kind to be imported into Japan. The importance of the Mitchell cameras as well as Mimura, who quickly modified the studio's lightning set-up so that it would adhere to the latest Hollywood industry practices, to the development

10 For a detailed look at Shōchiku's attitudes towards expressive lightning, see Miyao *The Aesthetics of Shadow*.

11 'Nihon saidai no tōkī satsueijo', p. 14-15.

12 Yagi, 'Kimura Sotoji', p 105.

of P.C.L.'s visual aesthetics cannot be overstated, and the impact of this bright image in P.C.L.'s early films came to be seen as intimately connected to a specific mode of urban modernity.

Future P.C.L. director Yamamoto Kajirō, then still at Nikkatsu, described the effect that seeing P.C.L.'s third film, the manga adaptation *Tadano bonji – jinsei benkyō*/*The Average Man Tadano – Life Lessons* (Kimura Sotoji, 1934), had on him:

> The Tokyo street buildings around Marunouchi area, the trees lining the streets of Jingū Gaien, all emerged boldly one after another, this bright modern landscape, somehow an unbearable homesickness welled forth. And even more, when I saw the vibrant and energetic way of the modern style of life lived by actresses such as Tsutsumi Masako, Chiba Sachiko, Takehisa Chieko, with their modern femininity, laughing and moving with their whole being, this chest of mine, 'Aah!', it grew hot, and without realizing it, as I left the theatre lost in the crowd of people, I started to cry.[13]

Just as P.C.L.'s technological equipment and skilful adaptation of Hollywood-style methods of lightning and shooting were *sine qua non* for the creation of its bright and upbeat image, so too it was equally contingent on the choice of production material, scenery, and the actors who physically embodied this consciously constructed audio-visual modernity.

As Nikkatsu abandoned its collaboration with P.C.L. and no new viable long term partner emerged, Mori argued that the only option for P.C.L. was to turn to in-house movie production. However, a very specific problem faced the studio; its acute lack of actors. Initial attempts to borrow talent from other studios failed, leaving only the option of hiring little known or so-called 'new face' actors, or to recruit talent from other, non-cinematic, venues. This the studio did, recruiting voraciously, especially from the urban theatre and revue stages, resulting in the eclectic mélange of actors present at P.C.L., as well as frequent guest appearances from famous stage performers, singers, theatre troupes and variety acts (most notably, during the latter half of the 1930s, *manzai* comedians from theatre company and talent agency Yoshimoto Kōgyō's stable), alongside actresses who graduated from Kobayashi Ichizō's Takarazuka revue theatre.

In this way, P.C.L., more than any other studio, came to rely heavily on the world of the urban revue-stage and dance halls for its actors, story material, and musical inspiration. Naturally, the awareness of the box office success

13 Yamamoto, *Katsudoya jitaden*, p. 145.

of many foreign musical and operetta films in Japan created an incentive to tap into this so far unexplored market of domestic production. Head producer Mori Iwao had both in his voluminous theoretical writing on talkie/sound cinema and in his past involvement with sound film production, previously advocated the utilization of talent from the revue and theatre stage, as well as elaborated on the importance of cinemas musicality for the future success of the Japanese sound film.[14]

P.C.L. was also instrumental in shaping the sound track of the Japanese sound cinema. Naturally, the multifaceted and urban experience of P.C.L.'s actors augmented the studios bright and up-beat identity, while simultaneously the actors' enunciation and musicality helped shape the diegetic aural part of the talkie soundtrack. Yet even more importantly, whereas Shōchiku and other studios at that time outsourced the composing of music for their early talkies, P.C.L. permanently hired Kami Kyōsuke, one of Japan's most famous jazz composers, and established the jazz ensemble P.C.L. Symphonic Jazz Orchestra. Both are considered to have had a major impact on the early music history of the Japanese sound film.[15] Furthermore, P.C.L.'s roots as a research laboratory and its connection to its mother company Orientaru Shashin Kōgyō meant that P.C.L. continued to seek out new technological innovations and to acquire patents throughout the 1930s. Among these were early innovations to facilitate soundtrack mixing, sound silencing technology, and further refinements to the P.C.L. shiki sound technology. Additionally, P.C.L. was the first Japanese studio to film on domestically made sound film stock, created by Orientaru Shashin Kōgyō.

Music, Operetta Films and the Virtual Revue Stage

The film industry's conversion from silent to sound in the United States had been partially motivated by the goal of producing sound films as low-cost substitutes for live musical, stage and radio acts. Therefore, as Charles O'Brien has pointed out, one of the salient features of early American sound films was their simulation of the experience of the popular stage,

14 Especially through his involvement with the *Nikkatsu*-tied think tank the *Friday Society/Kinyōkai*, which was heavily involved in the Nikkatsu-Mina Talkie co-production *Hometown/Furusato* (Mizoguchi Kenji, 1930), and his involvement with the short-lived Oriental eigasha, and their sound film production *Namiko* (Tanaka Eizo, 1932). For more on Mori Iwao's writing on the coming of the sound cinema, see: Johan Nordström, 'Mori Iwao to shoki saundo eiga', and Karl Johan Nordström, '"Tōkī ha P.C.L"'.

15 Akiyama, *Nihon no eiga ongakushi* (1), p. 37.

the concert hall, and the radio broadcast.[16] Actors, often with a vaudeville or revue- background, such as Al Jolson, Maurice Chevalier, and directors such as Ernst Lubitsch, and somewhat later the choreography of Busby Berkeley, and the films of Fred Astaire and Ginger Rogers, were creating films infused with song and dance numbers. In Germany, the operetta film was born with *Melodie des Herzens/Melody of the Heart* (Hanns Schwarz, 1929), the popularity of which spawned a new genre of music and dance films that came to continue well into the 1930s and influence other national cinemas, not least the Japanese.

However, beyond the influence of western musical films it is also possible to trace strands of the Japanese musical cinema back to the 'kouta eiga' of the silent era, and to non-cinematic sources of influence, such as the Asakusa opera musical comedy revues, the all-girl troupe of Takarazuka revue, and the Japanese record industry. Indeed, the development and growth of popular revue entertainment, first on the stages of Asakusa, later in Yūrakuchō, were closely connected to various forms of imported Western music, the development of hybrid forms of Japanese popular music, and the burgeoning Japanese record industry. The early Japanese musical films came to reflect both the economic situation represented by large corporate investments and the multiplicity of musical and sound forms that existed at the time. The resulting films were very much a composite product: the result of a self-aware appropriation of modes and conduct from the world of Hollywood musicals, the popular stages of urban Tokyo, and tried and tested commercial film practices of combining song and film.

P.C.L.'s two first feature films, *A Tipsy Life* and *Junjō no miyako/The Capital of Innocence*, came to illustrate these ties as well as the eclectic background of its actors. *A Tipsy Life* was marketed in the trade press as Japan's first 'ongaku kigeki', or 'musical comedy', and '*operetta eiga*', and P.C.L. emphasized the cast's connection to the revue stage through its advertisement which boldly stated that the film 'gorgeously gathers the finest talents from the world of revue'. Indeed P.C.L. had mobilized such revue stars as Furukawa Roppa, who brought with him members of his ensemble (among them Dekao Yokō, who had worked with Roppa on his show *Warai no ōkoku/Kingdom of Laughter* (April 1933 – June 1934), alongside other performance celebrities such as the *benshi* Tokugawa Musei, to appear in supporting roles in the film.

The narrative centres around the female protagonist Emiko, played by P.C.L.'s leading lady Chiba Sachiko, who works as a train station beer vendor,

16 O'Brien, *Cinemas Conversion to Sound*, p. 3.

Figure 6.1 *Tipsy Life* advertisement, the caption reads 'A Comedy with Laughter and Song' *Kinema junpō* 478 (1 August 1933).

and her relationship with the aspiring music student Asao, played by Ōkawa 'Henry' Heihachirō, who had just returned from the United States where he had studied acting at Paramount's New York acting school. *A Tipsy Life's* strongest evocation of stage revue aesthetics occurs towards the films end, when Furukawa Roppa's character gives a revue-like song performance while he stands on top of a large beer keg in a beer hall, his song backed up by a complete diegetic orchestra, and the customers in the establishment all move rhythmically to and fro with their beer glasses raised. Although the scene is presented diegetically, the atmosphere and the visuals are closer to that of the Asakusa revue stages.

For the shooting of P.C.L.'s second film, producer Mori Iwao sent a request to the Moulin Rouge Shinjukuza to 'borrow' their stage star Takehisa Chieko for three months, to star in the movie version of the their revue play *Reiai toshi Tokyo/City of Love, Tokyo*. Although the movie version was originally marketed under the same title as the play, it was subsequently changed to *Junjō no miyako/The Capital of Innocence* two weeks before its release, due to objections by the state censors on using the word *reiai*, 'romantic love', in combination with the name of the capital. In the film, Takehisa Chieko plays the street-savvy '*moga*', or 'modern girl', Kyōko, who shares an apartment and works as a secretary together with Michiko, played by Chiba Sachiko, a jovial but innocent girl from the country. In the film's climactic final scene, the playboy son of the company head where Michiko works invites himself back to her apartment and rapes her. Its stark ending seemingly suggests that the kind of innocence that Chiba's character symbolizes is doomed to be corrupted by the city, where in order to survive, you have to be tough, like Kyōko.

Takehisa Chieko stayed on at P.C.L. and became the studio's second star actress, and her image as the ultimate modern girl became the counterweight to the innocence and purity of Chiba Sachiko. Takehisa, with a distinctly erotic stage persona, became affectionately known as the studio's '*ero-anego*', or 'erotic big sister', a continuation of the image that she had cultivated on stage, first as a member of Enomoto Ken'ichi (Enoken)'s theatre troupe during their *Casino follies* show, but later and more specifically during her time at the Moulin Rouge.

More Real than the Real: *Diary of a Dancer*

P.C.L. continued and intensified their conscious borrowing of material and stars from the world of the theatre and revue stage in their fourth film *Odoriko nikki/Diary of a Dancer* (Yagura Shigeo, 1934). It was released in cinemas on 15 March, but had a pre-release screening event (entitled *Eiga to jitsuen no yū/An Evening of Film and Performance*), on the evening of the 12th at the prestigious concert, revue and event hall Hibiya Kōkaidō. Based on an original story by popular review writer Shimamura Ryūzō, the film starred Chiba Sachiko and Heihachirō Ōkawa in the romantic lead roles of Reiko and Kenji, and featured an impressive line-up of famous artists from the world of the revue stage appearing in performance. As the film opens, Kenji leaves for Tokyo to become a musician, however, he ends up as a stagehand at a small revue-company, eventually getting fired and finding work as a cook. Reiko, not hearing anything from Kenji, leaves for Tokyo as well, and ends up working as a dancer at the revue company where Kenji was previously employed. The main plot of a *Diary of a Dancer* takes place inside the revue theatre where first Kenji and later Reiko comes to work, and the audience are treated to a veritable who's who of famous Tokyo stage entertainers seen rehearsing in the background or performing. In the film's finale, as the revue theatre puts on a 'grand performance', the lovers are reunited.

In the marketing of *Diary of a Dancer*, apart from its label as a 'revue romance' film, P.C.L. emphasized the origin of the film's story by famous revue writer Shimamura, the revue related elements of the plot, and especially the appearance of many famous contemporary revue performers such as Ōtsuji Shirō, Furukawa Roppa, chanson singer Awaya Noriko, and jazz singer Betty Inada. The studio's newsletter magazine *P.C.L. eiga* boldly states that:

> *Odoriko nikki* is based on a story by review writer Shimamura Ryūzō, and accordingly it features several gorgeous play-within-a-play revue sequences. Therefore, even if you have never seen a revue, if you see this one film, you will know what kind of thing an Asakusa revue is.[17]

The revue stars that appear in the film appear as 'themselves', doing their 'guest appearances' in the context of the film's overarching narrative structure, and their presence lends a sense of realism to the film's fictional characters. The studio advertisement material highlights how the studio enlisted between 50-100 'beautiful dancers' for the production, as well as ballroom dancers,[18] and the film's final sequence was marketed by P.C.L. as a '*geki-chū-geki*', or 'a play within a play'. To film it a complete three-storey Asakusa stage replica was built inside the P.C.L. main studio. The studio magazine comments that 'as many P.C.L. actors originally came from the

17 'Odoriko nikki no rebyū-bamen: fukidasu gekichūgeki no kazukazu: enshutsusha no kaobure ha tenka ni zuiichi', p. 2.
18 Ibid.

(二) 昭和九年二月十五日 P C L 映画 第二號

踊り子日記のレヴュー場面
ふき出す劇中劇の數々
出演者の顔振れは天下に隨一

踊り子日記 主題歌 ・・戀の月・・

Figure 6.2 Advertisement article for *Odoriko nikki*, showing the many revue artists performing in the film. The headline reads 'The Revue Scenes of *Diary of a Dancer*: Many play within a play [scenes] burst out: The Lineup of Performers is the Greatest in the World'. *'Odoriko nikki* no rebyū-bamen: fukidasu gekichūgeki no kazukazu: enshutsusha no kaobure ha tenka ni zuiichi', *P.C.L. eiga* 2 (15 February 1934), p. 2.

revue world, it was very nostalgic' and that 'the performers insisted on having the musicians present in the box while the performance was on', as otherwise 'the feeling wouldn't be right'. It was 'real' to the point that studio head Uemura, who was present during its filming, allegedly shouted out the name of Takehisa Chieko during her performance.[19]

In *Diary of a Dancer* we have in effect a spatial co-presence with the performances, embedded into the narrative of the film. Although these passages of the film are not recordings of real events, but a documentation of a pseudo-event, constructed for the sake of the film, their inclusion were heavily utilized in the film's marketing by P.C.L., who, on the basis of cultural economy, argued that someone who sees *Diary of a Dancer* no longer need to go to the Asakusa revues, as they will already have experienced it, effectively voiding the live on the level of rhetoric and granting equivalence to the recorded pseudo-event as real.

Marketing Musicality

The importance that P.C.L. put on musicality in its early productions can also be gleaned from the way that the studio created links, be it symbolic or semantic, between its studio output and various forms of performance and popular music, even when these were almost non-existent. Two such examples are *Namiko no isshō/The Life of Namiko* (Yagura Shigeo, 1934) and *Sakura ondo – namida no haha/Sakura Ondo – The Crying Mother* (Kimura Sotoji, 1934), both serious melodramatic stories and lacking any substantial connection to music, theatre, or the revue. *The Life of Namiko* was a filmatization of the popular Japanese novel *Hototogisu/The Cuckoo* by author Tokutomi Kenjirō (also known as Tokutomi Rōka), perhaps most famously made into the silent film *Hototogisu/The Cuckoo* (Ikeda Yoshinobu, 1922), starring Japan's first female star Kurishima Sumiko. Mori Iwao had previously worked on the more recent version for Oriental Eigasha called *Namiko* (Tanaka Eizō, 1932), incidentally shot by Mimura. Although the P.C.L. version was not a musical film and lacked song performances, it was still marketed in advertisements and information material as 'The Musical film *The Life of Namiko*' to emphasize the musicality of its symphonic jazz score by Kami Kyōsuke.

P.C.L.'s third film *Sakura ondo – The Crying Mother* was released as a *kyōsaku*, i.e. in competition with several other films by different film studios, who all released their own *Sakura ondo* films roughly around the same time. Before P.C.L.'s version premiered it was advertised heavily in the trade press, and one of the film's salient features that the ads emphasized

19 'P·C·L gekijo', p. 5

was the film's theme song, similarly titled 'Sakura ondo',and performed by the former geisha turned popular singer Katsutarō. Some of the smaller advertisements for the film actually only included the film's title in a stylized font, the name of the song, and its number in the Victor record catalogue. P.C.L.'s version is a melodrama, and as such actually has very little to do with the popular song-and-dance phenomena, and the use of the song in the film is rather spectacular in its detachment from the narrative of the actual film.

The film's opening shot starts with a close up of the 'Sakura ondo' Victor record on an Electrola gramophone as it starts spinning. The camera tracks out to show a young girl who places the needle on the record, close the lid of the gramophone box, then with a smile hugs the machine as the song starts to play. From there the film cuts to a static close up of the actual record, from which it fades out to the P.C.L. logo, and the start of the opening credits, all the while accompanied by Katsutarō's song. As the credits finish, the film cuts to a montage sequence consisting of a picture of Mount Fuji with cherry trees in bloom, a track-in shot on Katsutarō singing, cherry blossoms, two male singers, and the main cast of the film dancing in tune with the music around a blooming cherry tree. When the song has finished, after approximately six minutes, there is a cut and we are brought into the film's narrative. The song is not heard or used thereafter, although instrumental variations on the popular song are featured as background music in certain scenes of the film. However, even then, there is little or no discernible connection between the lyrics of the original song, its implied meaning, and the actual narrative of the film.[20]

If *Diary of a Dancer* constitutes an attempt to bring the world of the Asakusa revue stage into the cinema, then *Rajio no joō/Queen of the Radio* (Kimura Sotoji, 1935) attempts the same under the guise of radio. P. C.L. collaborated with both Furukawa Roppa's *Warai no ōkoku/Kingdom of Laughter* theatre group and Yoshimoto Kōgyō for the production. Marketed by the studio as 'A Harmony of Roaring Sounds and Radio Waves: A Masterpiece of Satire and Wit', the film's plot is centred on two lovers struggling to overcome the hurdles put by their parents in the way of their union.[21] Against this backdrop, Chiba Sachiko's romantic lead character receives a contract for a radio performance, which results in a virtual tour of a radio studio – in this case the P.C.L. facilities. The film shows several famous vocal performers,

20 For a detailed analysis of Katsutarō and the use of the Sakura ondo song in the film, see Hosokawa Shuhei's chapter in this volume.

21 'Bakuon to denpa no kanaderu: fūshi to kaigyaku no daisaku: "*Rajio no jō*" no miryoku', p. 2.

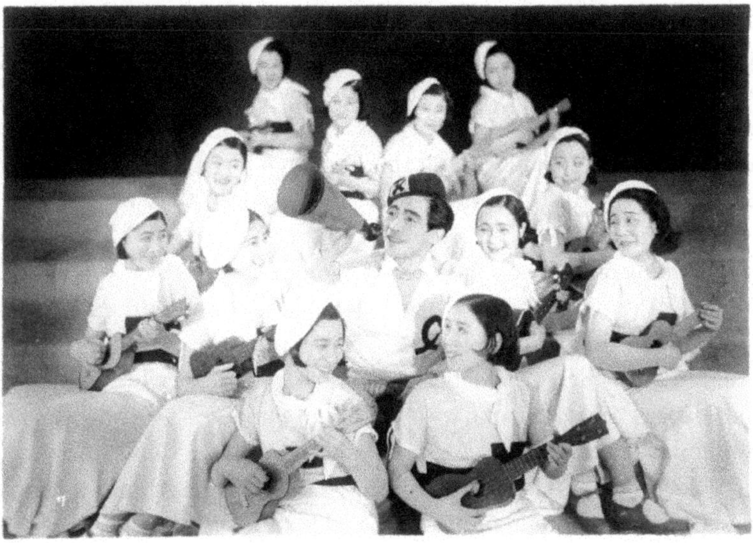

Figure 6.3 Promotional still from *Enoken's Youthful Water Margin*.

such as the *benshi* Ikoma Raiyū performing an '*eiga* monogatari', or 'film story', for the radio, and Yoshimoto Kōgyō talents, such as Ishida Ichimatsu, giving 'live' performances within the film's narrative. Through the course of the drama, P.C.L. playfully utilizes the soundscape of modern entertainment, and in the process once again incorporates recorded pseudo-events into its cinematic experience.

From Limited Stage to Unlimited Cinema – Enoken Goes to the Movies

Enoken no seishun suikoden/*Enoken's Youthful Water Margin* (Yamamoto Kajirō, 1934), P.C.L.'s 6th film, starred Asakusa revue megastar Enomoto Ken'ichi in the lead. The script was by written by the P.C.L. Geibun together with Enoken Gekidan's scriptwriting division, and the film became the directorial debut at P.C.L. for Yamamoto Kajirō, who was headhunted from Nikkatsu especially for the film.

Although Enoken previous to his success in revue had attempted a career in the movies, acting in several silent films produced by Teikoku Kinema, it was after seeing *A Tipsy Life*, which featured fellow Asakusa revue stage star Furukawa Roppa, that he decided to try once again. Contractually tied to Shōchiku, Enoken first approached their film production division with the idea of a revue style musical comedy but was turned down. Instead it was P.C.L. that signed with Enoken, stating in February 1934 that they would be going into production the following month with the goal of releasing their first Enoken film in April. The contract was for Enoken and his troupe, the Piēru Buriyanto Ichiza (later the 'Enoken Ichiza') to create two films a year. During the film's production, Mori Iwao stated that 'We will create a musical comedy like those of the Marx brothers' and that the film would feature many of Enoken's previous hit comedy scenes. Enoken himself is quoted as saying 'As it is my first talkie, I'll make sure to make a really entertaining, cheerful and fantastic film. With regards to talkies, I have absolute confidence, and there are several in my troupe who have previous talkie experience, so starting with myself, all of us are eager to do it'.[22] These, and similar statements, serve to highlight the optimistic and cosmopolitan attitudes prevalent at the studio, showing a rich international context against which the production studio and staff refer back to, and of course assuming the target audience awareness of the same.

At P.C.L., Mori Iwao at first lacked a suitable director for the film and confided to Enoken that 'right now there are only two directors at P.C.L. and both are saying that they don't have confidence in doing a musical film'.[23] However, two weeks later it was announced that a script for the film had been penned, and Yamamoto had been chosen as director, a move that Yamamoto attributed to Enoken, stating that 'It is fine to say that I joined Tōhō due to Enomoto Ken'ichi.'[24] Furthermore, Izaki Hiroyuki claims that 'when Enomoto-san wanted to do his first film part he had two conditions: 1) that the film be a musical, and 2) that it's director would be Yamamoto'.[25] The result was a long lasting creative collaboration between the star and director, lovingly dubbed 'Yamakaji', that came to stretch well into the post-war period.

In Japan, as in Hollywood, stars were of vital economic importance for the film industry. For many of P.C.L.'s major stars, like for instance Enoken, Furukawa Roppa, and Takehisa Chieko, there already existed a strong revue-based star image. Enoken was at this time the foremost entertainer of the Asakusa/Yūrakuchō revue world, and as such, for P.C.L. to sign Enoken meant the acquisition of an already established capital entity

22 'Eiga shinshutsu: Daikatsuyaku no P.C.L mōshin!!: Enoken ichiza to teikeiseiritsu: sangatsu no chōtokusaku kyōbakuteki daikigeki satsuei', p. 1.

23 Izaki, *Enoken to yobareta otoko*, p. 112-113.

24 Ibid, p. 113.

25 Ibid.

of great importance. Mori Iwao is quoted as having stated that 'Enoken was intrinsic to the success of the studio', a position reflected in the size of the budgets that P.C.L. invested in Enoken films, which were all at the higher end among their productions.[26]

As has been argued elsewhere, the fact that Enoken managed to make a contract together with P.C.L. not just for himself but for the whole of the theatre troupe is illustrative of the power of Enoken's star image.[27] It was also a testament to the unconventionality of P.C.L., as Shōchiku's film division had famously turned down Enoken's previous request for a similar contract. That the whole theatre troupe was contracted and appeared in the film together with Enoken was of course important for Enoken himself, who as the head of the troupe can be said to have filled not only the role of actor but also to a certain extent that of producer; but it was also important for the theatre troupe, since it is doubtful that they would have continued to be employed at Asakusa, at least in the troupe's current form, without Enoken, when he left for the movies.

Mori Iwao likened Enoken entering the world of film to that of Eddie Cantor and Maurice Chevalier leaving the stage for the cinema.[28] That Enoken was already a star was reflected in the marketing and advertisement for *Enoken's Youthful Water Margin*, the way that the studio emphasized the novelty of his presence in the medium of film, boldly announcing 'Japan's number one comedy actor and Japan's number one musical comedy', and stating that 'the Popular trio Enoken, Futamura Eiichi, and Kisaragi Kanta have jumped from the constrained stage to the unlimited silver screen, [creating] a horizontally and vertically inexhaustible rampage!'.[29] Another advertisement even feature two spurious quotes by the famous American

26 Ibid., p. 136. The budget for *Enoken's Youthful Water Margin* came in at 28,509 yen (eight reels, 6500 feet, 3 copies). In the budget the biggest outlay is for actors at 4,854 yen, of which 3,000 yen one to the Enoken P.B. Ichiza, which comparatively dwarfs the cost of the regular P.C.L. contracted actors, at a total of 856 yen, also a final 1,000 yen is budgeted for extras. This division of cost for the cast and staff is similarly reflected in the later Enoken films such as *Enoken no majutsushi/Enoken's Mysterious Magic* (Kimura Sotoji, 1934) in which once again the Enoken P.B. Ichiza received 6,000 yen out of a total cast budget of 7,300 yen, likewise in *Enoken juhachiban donguri tonbei/Enoken's Tonbei of the Acorns* (Yamamoto Kajirō, 1936) the P.B. Ichiza received 12,000 yen out of a total of 15,040 yen, and in *Enoken no Kondō Isami/Enoken's Kondō Isami* (Yamamoto Kajirō, 1935) P.B. Enoken ichiza is listed as receiving 12,000 yen out of a total of 14,180 yen. Furthermore, these figures do not include the fees that Enoken's script writing division also collected for some of these films that they collaborated on. For a detailed look at the budgets of P.C.L.'s films, see Nordström, '*Tōkī wa P.C.L*'.

27 Ibid.

28 Mori, 'Enoken eiga ni tsuite', p. 2.

29 'Enoken shueneiga *Seishunsuikoden*', p. 8.

comedians Groucho Marx (quoted as saying: 'This is like we have been surpassed by Enoken!'), and Eddie Cantor (quoted as saying: 'Anyone who doesn't laugh until their stomach hurts isn't human').[30]

The film lets us follow Enoken as he tries to graduate from university, gets married, works as a salaryman, and finally, in the climactic end bar room fighting sequence, saves a friend in need. The inclusion of modern urban localities such as the Hibiya Kōkaidō and the newly constructed Takarazuka Hall, including shots of actual performances, firmly locates the film within the sound-spectacle of modern Tokyo.

The film's script was co-written by the writing team at P.C.L. and Enoken's own writing team at the P.B. Ichiza, and the ensuing result is a kind of composite film where both foreign and domestic, stage-based and film-based, influences are merged into a self-conscious transnational multimedia work, balancing the aesthetics of the sound film with those of the stage revue. For instance, the university setting of the opening sequence of *Enoken's Youthful Water Margin*, as well as the trouble that comes from Enoken being found in the girls' dormitory, are heavily inspired by the beginning of Eddie Cantor's *The Kid from Spain* (Leo McCarey, 1932), in which he is found out hiding in the girls dormitory by the stern head matroness. Iwamoto Kenji comments that 'An "Enoken film" is a musical film that has the flavour of the Western romantic musical about the love between a beautiful boy and girl, together with that of a revue film where young healthy women reveal their shapely legs, with that of traditional song-based operetta films'.[31]

The borrowing of material from foreign sources is at its strongest in the custom of appropriating and adapting foreign songs and melodies. This kind of adaptation of Occidental music was common both in the context of film and revue, but also with the record companies in attempts to capitalize on famous foreign songs and artists. In the specific case of *Enoken's Youthful Water Margin*, all of the songs performed in the film are either old or new versions of foreign tunes, were the lyrics have been shifted and adapted.[32] For instance Enoken's song 'Boku wa yūutsu da'/'I'm bored', it is a version of 'My Baby Just Cares for Me' written by Gus Kahn, as sung by Eddie Cantor in *Whoopee* (Thornton Freeland, 1930). Many of these songs were instantly recognizable, carrying with them the cultural significance of the West, adapted and revised for the Japanese home market's sensibility. The songs and the song sequences are thematically connected to the plot, although

30 '*Enoken no seishun suikoden* [two-page advertisement]'.

31 Iwamoto, *nihon eiga to nashonarizumu*, p. 245.

32 Satō, *Utaeba tengoku*, p. 34-35.

their connection to the narrative impetus of the film are at best minimal. Instead they often create spectacle through appropriation of revue-like *mise-en-scène*, of which the acting and staging especially stands out. One key example is the opening sequence of the film where the girl students at the university that Enoken is attending break into synchronized dancing, flashing their legs, as well as contributing supporting vocals to the film's opening song.

Richard Dyer argues that 'The economic importance of the stars is of aesthetic consequence in such things as the centring of spectacle on the presentation of the star, and the construction of narratives which display the star's image'. The song numbers and the use of song in this film can be said to illustrate the importance of Enoken's star image, as the music and spectacle of the film are centred around him. This can be seen throughout the films narrative in various scenes, such as for instance when the girl students in the film's opening scene demonstrate the status of Enoken by breaking into supporting vocals and visual spectacle/dance.

Enoken's Youthful Water Margin also displays a for the time in Japan unusual degree of self-reflexivity within the film which, taken together with the films tongue-in-cheek emphasis on his stage persona, serves further to emphasize Enoken's star status. Dyer, commenting on the acting style of stars with a background in vaudeville and music hall, writes that:

> Their stylization, their use of non-realist, even distanciating, devices aimed at 'pointing' a gag or a number tend to render them problematic in relation to novelistic character. Even in comedies and musicals they are virtually used only to be actually funny or for numbers. Thus, there are shifts of performance gear between comic and/or musical sections of a film and the rest of it.[33]

In the case of Enoken, he repeatedly pauses the diegetic flow of the film to interact with the audience. For example, the first shot of the *Enoken's Youthful Water Margin* is a nonsensical greeting by Enoken dressed up in evening attire, after which the title of the film appears. At the end of the film Enoken, once again in evening attire, bids the audience goodbye on stage in front of the curtain, as if in a stage production. Most importantly though, at a key moment in the film when Enoken is having an argument with his wife, he turns, tongue in cheek, to the camera to directly address the spectators, asking for guidance from a 'fictional' audience whose voices

33 Dyer, *Stars*, p. 137.

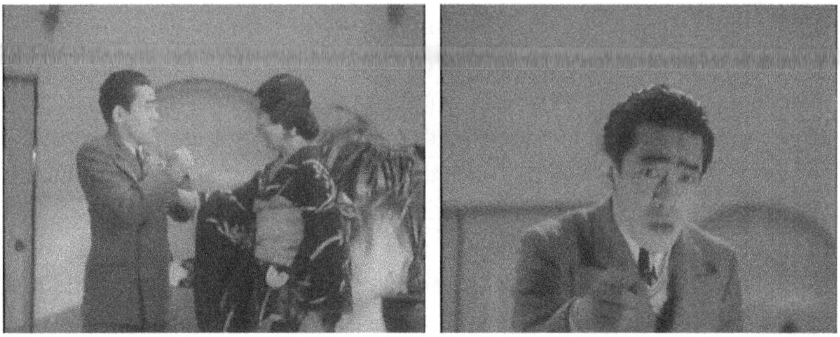

Figure 6.4 Enoken fighting with his wife turns to the audience for advice.

shout back various pieces of advice and encouragement, effectively breaking the fourth wall and wreaking havoc on the film's self-contained narrative integrity.

These diegetically disruptive scenes work to emphasize Enoken's stage personality over the film's diegetic narrative. Furthermore, as the star, it is only Enoken who is allowed to step out of the narrative in this way, setting him aside from the other actors who thus remain in the diegetic flow, captive of the narrative. As is often the case with star comedies, it is as if the stage personality of Enoken and the narrative of the film finds themselves in an aesthetic competition. Furthermore, in the film's climatic end fighting sequence, which takes place in a beer hall, the film turns again to the aesthetics of vaudeville and the revue stage, as Enoken with ferocious intensity battles innumerable opponents, a performance that displays his physical agility and was highly praised by the trade press at the time of its release.[34]

Many of the traits of early sound comedy, such as a de-emphasis on psychological motivation, display of visual spectacle, including physical performance, and non-realist devices are to be found in *Enoken's Youthful Water Margin*, and although to a certain extent present in later Enoken films as well, they are especially strong in this, his first feature film. Henry Jenkins argues these vaudeville characteristics of self-contained performances threaten the centrality of narrative, while performer virtuosity potentially undermines character consistency.[35] This vaudeville-like aesthetic taken together with anarchic gags, and songs that often work more along the guidelines of revue aesthetics than those of film, makes *Enoken's Youthful*

34 Izaki, 'Enoken to yobareta otoko', p. 114-117.
35 Jenkins, 'What Made Pistachio Nuts?', p. 98.

Water Margin a unique offering in the contemporary Japanese landscape of musical films.

This strength comes from the fact that at the moment of his first film, Enoken's was foremost a stage persona, which had to be emphasized in order to transfer his celebrity from stage to screen. In later Enoken films, this was not necessary to the same extent due to his then already successfully established screen personality, which resulted in the narrative structure of his later films often asserting itself over his revue style of acting, effectively reining in many of his more anarchic idiosyncrasies.

Conclusion

P.C.L. appeared at a juncture in time where the film industry was in a state of rapid change, while at the same time the intermediality of Japan's audio-visual culture brought with it new connections and synergies between music publishers, record companies, radio networks, and film companies. In P.C.L. we are able to see how the priorities of musicality and song of the pre-war sound cinema were tried and tested, and finally came to fruition, and the importance of songs and musicality for both the artistic expression as well as the marketing of early sound cinema in Japan. These early examples of Japanese musical films illuminate the aesthetic modes through which Japanese cinema incorporated and utilized the new sound film technology, as it sought to maximize the commercial appeal of the new films. Furthermore, P.C.L.'s tactic of aligning itself with the urban modernity, by being connected to places of consumer spectacle, and catering to a burgeoning 'salaryman' audience, proved to be a successful strategy. With light upbeat films centring around the new salaried middle class, which incorporated elements of urban modernism and musicality, P.C.L. carved a niche for itself in the Japanese cinematic arena, from which it would later be able to expand and grow. By importing stage personalities from the world of the Asakusa opera and revue P.C.L. succeeded in acquiring star personalities, as well bringing something new, and until then unexploited, to the Japanese cinema. First with Furukawa Roppa, and then with Takehisa Chieko and Enoken, the studio brought this strategy to its zenith, and managed to bring forth a new type of musically infused cinema that had previously not been seen in Japan.

Bibliography

Akiyama Kunihara. *Nihon no eiga ongakushi (1)* (Tokyo: Tabata Shoten, 1974).

Richard Dyer. *Stars* (London: British Film Institute; 2nd edition, 1998).

'Eiga shinshutsu: Daikatsuyaku no P.C.L mōshin!!: Enoken ichiza to teikeiseiritsu: sangatsu no chōtokusaku kyōbakuteki daikigeki satsuei', *P.C.L. eiga* 3 (15 February 1934), p. 1.

'*Enoken no seishun suikoden* [two-page advertisement]', *Kinema junpō* 501 (1 April 1934), between pp. 156-157.

'Enoken shueneiga *Seishunsuikoden*', *P.C.L. eiga* 6 (15 April 1934), p. 8.

Iwamoto Kenji. *Nihon eiga to nashonarizumu: 1931-1945* (Tokyo: Shinwasha, 1991).

K.O.T. 'Kenkyushitsu haikingu (1) P.C.L. hōmon'. *Kagaku pen* 1 (October 1936).

Mori Iwao. 'Enoken eiga ni tsuite'. *P.C.L. eiga* 6 (15 April 1934), p. 2.

Mori Iwao. *Watakushi no geikai henreki* (Tokyo: Seiabō, 1975).

Izaki Hiroyuki. *Enoken to yobareta otoko* (Tokyo: Kōdansha, 1985).

Henry Jenkins. *What Made Pistachio Nuts?: Early Sound Comedy and the Vaudeville Aesthetic* (New York: Columbia University Press, 1992).

'Nihon saidai no tōkī satsueijo Shashin Kagaku Kenkyujo (PCL): Sono soshiki to jinyō'. *Kinema shūhō* 138 (16 December 1932), pp. 14-15.

Johan Nordström. 'Mori Iwao to shoki saundo eiga'. *Engeki eizōgaku: Engeki Hakubutsukan Gurōbaru COE kiyō 2011* 1 (2011), pp. 97-112.

Karl Johan Nordström. *'Tōkī wa P.C.L' eiga satsueijo P.C.L o shikō suru* (PhD Dissertation, Waseda University, 2014).

Charles O'Brien. *Cinema's Conversion to Sound* (Bloomington, Indiana University Press, 2005).

'*Odoriko nikki* no rebyū-bamen: fukidasu gekichūgeki no kazukazu: enshutsusha no kaobure ha tenka ni zuiichi'. *P.C.L. eiga* 2 (15 February 1934), p. 2.

Ōmura Einosuke. 'Ōmura Einosuke shikikisho (2)'. *Kiroku eiga* 279 (February 1986), pp. 7-9.

'P·C·L gekijo', *P.C.L. eiga* 2 (15 February 1934), p. 5.

'Bakuon to denpa no kanaderu: fūshi to kaigyaku no daisaku: "*Rajio no jō*" no miryoku'. *P.C.L. eiga* 32 (15 June 1935), p. 2.

Satō Toshiaki. *Utaeba tengoku: Nippon kayō eiga derakkusu ten no maki* (Tokyo: Media Factory, 1999).

Satō Toshiaki. 'Eiga no naka no Enoken - Yamamoto Kajirō to no koraborēshon'. In *Enoken to Tokyo kigeki no ōgon jidai* (Tokyo: Ronsōsha, 2003).

Steve Wurtzler. '"She Sang Live but the Microphone was Turned Off": The Live, the Recorded, and the Subject of Representation'. In *Sound Theory, Sound Practice*, edited by Rick Altman (New York: Routledge, 1992).

Yagi Nobutada. 'Kimura Sotoji'. In *Kojinbetsu ryōiki betsu danwa shūroku ni yoru eigashi taikei. sono 2* (Tokyo: Nihon Daigaku Geijutsugakubu Eiga Gakka, 1986), pp. 93-128.
Yamamoto Kajirō. *Katsudōya jitaden* (Tokyo: Shōbunsha Shuppanbu).
Yomota Inuhiko. *Nihoneigashi 100 nen* (Tokyo: Shūeisha, 2000).

About the Author

Johan Nordström is Lecturer at the Department of Global Education, Tsuru University. He has written on various aspects of the Japanese cinema's transition to sound, and is currently working on a book on Tokyo based early sound film studio P.C.L., later Tōhō.

7 The Dawn of the Talkies in Japan

Mizoguchi Kenji's *Hometown*

Nagato Yohei
Translated by Michael Raine

Abstract

This chapter questions the historical judgment that *Madamu to nyōbō/The Neighbour's Wife and Mine*, made with the Tsuchihashi Shōchikuphone system and released in 1931, was the first commercially and aesthetically successful sound film in Japan. It shows that *Furusato/Hometown*, a part-talkie starring Fujiwara Yoshie made with the Mina Talkie system and directed by Mizoguchi Kenji for the Nikkatsu studio, played for weeks in major cinemas in 1930 and was widely praised by film critics. The subtle sound design of the film utilizes a concept of 'counterpoint' and a technique of 'cutaway within the shot' that anticipates Mizoguchi's intense 'one scene, one shot' long take style in his later films, in which the moving camera articulates an undivided *mise-en-scène*.

Keywords: transition to sound, sound aesthetics, counterpoint, image/sound cutaway, cutaway within the shot, film style

Introduction

The oldest surviving talkie feature film in Japan is Mizoguchi Kenji's *Furusato/Hometown* (1930).[1] This part-talkie (partly shot as a talkie with synchronized dialog and partly as a 'sound version' with only music and

1 When it was first released the film was titled *Hometown*, but on its rerelease it was retitled as *Fujiwara Yoshie no Furusato/Fujiwara Yoshie's Hometown*. This text will refer to the film throughout as *Hometown*. For information on Japanese talkies before *Hometown*, see Okabe, *Nihon eigashi*, Tanaka, *Nihon eiga hattatsushi I* and *II*, Sasō, 'Shoki tōkī ni tsuite', *Mizoguchi Kenji zensakuhinkaisetsu 7 – Furusato*, and Sasagawa Keiko's chapter in this volume.

Raine, M. and J. Nordström (eds.), *The Culture of the Sound Image in Prewar Japan*.
Taylor & Francis Group 2020
DOI: 10.5117/9789089647733_CH07

Figure 7.1 Poster for the film *Furusato/Hometown* (Mizoguchi Kenji, 1930). Image courtesy of the National Film Archive of Japan.

sound effects) film has almost never been subjected to serious close analysis, overshadowed as it is by the film usually acclaimed at 'the first true Japanese talkie', *Madamu to nyōbō/The Neighbour's Wife and Mine* (1931). By 1930 the lost aesthetic values of the silent film – complex camera positions and movement – was already widely discussed. *Hometown* was made as a part-talkie because the producers wanted to preserve the established qualities of the silent film. In fact, at the time of its release those parts of the film were widely praised. It was also a very successful film, playing to packed houses for three weeks instead of the usual one week at first-run houses such as the Asakusa Fujikan and the Kanda Nikkatsukan.[2] *Hometown* was also the first film to be called 'the first true Japanese talkie'.[3] However, the quality of the film's sound reproduction was roundly criticized. Dialog was described as incomprehensible and the musical accompaniment unfavourably compared to the 'squealing of pigs'.[4] In that sense, *Hometown's* eclipse by *The Neighbour's Wife and Mine* has more to do with the relative improvement in sound playback in Japanese cinemas between 1930 and 1931 than with the quality of the film's sound design itself. This chapter subjects the 'imperfect talkie' *Hometown* to a detailed examination, using concepts such as 'sound counterpoint' and 'image/sound cutaway' to re-evaluate its place in Japanese film history and make clear its significance for Mizoguchi's later film style.[5]

The dissolve between diegetic and non-diegetic worlds

Hometown's story and script were written by Mori Iwao, Hatamoto Shūichi, Kobayashi Tadashi, and Kisaragi Bin. Cinematographers were Yokota Tatsuyuki and Mineo Yoshio. Sound effects were by Nariu Toshio and Urashima Yoshikatsu. Tanaka Toyoaki conducted the musical accompaniment for the sound part and the music for the rest of the film was chosen in the main by Mori Iwao.[6] The narrative has to do with Fujimura Yoshio (Fujiwara Yoshie), an aspiring opera singer who wavers between his devoted wife Ayako (Natsukawa Shizue) and his scheming and beautiful patron Natsue (Hamaguchi Fujiko). As Fujimura's star rises, he spends more and more time enjoying the high life with Natsue. To reprove Fujimura for his dissipated lifestyle – or perhaps to win back his affections, which have strayed toward Natsue – Ayako gains the help of Sankichi (Tamura Kunio) in faking an affair at the Imperial Hotel. The somewhat foolish Fujimura completely falls for this ruse and when he returns home verbally attacks Ayako: 'I never thought you were the type to fly over there like a butterfly while I was out!'

2 Sasō, *Furusato*, p. 209.

3 Tanaka, 'Furusato sansoku', p. 17.

4 Sasō, *Furusato*, p. 212, 216.

5 Satō, *Mizoguchi Kenji no sekai*, p. 320.

6 Mori, 'Sakisofon to hana', p. 19; Mori et. al., '*Furusato* zadankai', p. 49-50.

With those parting words, Fujimura goes to a party at a mountain lodge with Natsue. Left all alone, the sobbing Ayako writes a letter of separation. Later, Natsue prevents Ayako from seeing Fujimura at the hospital after he is hit by a car, but then abandons the young singer when she learns that his continued career is in doubt. Although Fujimura survives, he ends up living in a tenement, racked with guilt for what he has done to Ayako. By coincidence, Ayako also lives nearby – they are reconciled when Sankichi brings them together. At the end of the film, Fujimura joins hands with Ayako and sings at a mass gathering, hinting at a kind of hybrid of the contemporary genres of *shinpa* melodrama and the class-conscious tendency film (*keikō eiga*).

What of the film text of *Hometown*? As the credit 'A Mina Talkie film' appears, the introductory music begins to play. After this short credit sequence, the first image of the film is of the deck of a ship. This is followed by a shot from behind of the famous tenor Fujiwara Yoshie (playing a character named Fujimura Yoshio) standing on the deck of the ship. The sound of the piano prelude to the theme song 'Hometown' plays over this shot, and then we hear the beginning of Fujiwara Yoshie's solo performance. 'Hometown' continues to play over the following shots of sea, sky, trees, a fishing village, the shore, a river, a rural home, a waterwheel, and a storehouse – that is, a rural or hometown (*furusato*) landscape shown in a rapid montage. Katō Mikirō is surely correct that we can see here the outline of the *kouta eiga* (ballad film) genre.[7] Before this theme song ends we return to Fujimura, now in a close-up profile shot. As the song ends we cut to a shot of the funnel, accompanied by the strikingly loud sound of the ship's horn. After the sound of the horn ends, the film transitions to a sequence in which five women mistakenly think the singer we have heard is Satō Misao (Murata Kōju). They surround Satō, exclaiming 'that was wonderful!' and so on.

I will begin by analysing the opening of the film, from the shot of the ship's deck to the shot of the funnel (a little over two minutes). The following three points are particularly important:

- The film attempts to construct sound perspective.
- In the sound part, non-diegetic sound is treated as diegetic but off-screen sound.
- That 'diegetic sound' acts as a sound bridge spread across multiple shots.[8]

7 Katō, 'Eigakan to kankyaku no bunkashi', p. 239. For more on the ballad film see Hosokawa, 'Kouta eiga no bunkashi', Sasagawa, 'Kouta eiga ni kansuru kiso chōsa', and Lewis, 'Media Fantasies'.

8 By 'sound bridge', I mean not the narrow sense of the presence on the soundtrack of diegetic sound from a subsequent shot, or the continuation of diegetic sound from one shot into the

Sound perspective becomes salient as soon as the theme song 'Hometown' ends, with the shot of the funnel. The sequence is constructed of three shots accompanied by the sound of the ship's siren: 1) a close-up of the funnel emitting smoke; 2) a long shot of the ship's deck; 3) another close-up of the funnel. The shots take up only a few seconds of screen time but what is important is the reduction in the sound of the siren over the second shot. We may now feel that to change the volume in accordance with the distance from the subject of the shot is not needed but 'the industry's desire for a match between image scale and sound scale' that Rick Altman indicates was a compulsory consideration in the early days of the Hollywood talkie was a serious concern in Japan too.[9] From a technical standpoint, it is unclear whether this scene should be included in the 'sound part' or the 'talkie part' of the film. From my viewing of the film at the National Film Archive in Tokyo, it seemed that the 'sound signature', in which the sound gives a sense of space that matches the space visible on the screen, only began with the following scene of synchronously recorded dialog. It is likely that this siren noise was post-recorded, in which case the volume of the sound was deliberately changed in post-production. From the point of view of film aesthetics, this siren noise is clearly 'diegetic noise'. In other words, we should see this rather unnecessary sequence of three shots that appears immediately after the theme song as strongly impressing on the audience a sense of sound perspective at the moment that the film narrative starts. Mizoguchi wanted to show his audience from the beginning a sound design characteristic of the talkie.

Returning to the theme song, 'Hometown', in the opening scene we do not get a head-on shot of Fujimura so we do not see his mouth. We simply cannot tell if this 'Hometown' is purely non-diegetic music, outside the world of the film, or if Fujimura is really singing in the diegetic world. Only in the following sequence, when the female fellow passengers ask Satō if that was him singing on the deck, does it become clear that the 'Hometown' that we just heard was a song that could be heard in the world of the film, and that the women had mistaken this beautiful voice for Satō's. At the same time, there is no possibility that the musical accompaniment could be part of the world of the film. The scene is an example of what Rick Altman calls the 'audio dissolve' characteristic of the unrealistic sound design of the film

subsequent shot, but the broader sense of diegetic sound that bridges the time and space of multiple successive shots.

9 Altman, 'Sound Space', p. 47.

musical, in which a character begins singing in tune with a non-diegetic musical accompaniment.[10]

This sound design was not particularly original. By 1930 Hollywood musicals containing audio dissolves such as *The Singing Fool* (1928) and *Broadway Melody* (1929) had already been imported to Japan, and probably seen by the producers of *Hometown*, so we can surmise that this design would not have been regarded as unusual at the time.[11] The problem here is rather that it is unclear whether not the music but *Fujimura's singing voice* is diegetic or non-diegetic. Fujiwara Yoshie was so famous in Japan for his beautiful voice and handsome physique that he was known as 'our tenor' – the audience would have immediately connected the singing voice with this image of Fujimura's back.[12] However, they would not have been able to tell if this was non-diegetic accompaniment or if it was actually being sung on the deck of the ship. In that sense, the song 'Hometown' was incorporated into the film in the manner of a sound version film (through post-recording), probably to avoid revealing errors in lip-sync by not showing Fujimura's lips (not showing his face from the front).[13]

There are many other scenes in the sound part of the film based around the matching of the image with post-recorded sound. For example, the short scene that follows the sequence on the boat that lays 'street noise' over images of modern Tokyo, or the shot of the 'Satō Misao Grand Recital' poster overlaid with the sound of jazz. The latter in particular could be read as non-diegetic accompaniment but it could also be understood in context as music coming from offscreen. Also, in the scene in which Fujimura and Natsue meet at a record store, the several record players in the shop window, each playing 'Blue Sky' or some other piece of music all at the same time is after all something like a sound collage that could be understood as either diegetic or non-diegetic.

Returning to the sound bridge-like design of the opening scene of *Hometown*, there are other parts of the film that demonstrate the 'omnipotent

10 Altman, *The American Film Musical*, p. 62.

11 *The Jazz Singer* was not shown in Japan until 21 August 1930 so the makers of *Hometown* would probably not have seen it. *The Singing Fool*, though made later, was shown in Japan in April 1930. It might seem strange that it could have influenced the makers of *Hometown*, which opened on 14 March, but Kinoshita (p. 175) argues that they could have seen it at a special preview screening for members of the film world. *Broadway Melody* opened in January 1930. Most of the musical accompaniment is diegetic but the film contains two examples of the audio dissolve.

12 We can also see the tendency, for example with Al Jolson in *The Jazz Singer* and *The Singing Fool*, of turning popular singing stars into the protagonists of early Hollywood talkies.

13 Mineo Yoshio said the music in this scene was added later (i.e. post-recorded) in Mori et. al., '*Furusato* zadankai', p. 47.

power to permeate different spaces' of Fujimura's voice.[14] For example, his voice bridges two classes (proletarian and bourgeois) in the juxtaposed shots of Ayako listening to his vocal practice from beside him while Natsue looks on from another room in the Shōwa hotel. This is also true of the montage of people all over Tokyo hearing Fujimura's rendition of 'The Boatman's Song' over the radio.[15] However, it is neither the hotel nor the radio broadcast that presents us with a truly radical example of sound bridge-like sound but the sequence of the dance party at the mountain lodge.

Counterpoint: The Second Movement of Dvořák's Symphony No. 9: From the New World

The dance party scene is juxtaposed with Ayako writing her letter of separation through the technique of cross-cutting. The music in this sequence is the Second Movement of Dvořák's 'Symphony No. 9: From the New World', in an up-tempo 'jazz' arrangement. Around 1930, jazz was the 'petty bourgeois music of the machine age, the age of speed'.[16] This music is the non-diegetic accompaniment to the petty bourgeois party at the mountain lodge. However, it clearly functions in the film as diegetic but offscreen sound. The music matches the lively party and the violent camera movements, as if the cameraman himself is dancing. In addition, although this is the sound part of the film, there are no intertitles representing important dialog in the scene, which weakens the sense that the music is non-diegetic. It is as if everyone here is dancing *in time with* this jazz arrangement of the 'New World' symphony.

The following shot is of Ayako writing the letter of separation, followed by a close-up of the writing itself. After that comes a shot of Fujimura and Ayako enjoying a game of cards, people dancing, a close-up of Ayako with tears in her eyes, the writing in the letter, Ayako's face, the tear-stained letter, a happy Fujimura and Natsue dancing, and finally a fade out. The party music continues over all these shots.

What effect, then, does the jazz version of 'New World' have on the image and the narrative? Most importantly, the cheerful party music that 'crosses over different spaces' forms a sharp contrast with Ayako's emotions, making her sadness stand out all the more. There is nothing particularly unusual

14 See Kinoshita, *Mise-en-scène of Desire*, p. 180 for a similar discussion.

15 See Kinoshita, *Mise-en-scène of Desire*, pp. 177-180; Sasō, *Furusato*, p. 233.

16 Hosokawa, 'Seiyō ongaku no Nihonka/taishūka 33' p. 150.

about this technique today, but how about in 1930? In the history of Japanese film music, this technique has been called counterpoint (*taihō*). The first work that intentionally used this technique is usually held to be Kurosawa Akira's collaboration with composer Hayasaka Fumio in *Yoidore tenshi/ Drunken Angel* (1948).

Theories of counterpoint between image and sound have often been confused so that the concept becomes difficult to understand but in general there are two ways that it can be understood:

1. The contrast between image and music
2. The method of making a functional connection between the image and either offscreen or non-diegetic sound.

Counterpoint is usually used as the first meaning but Chōki Seiji points out that this sense of counterpoint as 'contrast' is a mistake from the perspective of music theory, one that has persisted in particular in film discourse.[17] In Europe and America, especially in Europe, 'counterpoint' (= contrast) was a basic stage technique, but since Japan had no opera culture, nor a tradition of such stage techniques, such a connection between music and film, which spread in Japan before opera, was perceived as strikingly original.[18] If Chōki is correct then in a Japan that lacked an opera tradition, and even more during the early talkie period in the 1930s, can we not say that *Hometown's* experiments with the contrast between sound and image were fresh? At least on that score, the sound design of this film was by no means 'undistinguished'.[19] Nevertheless, there are also grounds to doubt whether contemporary audiences would have perceived this concept of contrast as an overwhelmingly novel technique, simply because Japan lacked an opera tradition. For example, the film *Kanaya Koume* (1930), which preceded *Hometown*, was discussed in the following way:

> In the early scene in which Chōji attempts suicide with a razor and Hamamoto stops him, the strongly melodramatic tension is undercut by the contrasting effect of lively music coming from offscreen. This technique is often used on the stage but it could not be done until now in the silent film. In the past they would have used a cutaway (*katto bakku*), but these days many foreign films juxtapose the mood of what we see with the mood of a completely contrasting sound. New terms such as

17 Chōki, *Sengo no ongaku*, p. 355.
18 Ibid. p. 357.
19 Shindō, *Aru eiga kantoku*, p. 114.

> 'sound counterpoint' (*oto no taiihō*) have been created to describe these things that I think can only be created in the talkie.[20]

It was also said of the scene: 'the opposite effect of sound and image in the scene in which Chōji attempts suicide with a razor, a kind of simultaneous cutaway, is of the type called by Walter Ruttmann "sound counterpoint"'.[21] Although it is not clear exactly what 'on the stage' referred to, it seems that this 'opposite effect' in *Kanaya Koume* would perhaps not have been seen as a wholly new technique at the time. In any case, we would do well to remember that this technique was already present in the oldest surviving talkie in Japan, *Hometown*. That would lead us to question the received wisdom of standard film histories that the concept of the 'counterpoint of image and sound' originates with the Hayasaka-Kurosawa collaboration.

The discussion to this point has concerned the first definition of counterpoint listed above, the contrast between music and image. The next section will consider the second definition, the 'image/sound cutaway' (*gamen to oto no katto bakku*) proposed by Walter Ruttmann.

The image/sound cutaway

Consider the following review of *Hometown*:

> Takeda: This is a fine point, but in the second half of the film Mr. Fujiwara decides to sing and comes back. In a jet-black image there is an iron kettle – it is placed on the bottom left edge of the frame, the image is almost completely black. That was a bold composition that I think had a strong psychological effect.
> Mineo: I thought perhaps they were trying to overlay a weak image of Mr. Fujiwara's shadow...
> Takeda: It would be better not to. They already superimposed a grey shadow in the hospital scene. Besides, we can hear sound in the scene, so the image and sound produce the effect of a simultaneous cutaway.[22]

20 'Gijutsuka ni yoru Nihon saisho no tōkī hihyō' *Eiga kagaku kenkyū* 5 (1930), p. 258 (quoted in Sasō, *Furusato*, p. 256).

21 Horino et. al., 'Gijutsuka ni yoru', p. 73.

22 Mori et. al., '*Furusato* zadankai', p. 47.

If we read this alongside the *Kanaya Koume* review quoted earlier, we can see that this concept of a 'simultaneous cutaway' presents the grounds for a great deal of confusion. The concept of 'sound counterpoint' in *Kanaya Koume* incorporates the Hayasaka Fumio-style meaning of counterpoint as contrast, but the same-named concept in *Hometown* contains no sense of contrast. How should we best understand this phrase?

In later years, Iwasaki Akira explained counterpoint in the follow way:

> In the talkie, instead of seeing an object on the screen and simultaneously hearing the sound of the object, one sometimes sees an object on the screen and simultaneously hears the sound of another object. The talkie style that uses this method has come to be called counterpoint.
> The German avant-garde filmmaker Walter Ruttmann, who I introduced earlier, also had an avant-garde approach to the talkie [...] and came to the same way of thinking. He wrote that in film, instead of seeing a shell explode and hearing the sound of the explosion one could hear the roar of the blast and at the same time see the face of a new recruit, ashen with fear – that is a sound film.[23]

This explanation is extremely easy to follow. The method has become so common that it is difficult for us now to regard it as special. In a word, it is what we mean by 'offscreen sound'.[24] When we consider the term counterpoint we should not confuse 'opposite effect of sound and image' (= contrast) and 'simultaneous cutaway' or 'image/sound cutaway' (= the effect of a cutaway created by the relation of image and sound).

Considering Iwasaki's explanation above, we can formulate the concept of a 'image/sound cutaway' in the following way: as the method of using offscreen sound to *represent in one shot what in a silent film would have been a scene consisting of multiple shots, including cutaways*. Keeping that point in mind, let us now investigate *Hometown's* sound design.[25]

23 Iwasaki, *Eiga no riron*, pp. 156-157.

24 Sasō also discusses this question at Sasō, *Furusato*, p. 255-260.

25 We might ask whether Mizoguchi had this second sense of 'counterpoint' in mind when he directed *Hometown*. Already by 1928 Soviet talkie theory had been widely discussed in Japan. See for example, Iijima, 'Kaigai eiga shōsoku', Takahara, *Tōkī gikō gairon*, p.223, and Kinugasa, *Waga eiga no seishun*, p.102-103. Also, in 1929, the year before *Hometown*, Mizoguchi had directed *Tokyo March*, which was intended to be a talkie, and the tendency (left wing) film *Metropolitan Symphony*. It is inconceivable that Mizoguchi would not have thought about Soviet talkie theory in this year in which his head was full of thoughts of 'talkies' and 'Soviet film'. The use of phrases, without explanation, such as 'produced the effect of a simultaneous cutaway'

There are several instances of offscreen sound in *Hometown* (omitting the non-diegetic music that is rendered as 'offscreen' sound).

1. An economy room in the Shōwa Hotel: Fujimura is doing his vocal practices ➔ a shot of Natsue viewing that scene from another room, over which Fujimura's voice is rendered as offscreen sound.
2. The same sequence: Fujimura singing 'Shikararete' (this is diegetic sound) ➔ Fujimura's voice as offscreen sound over a shot of Ayako standing behind Fujimura and looking at him in rapt admiration.
3. The same sequence: the offscreen sound of Higuchi (Kosugi Isamu) knocking at the door.
4. Fujimura's house: over a medium close up of Ayako waiting on Fujimura's return, the sound of a clock striking three (this is in the "sound version" part of the film and so is post-recorded non-diegetic sound converted to offscreen sound).
5. The fake 'affair' at the Imperial Hotel: over a medium close up of Ayako bowing her head, Sankichi's line of dialog 'with Fujimura-san at the Shōwa Hotel when we were poor [...]'
6. Fujimura returns to his new home, having completely bought Ayako's pretence [of infidelity]: over a medium close up of Ayako, Fujimura's line of dialog 'you think I can be fooled by that?'
7. In the hospital: over a long shot of Ayako and Sankichi sitting in the waiting room, the conversation between Natsue and Hattori (Doi Heitarō).
8. Ayako's home: over the image of a completely dark room (only an iron kettle is visible), Fujimura's line of dialog 'Ayako! Ayako!'

Although in a typical early talkie such as *The Singing Fool* there is almost no offscreen sound apart from music and street noises – with a very few exceptions, only characters within the frame speak – the use of offscreen sound in *Hometown* is a highly conscious aspect of its design.

It is somewhat paradoxical but the use of music (and song) in the first and second instances listed above is not impossible in the silent cinema. One can *imagine* that after an image of music being produced in a certain place the (live) music could continue as offscreen sound over a montage of images of that place. However, the other examples (in particular the cases involving dialog) would be impossible, or at the very least difficult, in the silent film. As a rule, the silent film intertitle must be *immediately preceded* (not followed) by a face speaking the line of dialog or an action that suggests

in the *Hometown* round-table discussion in which Mizoguchi took part also indicates that he was familiar with it.

the title. Breaking that rule makes the plot hard to follow. Except in special cases, a shot of person A is not followed by an intertitle of person B's line of dialog. Typically, you would have to cut back to person B, followed by their line of dialog. That is, two shots are necessary. However, in the talkie it is possible to represent in one shot an image of person A while hearing person B's line of dialog. In the shots listed above 3, 4, 5, 6, 7, and shot 8 (discussed in the round-table mentioned above) are clear examples of the technique of 'image/sound cutaway'. For the sake of convenience, let us call this technique using sound to create a 'cutaway within the shot'. We can say the shots listed above are the result of serious reflection on talkie technique. So why is it the received opinion of film historical discourse that in *Hometown* 'sound is applied to the image in a redundant manner'?[26]

Let us pay closer attention to shot 7 from the list above. A shot of Ayako and Sankichi sitting in the waiting room is overlaid by the *shadow* of Natsue and Hattori. We hear their conversation from offscreen. What is important here is that at the same time that the voices produce a 'cutaway within the shot', the *shadow* also produces a 'cutaway within the shot'.

Shadows are used very often in *Hometown*. This striking – perhaps rather excessive – use of shadows can also be seen in the following examples.

- The maids' room of the Shōwa Hotel: a light similar to a spotlight illuminates Ayako packing, creating a shadow on the wall behind her.
- The maids' room of the Shōwa Hotel: when Ayako is attacked by the hotel manager they are offscreen right and all that we see within the frame is their shadows, moving violently.
- The hospital: Ayako hangs her head as she sits alongside the sleeping Fujimura. 'Hometown' plays as non-diegetic music. On the left of the image we see the shadow of a nurse (the nurse does not appear in the image).
- The hospital: Ayako comes toward Sankichi as he turns over while sleeping in the waiting room. Her shadow is cast on the wall.

It is clear that this use of shadows in *Hometown* is deliberate. Had Mizoguchi continued to cling to the German Expressionist use of shadows since he had directed the first fully expressionist film in Japan, *Chi to rei*, in 1923? The films he made between 1923 and 1930 have been almost completely lost so it is difficult to say. However, in the oldest surviving Mizoguchi film, *Furusato no uta/Song of Home* (1925), this excessive use of shadows does not appear at all. Also, in the surviving prints (which are missing large parts) of *Asahi*

26 Iwamoto, *Sairento kara tōkī e*, p. 48.

wa kagayaku/The Morning Sun Shines and *Tokyo kōshinkyoku/Tokyo March*, both made in the previous year, shadows are barely used. At most, we can point to a shot at the beginning of *Tokyo March* in the deathbed scene with Michiyo's mother, in which Michiyo's shadow is cast on the wall, or a shot in which the shadow of deer antlers overlaps with Fujimoto (Takagi Eiji)'s head as he anguishes over the depth of his sin.[27] Also, in the films that follow *Hometown* such as *Taki no shiraito/The Water Magician* (1933) there are no shots that give the impression of an excessive use of shadow as in *Hometown*. In sum, this extreme attention to shadow is not necessarily typical of Mizoguchi's films of this period.

As clearly indicated by the examples listed above, 'shadow' in *Hometown* performs the same function of 'cutaway within the shot' as sound. That this use of 'cutaway within the shot' is deliberate in *Hometown* is made all the clearer if we pay attention to the three posters that appear in the film.

The first poster, of the 'Satō Misao Grand Recital' appears at the beginning of the film, the second poster is for the 'Hometown' solo concert, which appears just after Fujimura passes his audition, and the third poster is also for the 'Hometown' recital, and appears just before Fujimura gets in an accident and is taken to hospital. What I would like to focus on here is the image of the streetcar that appears in each of these three shots. It cannot be accidental that the streetcar appears in all three shots: surely it was timed deliberately to be so. The first and second times a poster is shown, it is shown through glass. The image of the streetcar appears in this image as a *reflection*. That is, the poster pasted to a wall and the image of the streetcar that runs in the *reverse field* are represented in the same shot. It is filmed exactly the same way in the first two instances: the 'cutaway within the shot' is created through a reflection.[28]

In *Hometown*, the effect of 'cutaway within the shot' is strongly foregrounded by the film's expressionist use of shadow, reflection in glass, and offscreen sound. And surely the basis of this idea is the concept of the 'image/sound cutaway' that was emphasized only in early sound discourse. The reason why the wide discussion of this concept was limited to this period is obvious: the technique of organically relating offscreen sound to the image

27 Incidentally, this latter image exists only in the French Cinémathèque version of *Tokyo March*.

28 Consider also the scene that occurs relatively soon after the second shot of a poster, in which Fujimura returns home by car. Ayako waits alone for Fujimura, who is late returning home to his new house. A car headlamp approaches. The chauffeur says, 'I brought him from the Imperial Hotel'. When Ayako looks into the returned car, she sees Fujimura in a drunken stupor. I would like to call attention to the glass in the car door: here, too, Ayako's face appears as a *reflection*.

became commonplace, and no longer needed over-the-top labels such as 'image/sound cutaway'. In the early talkie period, simultaneous with the praise for Soviet sound theory, the concept of the 'image/sound cutaway' was inflated in *Hometown* into the form of the 'cutaway within the shot', producing a kind of excess. This 'cutaway within the shot' was then extended to greatly influence the development of Mizoguchi's future 'one scene, one shot' mode of representation.

One scene, one shot

Mizoguchi's 'one scene, one shot' style is usually thought of as the intent gaze of the camera on an embodied subject over a long duration. Mizoguchi himself said, 'human psychology builds over the movement of a single composition. It would be a shame to suddenly cut that off. I want to keep pressing as much as possible'.[29] But in the film that exhibits the most extreme 'one scene, one shot' style, *Zangiku monogatari/Story of the Last Chrysanthemums* (1939), what is captured in the long take is not only the actions of the actor. Distinct spaces are connected through the movements of the camera and offscreen space is represented through voice and other sounds. As Chika Kinoshita writes of *Saikaku ichidai onna/Life of Oharu* (1952): 'What was decisive to Mizoguchi was that the subject and object of some action – of some desire or gaze – were contained within the same frame'.[30] This description surely fits the various shots from *Hometown* described above. Later in the article, Kinoshita refers to Andre Bazin's argument that 'editing is forbidden': 'Whenever the essential aspect of an event depends upon the simultaneous presence of two or more agents, editing is prohibited'.[31] To Mizoguchi, the 'essential aspect of an event' is an extension of embodiment, and that extension developed out of the 'simultaneous presence of two or more agents'.

If we started this essay with theories of Soviet (or Ruttmann-style) montage headed by Eisenstein, how did we end up with Bazin, for whom 'editing is forbidden'? Eisenstein is often taken as 'a theorist who in every respect… is antagonistic' to Bazin.[32] However, the following quotation from Bazin explains his defence of a 'depth-of-field découpage':

29 Mizoguchi, 'Eiga, jinsei, geijutsu', p. 49.
30 Kinoshita, *Mise-en-scène of Desire*, p. 128.
31 Bazin, *What is Cinema?*, p. 81.
32 Aumont, p. 98.

> In other words, modern filmmakers who use long takes and depth of field do not renounce the use of editing (how could they without reverting to primitive babbling?); they make it a part of their style.[33]

Strictly speaking, Bazin did not forbid montage. Rather, to the extent that it was contained within a single shot, he came to defend it. From the point of view of sound counterpoint (the 'cutaway within the shot') Bazin's theory, which is often connected to Mizoguchi's deep space compositions and long takes, begins to take on a strange affinity with Eisenstein. At the same time, it is clear that Mizoguchi's direction, which has been understood as the perfect embodiment of Bazinian aesthetics, cannot be understood only from visual (deep space composition) and temporal (long take) perspectives. Is it really an accident that Mizoguchi consciously began his one scene, one shot directorial style with the film he made after *Hometown*, *Tōjin Okichi* (1930)?[34] It seems not entirely mistaken to regard Mizoguchi's one scene, one shot as originating in the idea of the 'image/sound cutaway' found in *Hometown*.

Conclusion

At the start of this essay I claimed that the reason *Hometown* has been described as an 'incomplete' talkie was that, in addition to its poor quality, the sound had no 'design'. The film gained that reputation in comparison to *The Neighbour's Wife and Mine*, which was regarded as the first Japanese film successfully to connect image and sound, in particular offscreen sound. For example, Iwamoto Kenji writes that what is 'not seen in *Hometown* that is in *The Neighbour's Wife and Mine* is the use of off-scene [offscreen] sound that does not accompany the image'.[35] However, as I have argued, it is clear that not only is there no basis for that judgment but that offscreen sounds in *Hometown* are connected to the image in a richly organic way. Moreover, *Hometown* should be regarded as pioneering many aspects of sound design in the Japanese feature film, such as the use of sound perspective, the ambiguification of non-diegetic and offscreen sound, and the use of counterpoint – both as contrast and as a 'image/sound cutaway'. Finally, I have argued in this chapter that

33 Bazin, *What is Cinema?*, p. 98, 100.

34 In Mizoguchi's words, 'I've been doing that way of shooting [one scene, one shot] for a long time. From the time of *Tōjin Okichi*, starring Umemura Yoko'. See Yomota, *Eiga kantoku Mizoguchi Kenji*, p. 352. See also Yoda, *Mizoguchi no hito to geijutsu*, p. 37

35 Iwamoto, *Sairento kara tōkī e*, p. 51.

the idea in *Hometown* of the 'image/sound cutaway', or the 'cutaway within the shot', is a possible impetus for the development of 'Mizoguchi style'. This earliest genuine talkie in Japan, *Hometown*, is deeply significant as a way to understand the development of the talkie in Japan and as a way to rethink the cliché in film history of 'one scene, one shot' Mizoguchi.

* This chapter was first published as 'Nihon Tokii jidai no reimei: Mizoguchi Kenji Furusato (1930) o megutte' in *Engeki eizōgaku* (Waseda Daigaku Engeki Hakubutsukan, 2011). We are grateful to the Waseda University Tsubouchi Theatre Memorial Museum for permission to edit and translate the original essay.

Bibliography

Rick Altman. 'Sound Space'. In *Sound Theory Sound Practice*, edited by Rick Altman (New York: Routledge, 1992), pp. 46-64.

———. *The American Film Musical* (Bloomington: Indiana University Press, 1987).

André Bazin, *What is Cinema?*, translated by Timothy Barnard (Montreal: Caboose Press, 2009).

———. *Eiga towa nanika II: Eizō gengo no mondai*, translated by Kokai Eiji (Tokyo: Bijutsu Shuppansha, 1974).

Jacques Aumont. *Eiga riron kōgi: Eizō no rikai to tankyū no tameni,* translated by Takeda Kiyoshi (Tokyo: Keisō Shobō, 2007).

Chōki Seiji. *Sengo no ongaku: geijutsu ongaku no poritikusu to poetikusu* (Tokyo: Sakuhinsha, 2011).

Horino Masao et. al. 'Gijutsuka ni yoru hitotsu no Nihon tōkī hihyō – "Kanaya koume" gappyō kiroku yori'. *Eiga ōrai* 6.3 (March 1930), pp. 72-76.

Hosokawa Shuhei. 'Kouta eiga no bunkashi'. *Shinema dondon* 1 (2002), pp. 12-13.

———. 'Seiyō ongaku no Nihonka/taishūka 33' *Myūjikku magajin* (December 1991), pp. 148-153.

Iijima Tadashi. 'Kaigai eiga shōsoku'. *Shinchō*, 1 December 1928, pp. 65-67.

Iwasaki Akira. *Eiga no riron* (Iwanami Shoten, 1975).

Iwamoto Kenji. *Sairento kara tōkī e: Nihon eiga keiseiki no hito to bunka* (Tokyo: Shin'washa, 2007).

Katō Mikirō. *Eigakan to kankyaku no bunkashi* (Tokyo: Chūōkōron Shinsha, 2006).

Kinoshita Chika. '*Saikaku ichidai onna* shiron – Andore Bazan no "ofusukurīn"'. In *Eiga no jiogurafī* (Tokyo: Keisō Shobō, 1996), pp.121-132.

———. *Mise-En-Scène of Desire: The Films of Mizoguchi Kenji.* (Ph.D. diss., University of Chicago, 2007).

Kinugasa Teinosuke. *Waga eiga no seishun* (Tokyo: Chūōkōronsha, 1977).
Diane Wei Lewis. 'Media Fantasies: Women, Mobility, and Silent-Era Japanese Ballad Films'. *Cinema Journal* 52:3 (Spring 2013), pp. 99-119.
Mizoguchi Kenji. 'Eiga, jinsei, geijutsu'. *Eureka* (October 1992), pp. 48-55.
Mori Iwao. 'Sakisofon to hana'. *Kinema shūhō* 5 (14 March 1930), pp. 18-21.
Mori Iwao, et.al. '*Furusato* zadankai'. *Eiga ōrai* 6.5 (May 1930), pp. 45-56.
Johan Nordström. 'The Emergence of the Sound Film in Japan: Mina Talkie and the Reception of Its Early Works'. *Engeki eizōgaku 2010* 5 (2011), pp. 1-17.
Okabe Ryū. *Nihon eigashi sokō 10: Shiryō Nihon hassei eiga no sōseiki* (Tokyo: Firumu Raiburari Kyogikai, 1975).
Sasagawa Keiko. 'Kouta eiga ni kansuru kiso chōsa: Meiji makki kara Shōwa shoki o chūshin ni'. *Engeki Kenkyu Senta kiyo* 1 (2003), pp. 175-196.
Sasō Tsutomu. 'Shoki tōkī ni tsuite no kijutsu'. In *Nihon eigashi tanbō: eiga e no omoi 4* (Nittamachi [Gunmaken]: Tanaka Jun'ichirō Kinen Daiyonkai Nihon Eigashi Fesutibaru Jikkō Iinkai, 2001), pp. 149-157.
———. *Mizoguchi Kenji zensakuhin kaisetsu 7: Furusato* (Tokyo: Kindai Bungeisha, 2010).
Satō Tadao. *Mizoguchi Kenji no sekai* (Tokyo: Chikuma Shobō, 1982).
———. *Zōhoban Nihon eigashi 1* (Tokyo: Iwanami Shoten, 2006).
Shindō Kaneto. *Aru eiga kantoku: Mizoguchi Kenji to Nihon eiga* (Tokyo: Iwanami Shoten, 1976).
Takahara Fujirō. *Tōkī gikō gairon: eiga no bunshōhō* (Tokyo: Shorin Kentendō, 1930).
Tanaka Jun'ichirō. 'Furusato sansoku: Hakkan ni sai shite'. *Kinema shūhō* 5 (14 March 1930), p. 17.
———. *Nihon eiga hattatsushi I: Katsudō shashin jidai* (Tokyo: Chūōkōron Shinsha, 1980).
———. *Nihon eiga hattatsushi II: Katsudō shashin jida* (Tokyo: Chūōkōron Shinsha, 1980).
Yoda Yoshikata. *Mizoguchi Kenji no hito to geijutsu* (Tokyo: Tabata Shoten, 1983).
Yomota Inuhiko. *Eiga kantoku Mizoguchi Kenji* (Tokyo: Shinyōsha, 1999).

About the Author

Nagato Yohei is an Assistant Professor in Film Studies at Rikkyo University, specializing in film and sound studies. He has contributed to books on film studies and film soundtracks, and his book *Eiga onkyōron: Mizoguchi Kenji eiga o kiku* (Tokyo: Misuzu Shobō, 2014) won the 36th Suntory Prize for Art and Literature.

8 The Early talkie frame in Japanese cinema

Itakura Fumiaki

Abstract
This chapter approaches the transition to sound from the perspective of its material substrate. It shows how the 'early talkie frame', in which the soundtrack was added to 35mm silent film without modifying the top and bottom of the frame, changes the aspect ratio of the image. Arguing for the importance of a concept of 'authenticity' in archival studies, the chapter shows that many well-known films, including Japanese films, cannot now be seen in the correct aspect ratio without access to archival sources. Through a close analysis of the original negatives, it shows that Ozu Yasujirō's use of the early talkie frame coincided with his increased interest in visual composition, in particular with arranging objects along the bottom frame line.

Keywords: visual style, composition, archival studies, authenticity, Ozu Yasujirō, framing

> Recently much concern was aroused among Hollywood studio technicians by the fact that in some theatres the heads and feet of characters, important words in titles, and other vital elements of the picture were being cut off in projection of sound-on-film pictures.[1]

This study investigates the 'early talkie frame', a neglected but once dominant aspect ratio of 35 mm film that flourished in the early talkie era, around 1927–1934. The inclusion of the soundtrack created a different frame shape

Acknowledgement: I would like to thank Okada Hidenori and Daibō Masaki of the National Film Archive of Japan, and the Shōchiku Company for the frame enlargements of the Ozu films.

1 Cowan, 'Camera and Projector Apertures', p.108.

Raine, M. and J. Nordström (eds.), *The Culture of the Sound Image in Prewar Japan*.
Taylor & Francis Group 2020
DOI: 10.5117/9789089647733_CH08

to that of the full-frame image. Due to resulting technical and economic problems, the US film industry introduced the standardized 'Academy Ratio' of 1:1.37 in 1932. This study focuses on the extent of the use of the early talkie frame in Japan and establishes that the transition to the Academy Ratio was delayed by some years. This essay has two purposes: to argue for the importance of 'authentic' restoration and projection of films that used the early talkie frame as their original film format; and to argue that knowing the original film format and aspect ratio leads us to a better understanding of characteristics of a film directors' style, drawing examples from Ozu Yasujirō's films. By examining prints in the National Film Archive of Japan, key Japanese films are analysed in terms of frame composition, finding evidence of image cropping that shows that important directors (in particular, Kinugasa Teinosuke, and Ozu Yasujirō) had originally intended their films to be shown in the early talkie frame. The findings highlight the vital importance of showing these films in their intended aspect ratio, and have significant implications for promoting authentic projection and recording practices in the future.

The standard aspect ratio of the recorded image on 35 mm film has changed throughout the history of cinema. The dominant aspect ratio in each period can be summarized as follows:

1. Full frame (1:1.33): used from the beginning of cinema to the end of the silent period.
2. Academy Ratio (1:1.37): the Academy of Motion Picture Art and Science standardized this aspect ratio in 1932 and it spread throughout the world. This format was generally used until the 1950s.
3. CinemaScope (1:2.35): the most famous widescreen frame using an anamorphic lens. This format was mostly used during the 1950s and 1960s.[2]
4. Widescreen (European Widescreen: 1:1.66, American Widescreen 1:1.85): this has been dominant approximately after the 1970s to the present.

However, another short-lived but dominant aspect ratio existed between the first period (full frame) and the second period (Academy Ratio). In this study, I will focus on this short-lived aspect ratio, which was used in various countries only in the early part of the talkie era, around the years 1927–1934. This aspect ratio involves the removal of a part of the left-hand side of the full-frame image in order to insert the soundtrack.

2 The most important prior study of widescreen including cinema scope is Belton, *Widescreen Cinema*.

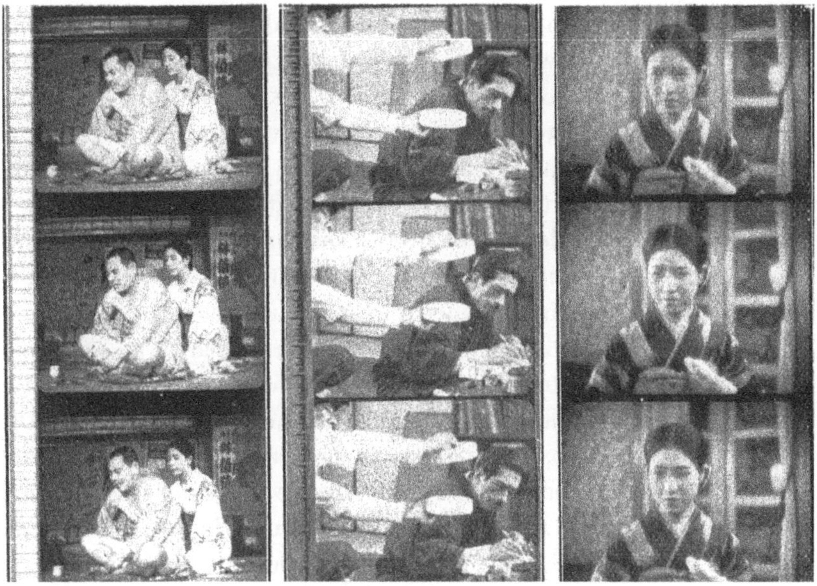

Figure 8.1 Left: Academy Ratio. Centre: Early talkie frame. Right: Full frame.[3]

This early talkie aspect ratio has been given different names. Film historian Barry Salt refers to this ratio as 'early sound aperture' while film projection consultant Torkell Saetervadet calls it 'Movietone format' after the aspect ratio of the 'Movietone system', the first commercial system of sound-on-film used in the US by the Fox Company, which had an aspect ratio of 1:1.19.[4] However, in reality, the aspect ratio during the early talkie period varied in each Hollywood studio, and for each cameraman.[5] Therefore, in this study, we shall use the term 'early talkie frame' as being a frame that has a higher height than the Academy Ratio with an aspect ratio of approximately 1:1.19. Other than the brief mentions by Salt and Saetervadet, we can find only a few previous studies that refer to this early talkie frame,

3 Takahara Fujirō. *Tōkīgikō gairon*. (Tokyo: Shorin kentendō, 1935). The film titles are *Ukikusa monogatari/Story of Floating Weeds* (1934) (left), *Madamu to nyōbō/The Neighbour's Wife and Mine* (1931) (middle), Unknown (right).

4 Salt, *Film Style and Technology*, p. 211. Saetervadet, *The Advanced Projection Manual*, pp. 69-70. This book is a practical manual for film projectionists. Thus, the explanation of the historical background is limited to only two pages.

5 Cowan, 'Camera and Projector Apertures', pp. 246-247. Actual research has established the following ratios: Paramount 1:1.3, Fox 1:1.28, MGM 1:1.15, Columbia Pictures 1:1.13, Universal 1:1.34 or 1:1.15. These data denote the size of the actual film frame, not the aspect ratio of projected images on the screen. The image on the screen is generally cropped a little by screen masks.

for example John Belton's *Widescreen Cinema* and Leo Enticknap's *Moving Image Technology*.[6] However, these two studies mention the early talkie frame in only one or two paragraphs and they restrict their analysis to the context of US cinema. I will extend this discussion of the early talkie frame to its Japanese context and create a basis for further future exploration of the early talkie frame in an international context.

Before presenting a detailed analysis of the Japanese early talkie frame, let us summarize the history of early talkie frames mainly in the US by referring to previous studies. When the soundtrack was added on the left-hand side of the film strip, the width of the image was narrowed. This early talkie frame was repeatedly criticized by cameramen and directors, since they believed that it reduced the dynamism of the composition within the frame.[7] In January 1930, the magazine of the Academy of Motion Picture Arts and Sciences carried an article discussing the most suitable aspect ratio for cinema. This article applied statistical research to hundreds of fine art paintings, by artists such as Peter Paul Rubens, and criticized contemporary early talkie frames on an aesthetic basis.[8] Furthermore, in the same edition of the magazine, there was a report on how the cameramen at the studios shot images to cope with the early talkie frame and how the projectionists at the movie theatres projected these films. This report written by Lester Cowan of S.M.P.E. (The Society of Motion Picture Engineers) revealed that there was no standardized common aspect ratio during that time, and that actual projection conditions were highly variable. The main reason for the projectionists' confusion was an economic one. To correctly project the films of the early talkie aspect ratio using the standard projector for silent films, projectionists had to adjust the position of the screen curtains in the theatre, and also obtain a new projection lens and aperture plate for the projector. Thus, for economic reasons, some theatres were able to setup this new equipment, whereas others could not.

In these problematic circumstances, the American film industry began to solve this problem by standardizing the aspect ratio of talkie films. Lester Cowan recommended to the Hollywood film companies shooting the film with a standardized frame of 0.620 inches by 0.835 inches (1:1.35) and projecting the film using an aperture plate of 0.60 inches by 0.80 inches.[9] Finally, in 1932, the Academy of Motion Picture Arts and Sciences declared that it

6 Belton, *Widescreen Cinema*, p. 44. Enticknap, *Moving Image Technology*, pp. 51-53.

7 Belton, *Widescreen Cinema*, p. 44.

8 Jones, 'Rectangle Proportions in Pictorial Compositions', pp. 32-49.

9 Cowan, 'Camera and Projector Apertures', pp. 118-119.

Figure 8.2 Opening shot of *City Lights* (1930). Cropped version (DVD released by Asahi Shimbunsha, 2004)/Original version (DVD released by Criterion Company, 2013).

was appropriate for filmmakers to adopt the aspect ratio of 1:1.37, which was almost the same aspect ratio as full frame in the silent period. The major American studios agreed to adopt this new aspect ratio, which was later called the Academy Ratio.[10] This Academy Ratio was beneficial for filmmakers because the newly lowered horizontal height of this frame enabled 'the top light and microphone to descend to approximately six feet', which was closer to the actors.[11] Furthermore, this new Academy Ratio allowed projectionists to avoid adjusting screen curtain and aperture plates film by film.[12]

This supposedly linear 'history' of conversion from the early talkie frame to the Academy Ratio has obscured the historical importance of the early talkie period and its rich diversity of films. In fact, from the late 1920s to the beginning of the 1930s, most films around the world were made using a sound-on-film process, and were shot and projected with the early talkie frame. Those films include such masterworks as *City Lights* (Charles Chaplin, 1931 sound version), *Die 3 Groschen Opera/The Threepenny Opera* (G.W. Pabst, 1931), the talkie version of *Blackmail* (Alfred Hitchcock, 1929), *The Public Enemy* (William A. Wellman, 1931), and as I will discuss later, some of the films by Ozu Yasujirō and Mizoguchi Kenji. Demand from movie fans and scholars to see films in their original aspect ratios has increased, and recently several new DVD versions have been produced with the original early talkie frame, not cropped to the Academy ratio. For example, newly published DVD versions of films such as *M* (Fritz Lang, 1931) and *Vampyr*

10 It has not been possible to locate any empirical studies confirming whether all Hollywood film studios changed from the early talkie frame to Academy frame soon after the standardization in 1932 by AMPAS.

11 'Tōkī eiga no gamen', p. 10.

12 Cowan, 'Camera and Projector Apertures', pp. 109-113.

(Carl Theodor Dryer, 1932) have been transferred with the original early talkie frame intact. Let us examine one example of the importance of authentic recording in Chaplin's *City Lights*. The well-composed opening shot of this film would be disturbed if it is projected or transferred in the Academy Ratio because the top of the church tower in the background would be cropped (Fig. 8.2).

This essay explores the neglected field of the transition of Japanese aspect ratios during the early talkie period (from approximately 1930 to 1934), based on a comprehensive inspection of actual 35 mm prints, which are preserved in the National Film Archive of Japan (NFAJ).

Before examining them detail, let us look back briefly at the history of sound systems in the Japanese film industry.[13] In the latter part of the 1920s, both the sound-on disc system and the sound-on-film system were introduced in Japan. The sound-on-disc format was first introduced in 1928 by Tōjō Masao who established the Nippon Tōkī Company to make talkie films with the technology system called Īsutofon tōkī (usually referred to in English as 'Eastphone'). The most famous title was *Modoribashi/The Modori Bridge* (Makino Masahiro, 1928) but none of the Eastphone films have survived. The first sound-on film format in Japan was Mina Talkie by Minagawa Yoshizō. Minagawa bought the exclusive Japanese rights for Lee De Forest's Phonofilm system, which he renamed Mina Talkie. Minagawa made Mina Talkie films from 1927 to 1930. The oldest surviving film with Mina Talkie is *Seiyūkai sōsai Tanaka Giichi-shi enzetsu/The Speech of Prime Minister Tanaka* (1927), preserved by the National Film Archive of Japan, and the most famous surviving Mina Talkie film is Mizoguchi Kenji's *Furusato/Hometown* (1930). Both films were shot with the early talkie frame.

The major film company Shōchiku succeeded in making a sound-on-film feature in 1931 with *Madamu to nyōbō/The Neighbour's Wife and Mine* (Gosho Heinosuke), utilizing the Tsuchihashi system, which was invented by Tsuchihashi Takeo. *The Neighbour's Wife and Mine* was also shot with the early talkie frame (see the centre image of Fig. 8.1). The Shashin kagaku kenkyūjo/'Photo Chemical Laboratory', or P.C.L. for short, was established in 1932 as a specialized sound recording studio that started making films the following year (it later merged with the J.O. studio to become Tōhō in 1937). The oldest surviving film utilizing the P.C.L. sound system is *Tabi wa Aozora/Travel Under a Blue Sky* (Inagaki Hiroshi, 1932) which was produced by Kataoka Chiezō production, and P.C.L.'s first production under its own

13 On the introduction of talkie systems in Japan, see Nagato, *Eiga onkyōron*, pp. 59-72; Nihon Eiga Terebi Gijutsu Kyōkai, *Nihon eiga gijutsu shi*, pp. 153-158.

studio name was *Ongaku Kigeki: Horoyoi jinsei/A Tipsy Life* (Kimura Sotoji, 1933). Both films were shot with the early talkie frame. The other major company, Nikkatsu, started utilizing the Western Electric sound system from 1933. The first production film was *Tange Sazen* (Itō Daisuke, 1933), which was also shot with the early talkie frame.

The most important reason for us to focus on the aspect ratio of films is that the transition of technology and the film author's style can be interrelated. Nagato Yohei, a specialist on the films of Mizoguchi Kenji, mentions that Mizoguchi's first talkie film *Furusato* made the director aware of off-screen space, which he developed as part of his *mise-en-scène* in the latter part of the 1930s in films such as *Naniwa erejī/Osaka Elegy* (1936) and *Zangiku monogatari/Story of the Last Chrysanthemums* (1939).[14] The transition from full frame to the early talkie frame seems to be a slight change, but for some directors this transition was a crucial one for their composition and framing. In the latter part of this essay, I will take up Ozu Yasujirō's films, as the introduction of the early talkie frame made Ozu more conscious of framing and his composition, which in turn led to the development of his characteristic *mise-en scène.*

What is 'authentic' film projection?

For the film scholar who analyses film style and the *mise-en-scène* of individual films, it is necessary to see the film in their original aspect ratio. However, most of the past screenings and recordings of films shot in the early talkie frame have neither been screened nor re-recorded in their original aspect ratio. This lack of understanding of the early talkie frame is demonstrated by the fact that practically no previous studies have focused on this theme. Before analysing actual Japanese films using the early talkie frame, it will be useful for us to discuss exactly what is meant by authentic projection and recording. Authentic projection can be defined as the practice of screening which tries to recover the original screening methods and the context of the film's first screening venues as much as possible.[15] The term

14 See the previous chapter in this volume.

15 'Authenticity', has been much discussed in the fields of early music in musicology and in museum studies in terms of preserving cultural heritage. See Levinson, 'Authentic Performance and Performance Means', pp.393-408; and 'The Nara Document on Authenticity'. In the field of film studies, 'authenticity' has been discussed in relation to film restoration. See Usai et. al., *Film Curatorship*, and Fossati, *From Grain to Pixel*, pp.117-123; and Itakura, 'Yottsu no kachi no hyakubunritsu', pp. 269-290.

'original' and 'authentic' have been discussed in the field of film restoration because film restoration needs to duplicate film materials. The International Federation of Film Archive (FIAF) made a declaration on the ethics of film archives in 1993 the defined film restoration as follows:

> When restoring material, archives will endeavour only to complete what is incomplete and to remove the accretions of time, wear, and misinformation. They will not seek to change or distort the nature of the original material or the intentions of its creators.[16]

The most important points are to project the proper and original aspect ratio, and to project at the right speed (frames per second).[17] If the aspect ratio intended by the director and cameraman has been partly cropped to facilitate ease of screening in the theatre, it cannot be called an authentic projection. Cropping the aspect ratio disrupted the designated composition and *mise-en-scène* that the director and cameraman carefully created. In previous decades, there were many TV broadcasts and commercial VHS tapes in which CinemaScope films of the 1950s and 1960s were cropped on both sides. However, in the last twenty years or so, the increased resolution of TV has enabled CinemaScope films to be broadcast without cropping.[18]

One controversial example, in which a film's original aspect ratio was changed by its director, is the film *Kurutta ichi pēji/Page of Madness* (1926) directed by Kinugasa Teinosuke. This film has been recognized as one of the first experimental silent films in Japan. *Page of Madness* was originally shot in full frame at 18 fps.[19] This film was considered to have been lost until the original nitrate negative was found in a warehouse at Kinugasa's house in 1971 and was restored under Kinugasa's direction. Crucially, Kinugasa restored the film not as the original version but as a 'new sound version', which added a soundtrack of instrumental music composed by Kurashima Tōru. The problem was that the newly recorded soundtrack on the film print cropped the left-hand side of the original full frame. Furthermore, to complicate things further, in order to play the soundtrack effectively this

16 FIAF Code of Ethics <http://www.fiafnet.org/pages/Community/Code-Of-Ethics.html> (Accessed 20 April 2020).

17 Moreover, in the case of silent films, we must consider live musical accompaniment, and *benshi* narration in the contexts of Japanese film screenings.

18 The problem that the original aspect ratio tended to be cropped in VHS and DVD is mentioned in Bordwell and Thompson, *Film Art*, pp. 44-45.

19 Kinugasa, *Waga eiga no seishun*, pp.73-74.

new sound version had to be projected at 24 fps, rather than the original 18 fps, with the effect that the images moved too rapidly.

From the standpoint of respecting 'authenticity' (the originality of film format and the original context of a film's first screening), Kinugasa's 'new sound version' was far from being an authentic film restoration or reflecting authentic screening practice (although this 'new sound version' can be authorized as a 'director's cut').[20] Another problem with the screening of the 'new sound version' was that the aspect ratio projected on the screen was different from that recorded on the film itself. The aspect ratio of the 'new sound version' raises similar problems to Academy ratio rereleases of films shot in the early talkie frame, since the original full frame was cropped by the soundtrack. However, when Kinugasa's new version was screened after 1971, there was no choice but to project this film in the Academy Ratio because most of the projectionists were unaware of the history of the early talkie frame. In fact, at the screening of this 'new sound version' at Iwanami hall, Tokyo, in 1975, the brochure described the aspect ratio of this film as Academy Ratio.[21]

As Chart 1 indicates, full frame has an image height of 18 mm, whereas Academy Ratio is only 15.75 mm. Therefore, it is likely that the screened image of the 'new sound version' of *Page of Madness* has been cropped, on the left-hand side by the soundtrack and on the upper and lower sides by the projection aperture plate. If the projectionist at Iwanami Hall had noticed the aspect ratio on the print of this 'new sound version' (which has the Full Frame height) and wanted to project it correctly, they would have had to use the appropriate lens and aperture plate suitable for the early talkie frame.[22]

This case study of *Page of Madness* shows us that authentic projection tends to be restricted by each decade's dominant projection machine and the duplication machines in film laboratories. There is no doubt that Kinugasa knew that the original format was full frame; thus, he must have noticed

20 Aaron Gerow assumes that the surviving materials of *A Page of Madness* is a shortened version of the original material that was reedited by Kinugasa after rediscovering the film in 1971. But the shortened version was already produced and passed through censorship in 1927 and there is a nitrate print of the shortened version which is preserved in the NFAJ (nitrate films were circulated until the first half of the 1950s). See Itakura, '*Review*', pp.86-89.

21 'Kurutta ichipeji/Jūjiro', *Ekipu do shinema* 8, pp. 33, 39.

22 Saetervadet has advised film projectionists to combine a CinemaScope aperture plate with CinemaScope base lens (i.e., without anamorphic attachment) to project early talkie frame films (Saetervadet, op. cit., pp. 70.). However, the actual height of early talkie frames varies. Therefore, differences in the actual films must be carefully inspected.

the change to the original image in the 'new sound version'. It is possible that Kinugasa reluctantly selected the inadequate image because he knew the technological limitations of both laboratories and movie theatres in Japan during the early 1970s. However, today archivists attempt to pursue authentic projection practices, reflecting the original aspect ratio and projection speed, by researching the contexts of each period.

Result of the inspection Japanese films

To achieve an authentic projection, we must first carefully inspect the image recorded on the film itself. After inspecting approximately sixty 35 mm prints, which were made from 1928 to 1942, it becomes clear that there are many Japanese films originally shot with the early talkie frame (Appendix 1).

This list is not comprehensive, since thousands of 1930s Japanese films have been lost. I have selected for inspection films in which the aspect ratios appear not to have been changed or cropped from the original format. Therefore, the inspected films were limited to 35 mm prints that originated from either a 35 mm nitrate print or a 35 mm nitrate negative. In other words, I limited the sample to those films that maintain their original aspect ratio. This means that I removed the 16 mm, 9.5 mm, and 8 mm films from the inspection because it is impossible to determine whether these small-gauge films preserve the original 35 mm film's aspect ratio.[23]

There was a short-lived talkie system in Japan from approximately 1928 to 1931, which was named Mina Talkie. The name of this system came from the inventor's name, Minagawa Yoshizō, who obtained a license to use Lee de Forest's Phonofilm talkie system. We do not have much information about this system; however, the movements of the images appear to be natural when these Mina Talkie films are projected at 21 fps. The surviving Mina Talkie films were all shot in the early talkie frame (see Fig. 8.3). The most famous Mina Talkie film is *Furusato/Hometown*, directed by Mizoguchi Kenji in 1930. This part-talkie sound film was clearly intended to be shot with the early talkie frame because there are many shots in which part

23 There is still the possibility that some of the surviving films with Academy frames might be cropped from the original early talkie frame during a previous duplication process. But in those cases we can often recognize traces of the original frame in 'clues' such as curves at the corners of the frame, and the balance of the composition within the frame.

Figure 8.3 *Hometown* (1930). Image courtesy of the National Film Archive of Japan.

of the images in the upper and lower edges have been cropped by the Academy Ratio frame. In the film, there is a shot that shows us the poster of Fujiwara's concert. However, if this shot is projected in the Academy Ratio, the image of Fujiwara's face on the poster is cropped. Another shot is one of the most important images for this narrative. Fujiwara's lover Ayako leaves a letter for Fujiwara because she is unhappy to see him corrupted by fashionable society. There is a shot of the letter, filled with Ayako's handwriting. However, if this shot is projected in the Academy Ratio, some of the characters are cropped and we cannot understand the important information in the letter.

Gosho Heinosuke's first talkie film *The Neighbour's Wife and Mine* is designated as the first commercially and critically successful Japanese all-talkie feature film. It was also shot with the early talkie frame and available 35 mm prints are reproduced as such. However, like *Furusato*, when this film is projected on to the screen or transferred onto VHS or DVD, the image is converted into the Academy Ratio and the tops of characters' heads are cropped. Unfortunately, all the available DVD or VHS versions of this film were reproduced by the Shōchiku Company in the Academy Ratio.

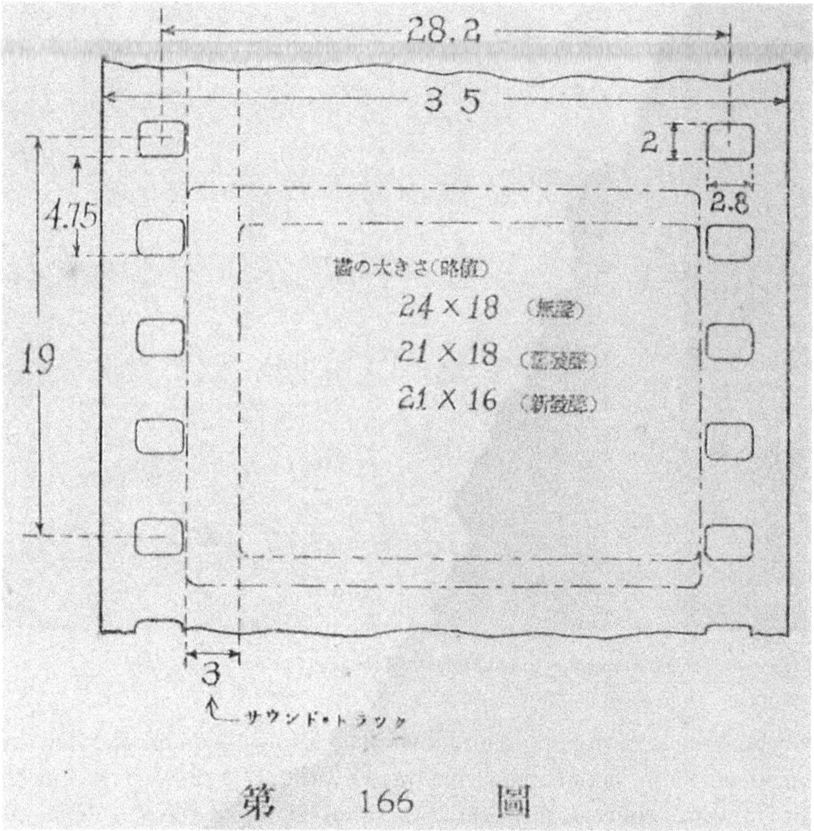

Figure 8.4 Kaeriyama Norimasa. *Eisha gishi kyōkasho* (Nikkan Kōgyō Shinbunsha, 1938).

The transition from the early talkie frame to the Academy Ratio

When did the aspect ratio in Japan change from the early talkie frame to the Academy Ratio? We currently have no information as to whether there was any agreement to standardize the aspect ratio in the Japanese film industry, as in the case of the Academy of Motion Picture Arts and Science (AMPAS). The frame standardization by AMPAS was reported in the Japanese trade magazine in May 1932.[24] However, looking at Appendix 1, we can see that the early talkie frame is still dominant until 1933. The number of early talkie frame films begins to reduce in 1934. After 1935, most Japanese sound-on-film films used the Academy Ratio.[25]

24 'Tōkī eiga no gamen', p. 10.

25 It is difficult for us to draw a clear boundary between the early talkie frame and Academy frame in the field of Japanese documentary films because the number of inspected sample films

In 1934, the American of projection equipment company Acme published a promotional book for the new talkie Simplex projector in Japanese. The book proudly announced the ability to slide the lenses horizontally in order to adjust the centre of both silent film and talkie film.[26] This book also explains that you have to change the aperture plate and the position of the lens to project silent and talkie films because the centre of each image is different.

There is some evidence confirming that Japanese films using the early talkie frame were still being projected during the latter half of the 1930s. Kaeriyama Norimasa, one of the Japan's most famous experts in film technology and the first influential film critics, wrote a technical textbook about film projection in 1938 that explained the three types of aspect ratio: full frame, early talkie frame, and Academy Ratio (Fig. 8.4).

Kaeriyama gave detailed information on the sizes of the three types of aperture gates for the benefit of contemporary projectionists. This suggests that Japanese projectionists in 1938 had to handle all three types of film format. Kaeriyama's 1942 book also explains these three types of format; even in 1942, this explanation of the three categories was useful for contemporary projectionists. However, the same author wrote a book in 1950, which contains no references to the early talkie frame and only mentions the Academy Ratio. This suggests that projectionists in post-war Japan no longer needed to use the early talkie frame and knowledge of its existence began to fade from the history of cinema.

Even though we can see only a limited sample, we can summarize from the inspection of Japanese films that Japanese sound-on-film features using the early talkie frame seem to have been dominant from the beginning of the sound-on-film period to approximately 1933. The films produced by the major film productions such as Shōchiku, Nikkatsu and P.C.L., used the early talkie frame around in 1933 but in 1935 almost all of them changed to use the Academy Ratio. The Academy Ratio began to be dominant in 1934 and most of the feature films produced by major studios were shot in Academy Ratio in 1935. It was in this year that more than half of new Japanese feature films were now talkie films. Therefore, we can assume that, from approximately 1934 to 1935, the double standard of early talkie frame and Academy Ratio was regarded as a problem in the Japanese film industry. The Shōchiku cameraman Sasaki Tarō wrote in a technical book on

is very limited. However, the aspect ratio of the early talkie frame was used until the early 1940s in some Japanese documentary films. There is no definite information or references regarding how these documentaries were projected.

26 Ōtaka, *Shinpurekkusu eisha sōchi*, pp. 25-26.

cinematography in 1935, describing only the Academy Ratio. This indicates that the early talkie frame was out of date and not recommended to the contemporary cameraman.[27] Compared to the American film industry, the dominance of the Academy Ratio in Japan appears to have been delayed by approximately two or three years.[28]

Ozu Yasujirō's silent films shot with the early talkie frame

There is something of a mystery in the history of the early talkie frame. There are two silent films by Ozu Yasujirō that were originally shot with the early talkie frame: *Tokyo no onna/Woman of Tokyo* (1933) and *Haha o kowazuya/A Mother Should Be Loved* (1934).[29] According to contemporary documents of national censorship by the Home Ministry, these two films were originally screened officially as silent films.[30] All the available DVD and VHS versions of these two films produced by Shōchiku were transferred using the Academy Ratio. Thus, the upper and lower sides of the frames in these two films are cropped and there are many shots in which the characters' heads and feet are unnaturally cut off. We can assume that this film was originally shot with early talkie frame (not with Full Frame) because letters in credit titles and intertitles are placed in the centre of the frame symmetrically.

It is very important for us to focus on the aspect ratios of these two films because it is well known that Ozu strictly composed the framing of each shot throughout his entire work, adjusting camera positions and actors' poses by a few inches. Several prior studies have focused on Ozu's films and it can be said that almost every shot and composition has been analysed. In 2013, a screening of *Woman of Tokyo* with the original early talkie format took place at the Cinema Ritrovato film festival in Bologna. However, most

27 Nakamura, *Saishin shashin kagaku*', pp. 10-13. On the other hand, the manual for film projectionists that was published in February 1932 titled *Katsudō shashin eisha hō* (Tōhō shoin) inserted images of 35mm Japanese film enlargement with only early talkie frames. There are no images of Academy Ratio.

28 Even in the latter part of the 1930s, some of the small production companies such as Daito, Kyokutō and Zenshō still produced silent films and sound version films with *benshi* narration. Unfortunately, there are no appropriate samples which maintain the original aspect ratio.

29 Gosho Heinosuke's *Izu dancer* (Izu no odoriko, 1933) was a silent film, but was also shot in the early talkie frame. It is likely that this film was originally planned as sound version; however, in the middle of production this film was somehow changed to a silent version. The VHS version of this film was reproduced in the Academy frame.

30 *Fukkokuban eiga ken'etsu jiho* 16, p.69; and *Fukkokuban eiga ken'etsu jiho* 18, p.303.

Table 8.1 List of aspect ratios in Ozu's films during the transition period from silent to talkie

Nr	Release date	Film title	Silent/sound/ talkie	Aspect ratio
1	24 November 1932	*Mata au hi made/ Until the Day We Meet Again*	Sound version	Unknown because film is lost. But probably Early talkie frame
2	09 February 1933	*Tokyo no onna/ Woman of Tokyo*	Silent	Early talkie frame
3	27 April 1933	*Hijōsen no onna/ Dragnet Girl*	Silent	Full frame
4	07 September 1933	*Dekigokoro/Passing Fancy*	Silent	Full frame
5	11 May 1934	*Haha o kowazuya/A Mother Should be Loved*	Silent	Early talkie frame
6	23 November 1934	*Ukikusa Monogatari/A Story of Floating Weeds*	Sound version (surviving version is silent)	Academy Ratio
7	20 January 1935	*Hakoiri musume/An Innocent Maid*	Sound version	Unknown. Film lost
8	21 November 1935	*Tokyo no yado/An Inn in Tokyo*	Sound version	Unknown (Only surviving print is a 16 mm film)
9	1935	*Kagami jishi/Kagami jishi*	Talkie	Academy Ratio
10	19 March 1936	*Daigaku yoitoko/ College is a Nice Place*	Sound version	Film lost
11	15 September 1936	*Hitori musuko/The Only Son*	Talkie	Academy Ratio

movie fans and scholars do not realize that an authentic reproduction has not yet been achieved and they have seen only the cropped DVD version.[31]

Table 8.1 shows the chronological list of Ozu's films, from his first sound version film to his first talkie film, with information on their original aspect ratios and sound format. *Ukikusa monogatari/A Story of Floating Weeds* (1934) is Ozu's first film using the Academy Ratio and his second sound version (although only the silent version survives). After *A Story of Floating Weeds*, Ozu appears to use only the Academy Ratio (though we cannot know the aspect ratio of the lost films).

31 *Passing Fancy* (1933) was originally shot in full frame. But unfortunately, the released DVD and VHS versions are presented in Academy frame.

Figure 8.5 Chikako's room in *Woman of Tokyo*. We can see the reporter's cane on the hat rack in the original 35mm print. Image courtesy of the National Film Archive of Japan. By special permission of the Shōchiku Company.

Among Ozu's surviving films, *Woman of Tokyo* is the first to use the early talkie frame. There is no clear indication why Ozu used the early talkie frame in this silent film. One might assume that Ozu changed the sound format of this film from talkie to silent in the middle of the production process. However, it would have been almost impossible for him to do so because Ozu was asked to make *Woman of Tokyo* on very short notice, during the production process of *Hijōsen no onna/Dragnet Girl* (1933); Ozu and his staff had to complete shooting *Woman of Tokyo* in only eight days.[32] Another clue is that the film contains some inserted footage of a 1932 Hollywood talkie, *If I had a Million* (James Cruze and seven other directors). *If I had a Million* was released in Japan on 1 February 1933. If *Woman of Tokyo* was shot in full-frame, the soundtrack image of this Hollywood talkie film would be exposed on the left-hand side of the frame. Thus, we can assume that it would be convenient for the staff of *Woman of Tokyo* to shoot with the early talkie frame from the beginning.

Another strong reason for analysing the aspect ratio of *Woman of Tokyo* and *A Mother Should be Loved* is that these films are very important in demonstrating

32 'This film was very rushed. I guess that the shooting period was only about eight days'. See Ozu, 'Ozu Yasujirō: jisaku o kataru', pp.126-127.

an inflection point in Ozu's cinematic style. Ozu himself recalled that *Woman of Tokyo* was the first film in which he positively utilized his 'low' camera position. Ozu wrote a recollection of his earlier works in 1952. He said, 'the position of framing seems to have become fixed at this time'.[33] One of the pioneering scholars of Ozu's work, Tanaka Masasumi, also mentions that contemporary critics had begun to mention the characteristics of Ozu's low camera position in relation to *Woman of Tokyo*.[34] Therefore, we can assume that Ozu's style and *mise-en-scène* might have been influenced by the changing circumstances of the Japanese film industry, particularly by the change in aspect ratio.

Having viewed the actual 35 mm print of *Woman of Tokyo* with the original early talkie frame, I can confirm that Ozu strictly composed his framing and *mise-en-scène* by taking account of the early talkie frame.[35] The contemporary film critic Kitagawa Fuyuhiko particularly admired the *mise-en-scène* in the last scene of this film, in which a newspaper reporter 'impudently enters Chikako's room and hangs his cane on the hat rack' (Fig. 8.5).[36] However, the image of the hat rack cannot be seen in the commercially available versions. Therefore, Kitagawa's article specifies that *Woman of Tokyo* was screened with the early talkie frame at the theatres in 1933.

There are many low position shots that show floorboards or tatami, on which items such as cups, kettles and floor cushions are placed on the foreground of the frame. These types of objects in the foreground at the bottom of the frame function to create depth within the frame and enhance the stability of each shot's composition. However, unfortunately, this utilization of the foreground at the bottom of the frame is lost when his films are screened in the Academy Ratio, as part of tatami and some properties become invisible. *A Mother Should be Loved* has the same problems because its DVD and VHS versions are transferred in the Academy Ratio. We only have to look at his first Academy Ratio film, *A Story of Floating Weeds*, to recognize this utilization of the foreground because this print is correctly transferred with the original aspect ratio. We can clearly see tatami or ground at the bottom of foreground within the frame sufficiently so that the stability of the composition increases in the whole film. This

33 Ozu, 'Ozu Yasujirō: jisaku o kataru', p. 127.

34 Tanaka, *Ozu Yasujirō sengo goroku shūsei*, p. 441.

35 Hasumi Shigehiko is the only critic who has mentioned the early talkie frame in Ozu's films. Hasumi interviewed the most prominent cameraman, Atsuta Yuharu, and asked about the existence of the early talkie frame. Atsuta answered that it was difficult to fix a proper composition of framing because they did not have the aperture plate for the early talkie frame in the camera. See Atsuta and Hasumi, *Ozu Yasujirō Monogatari*, p. 100.

36 Kitagawa, '*Tokyo no onna* hihyō', p. 76.

utilization of the foreground, which seems to become a characteristic of his composition after *Woman of Tokyo*, is what Ozu was struggling to achieve between *Woman of Tokyo* and *A Mother Should be Loved*. Changing the aspect ratio from full frame to early talkie frame seems to have made Ozu rethink his composition and framing techniques.

Cropped images also disturb other aspects of Ozu's *mise-en-scène*. There is a critical problem in the denouement scene of *Woman of Tokyo*, when Ryōichi slaps Chikako's face in anger. This scene obviously emphasizes the *mise-en-scène* of the characters' subtle hand movements. The detailed movements of both characters' hands and fingers represent their inner feelings, such as Ryōichi's anger and irritation and Chikako's restlessness and fear. However, parts of the images of their hands are hidden below the Academy Ratio line. This reduces the effectiveness of the *mise-en-scène* that Ozu had intended.

In analysing Ozu's early talkie frame films, it is essential for us to view his films in the original aspect ratio, in order to properly evaluate his cinematic style. Therefore, it is important that future commercial releases from this period should record the films in their original aspect ratio. Looking forward, it would be a very exciting project to collect information about the early talkie frame in different film industries to explore the influence of the early talkie frame on film style in the context of world film history.

Appendix 1 List of the early talkie frame titles preserved at the National Film Archive of Japan

Number	Release year	Film title	Director	Production company	Sound format
1	1928	*Seiyūkai sōsai Tanaka Giichi-shi enzetsu*	Unknown	Mina Talkie	Talkie
2	December 1930	*Nakayama shichiri*	Ochiai Namio	Mina Talkie	Talkie
3	1930	*Furusato*[37]	Mizoguchi Kenji	Nikkatsu, Mina Talkie	Talkie
4	August 1931	*Madamu to nyōbō*	Gosho Heinosuke	Shōchiku	Talkie
5	December 1932	*Chūshingura*	Kinugasa Teinosuke	Shōchiku	Talkie

37 The surviving version of *Hometown* seems to be reedited after the latter half of the 1930s and the title was changed to *Fujiwara Yoshie's Hometown*. Extra footage of Lee De Forest and Minagawa Yoshizō was added at the beginning of the film and was shot in Academy Ratio.

Number	Release year	Film title	Director	Production company	Sound format
6	April 1932	*Jōriku daiippo*	Shimazu Yasujirō	Shōchiku	Talkie
7	May 1932	*Chokuyu kasha gojūshūnen kinen rikugun daikōshin*	Shimizu Hiroshi et. al.	Shōchiku	Sound
8	July 1932	*Tabi wa aozora*	Inagaki Hiroshi	Chiezō production	Talkie
9	1932	*Umi no seimeisen waga nanyō shotō*	Aochi chūzo	Yokohama shinema	Talkie
10	January 1933	*Ureshii koro*	Nomura Hiromasa	Shōchiku	Talkie
11	January 1933	*Hanayome no negoto*	Gosho Heinosuke	Shōchiku	Talkie
12	Novem-ber 1933	*Tange sazen dai ippen*	Itō Daisuke	Nikkatsu	Talkie
13	February 1933	*Koi no hanasaku izu no odoriko*	Gosho Heinosuke	Shōchiku	Silent
14	February 1933	*Tokyo no onna*	Ozu Yasujirō	Shōchiku	Silent
15	July 1933	*Tenryū kudareba*	Nomura Yosimasa	Shōchiku	Sound
16	August 1933	*Ongaku kigeki: horoyoi jinsei*	Kimura Sotoji	P.C.L.	Talkie
17	February 1934	*Konjiki yasha*	Akazawa Daisuke	Akazawa kinema	Talkie
18	May 1934	*Haha o kowazuya*	Ozu Yasujirō	Shōchiku	Silent
19	June 1934	*Dai gōrei*	Yoshimura Misao	Daito eiga	Talkie (Docu-mentary)
20	January 1935	*Ongaku eiga hyakuman nin no gasshō*	Tomioka Atsuo	Nihon Bikutā	Talkie
21	January 1935	*Tetsu no tsume Hanayome ryakudatsu hen kanketsu hen*	Gotō Taizan	Etona eiga sha	Talkie
22	January 1935	*Orizuru Osen*	Mizoguchi Kenji	Daiichi eiga	Sound (*benshi* narration)
23	March 1935	*Haha no kokoro*	Negishi Toichirō	Akazawa kinema	Talkie
24	December 1934	*Seinen nihon o kataru*	Ozawa Tokuji	Chijō eiga sha	Talkie (Docu-mentary)

Number	Release year	Film title	Director	Production company	Sound format
25	1937	*Kaitaku totsugeki tai*	Akutagawa Mitsuzo	Man'ei	Talkie (Documentary)
26	1942	*Sora mamoru shōnen hei*	Watanabe Takashi	Shinseiki Eiga seisakusho	Talkie (Documentary)

Bibliography

Atsuta Yūharu and Hasumi Shigehiko. *Ozu Yasujirō monogatari* (Tokyo; Chikuma Shobō, 1989).

John Belton. *Widescreen Cinema* (Cambridge, Massachusetts: Harvard University Press, 1992).

David Bordwell and Kristin Thompson. *Film Art: An Introduction* (New York: McGraw-Hill, 2008).

Lester Cowan. 'Camera and Projector Apertures in relation to sound-on-film pictures'. *Journal of the Society of Motion Picture Engineers* 14.1 (January 1930), pp. 108-121.

Leo Enticknap. *Moving Image Technology* (London: Wallflower Press, 2005).

Giovanna Fossati. *From Grain to Pixel* (Amsterdam; Amsterdam University Press, 2009).

Fukkokuban eiga ken'etsu jihō (Tokyo; Fuji Shuppan, 1985).

Itakura Fumiaki. *'Review: Aaron Gerow, A Page of Madness: Cinema and Modernity in 1920s Japan'. Eizogaku* 87 (2011), pp. 86-89.

Itakura Fumiaki. 'Yottsu no kachi no hyakubunritsu'. In *Eiga to tekunorojī*, edited by Tsukada Yukihiro (Kyoto: Mineruba Shobō, 2015).

Kaeriyama Norimasa. *Eisha gishi kyōkasho* (Tokyo; Nikkan Kōgyō Shinbun, 1938).

Kinugasa Teinosuke. *Waga eiga no seishun: Nihon eigashi no ichi sokumen* (Chūō Kōronsha, 1977).

Kitagawa Fuyuhiko. '*Tokyo no onna* hihyō'. *Kinema junpō* 462 (21 February 1933).

Jerrold Levinson. 'Authentic Performance and Performance Means'. In *Music, Art, and Metaphysics* (Oxford: Oxford University Press, 1990), pp. 393-408.

Lloyd A. Jones. 'Rectangle Proportions in Pictorial Compositions'. *Journal of the Society of Motion Picture Engineers* 14.1 (January 1930), pp. 32-49.

Nagato Yohei. *Eiga onkyōron: Mizoguchi Kenji eiga o kiku* (Tokyo: Misuzu Shobō, 2014).

Nakamura Michitarō (ed.). *Saishin shashin kagaku taikei dai 6 kai* (Tokyo; Seibundō Shinkōsha, 1935).

Nara Conference on Authenticity in Relation to the World Heritage Convention, 'The Nara Document on Authenticity' (Nara Conference on Authenticity in Relation to the World Heritage Convention, Nara, Japan, 1994).

Nihon Eiga Terebi Gijutsu Kyōkai. *Nihon eiga gijutsu shi* (Tokyo: Nihon Eiga Terebi Gijutsu Kyōkai, 1997).

Ōtaka Keizaburō. *Shinpurekkusu eisha sōchi: Eisha miryoku no gensen* (Osaka; Akume Shōkai, 1934).

Ozu Yasujirō. 'Ozu Yasujirō: jisaku o kataru'. *Kinema junpō* (1 June 1952). Reprinted in Tanaka Masasumi (ed.). *Ozu Yasujirō sengo goroku shūsei: Shōwa 21(1946) nen – Shōwa 38 (1963) nen.* (Tokyo: Firumu Ātosha, 1989), pp.126-127.

Torkell Saetervadet. *The Advanced Projection Manual* (Oslo, Brussels: Norwegian Film Institute and FIAF, 2006).

Barry Salt. *Film Style and Technology: History and Analysis, 2nd. ed.* (London: Starword, 1992),

Takahara Fujirō. *Tōkī gikō gairon* (Tokyo: Shorin Kentendō, 1935).

Tanaka Masasumi (ed.). *Ozu Yasujirō sengo goroku shūsei: Shōwa 21(1946) nen – Shōwa 38 (1963) nen.* (Tokyo: Firumu ātosha, 1989).

'Tōkī eiga no gamen chōhōkei to naru'. *Kokusai eiga shinbun* 101 (1 May 1932), p. 10.

Paolo Cherchi Usai, David Francis, Alexander Horwath and Michael Loebenstein. *Film Curatorship: Archives, Museums, and the Digital Marketplace.* (Vienna; Filmmuseum Synema Publikationen, 2008).

About the Author

Itakura Fumiaki is Associate Professor of Film Studies at Kobe University, Japan. He spent several years working for the National Film Archive of Japan, and has published widely on Film Studies. His book on the reception of Japanese cinema by Japanese-Americans, *Eiga to imin: zaibei nikkei imin no eiga juyō to aidentiti* was published in 2016.

Index

For Product Safety Concerns and Information please contact our EU representative GPSR@taylorandfrancis.com
Taylor & Francis Verlag GmbH, Kaufingerstraße 24, 80331 München, Germany

www.ingramcontent.com/pod-product-compliance
Ingram Content Group UK Ltd.
Pitfield, Milton Keynes, MK11 3LW, UK
UKHW021428101225
465870UK00021B/626

* 9 7 8 1 0 4 1 1 8 7 5 9 2 *